HV6594 .S68 2002

Stalking and
 psychosexual obsessio
    c2002.

MW01120649

2003 11 26

Humber College Library

Stalking and
Psychosexual Obsession

Humber College Library
3199 Lakeshore Blvd. West
Toronto, ON   M8V 1K8

Wiley Series in

The Psychology of Crime, Policing and Law

Series Editors

Graham Davies   and   **Ray Bull**
University of Leicester, UK   *University of Portsmouth, UK*

The Wiley series on the Psychology of Crime, Policing and the Law publishes concise and integrative reviews on important emerging areas of contemporary research. The purpose of the series is not merely to present research findings in a clear and readable form, but also to bring out their implications for both practice and policy. In this way, it is hoped the series will not only be useful to psychologists but also to all those concerned with crime detection and prevention, policing, and the judicial process.

Stalking and Psychosexual Obsession

Psychological Perspectives for Prevention, Policing and Treatment

Edited by

Julian Boon and Lorraine Sheridan

University of Leicester, UK

160201

JOHN WILEY & SONS, LTD

Copyright © 2002 by John Wiley & Sons, Ltd.,
Baffins Lane, Chichester,
West Sussex PO19 1UD, UK

National   01243 779777
International (+44) 1243 779777
e-mail (for orders and customer service enquiries): cs-books@wiley.co.uk
Visit our Home Page on: http://www.wiley.co.uk or http://www.wiley.com

All Rights Reserved. No part of this publication may be reproduced, stored in a retrieval
system, or transmitted, in any form or by any means, electronic, mechanical, photocopying,
recording, scanning or otherwise, except under the terms of the Copyright, Designs and
Patents Act 1988 or under the terms of a licence issued by the Copyright Licensing Agency
Ltd, 90 Tottenham Court Road, London W1P 0LP, UK, without the permission in writing of
the publisher.

Chapter 4 Copyright © 1997 Gavin de Becker. Reprinted from *The Gift of Fear: Survival
Signals that Protect us from Violence* by Gavin de Becker. Reprinted 2002 by John Wiley &
Sons Ltd by permission of Little, Brown and Company, Inc.

Other Wiley Editorial Offices

John Wiley & Sons, Inc., 605 Third Avenue,
New York, NY 10158-0012, USA

WILEY-VCH Verlag GmbH, Pappelallee 3,
D-69469 Weinheim, Germany

John Wiley & Sons Australia, Ltd., 33 Park Road, Milton,
Queensland 4064, Australia

John Wiley & Sons (Asia) Pte, Ltd., 2 Clementi Loop #02-01,
Jin Xing Distripark, Singapore 129809

John Wiley & Sons (Canada), Ltd., 22 Worcester Road,
Rexdale, Ontario M9W 1L1, Canada

British Library Cataloguing in Publication Data

A catalogue record for this book is available from the British Library

ISBN 0-471-49458-5 (cased)
ISBN 0-471-49459-3 (paper)

Typeset in 10/12pt Century Schoolbook from the author's disks by TechBooks, New Delhi,
India
Printed and bound in Great Britain by Biddles Ltd, Guildford and King's Lynn
This book is printed on acid-free paper responsibly manufactured from sustainable forestry,
in which at least two trees are planted for each one used for paper production.

Contents

About the Editors

Dr Julian Boon (MA Hons, AFBPsS, PhD, C. Psychol. (Forens)) is a chartered forensic psychologist and senior lecturer in forensic psychology at the School of Psychology, University of Leicester. He has published and lectured widely in the area of offender profiling and psychological correlates of crime analyses. In addition he is an ACPO accredited offender profiler who has very extensive experience in advising police forces in the UK, Europe and Scandinavia. His specialist research interests lie in understanding the psychology of destructive and self-actualising behaviour.
Department of Psychology, University of Leicester, Astley Clarke Building University Road, Leicester LE1 7RH, UK

Dr Lorraine Sheridan (BSc Hons, IPD, PhD, C. Psychol.) is a lecturer in psychology at the University of Leicester. She has completed a PhD on psychological aspects of stalking, with particular reference to the course and nature of personal stalking, exacerbating and alleviating factors, and the effectiveness of various anti-harassment interventions. She has published and spoken widely on the psychology of stalking, harassment and violence.
Department of Psychology, University of Leicester, Astley Clarke Building University Road, Leicester LE1 7RH, UK

About the Contributors

Ella Arensman, *Leiden University, Stationsweg 46, P O Box 9500, 2399 RA Leiden, The Netherlands*
Ella Arensman PhD, is a lecturer at Leiden University. Her main field of research is suicide prevention.

Richard Badcock, *Rampton Hospital, Retford, Nottinghamshire DN22 OPD, UK*
Dr Richard J. Badcock works as a consultant forensic psychiatrist at Rampton Hospital, UK. In recent years, he has become more involved with working with the police during a variety of investigations. He also has a particular interest in the psychology of stalking, for both victims and offenders.

Timothy Baker, *University of Pennsylvania School of Nursing, Nursing Education Building. 420 Guardian Drive, Philadelphia, PA 19104-6096, USA*
Timothy Baker MSW, ACSW, PhD is an independent research contractor in the Washington DC Area and an Adjunct Professor at the University of Pennsylvania School of Nursing. He has his Bachelor of Science in Education and Masters in Social Work from the University of Pennsylvania, and his PhD from Bryn Mawr College. Dr Baker has done major studies in the area of the relationship between victims of rape and their significant others, child sexual abuse in day care centers, and stalking in domestic violence. He is currently working with Ann Burgess on violence in non-family infant kidnapping and on stalking and cyberstalking in collegiate populations.

Anna C. Baldry, *Department of Social and Developmental Psychology, University of Rome "La Sapienza", Via dei Marsi, 78, Rome 00185, Italy*
Anna C. Baldry obtained her first PhD in Social Psychology from the University of Rome "La Sapienza" and then one in criminology from the University of Cambridge, UK. She is currently doing research at the University of Rome. She is also an executive member of the NGO "Differenza Donna" that runs three shelters for battered and exploited women in

Rome. Here she practises her profession as a psychologist consultant. She has published extensively in journals and books on victimological issues and bullying in school.

Eric Blaauw, *Forensic Psychology Programme, Department of Clinical Psychology, Vrije Universiteit Amsterdam, Van der Boechorststraat 1, 1081 BT Amsterdam, The Netherlands*
Eric Blaauw, PhD, is senior lecturer and the coordinator of the Forensic Psychology Programme of the Vrije Universiteit Amsterdam. His main fields of research are in psychopathology of prisoners, stalking, offender profiling and guidance programmes in prisons.

Dr Julian Boon (*see* About the Editors)

Dr Ann Wolbert Burgess, *School of Nursing, Boston College, 140 Commonwealth Avenue, Chestnut Hill, MA 02465, USA*
Ann Wolbert Burgess, RN, DNSc, CS, FAAN is a professor of psychiatric nursing at Boston College. She has her Bachelor of Science and Doctor of Nursing Science degrees from Boston University and her Master of Science degree from the University of Maryland. She is recognised as a pioneer in the assessment and treatment of victims of trauma and abuse. Dr Burgess began her research with victims when she co-founded, with sociologist Lynda Lytle Holmstrom, one of the first hospital-based crisis counselling programmes at Boston City Hospital. She then worked with FBI Academy special agents to study serial offenders, and the links between child abuse, juvenile delinquency, and subsequent perpetration. Currently she and Dr Baker are studying cyberstalking in collegiate populations.

Gary Copson, *Metropolitan Police, London, UK*
Gary Copson is a Detective Superintendent with 23 years service in the Metropolitan Police, most of it served within the CID. He has conducted extensive postgraduate research into the usefulness of offender profiling, has published numerous academic papers on the subject, and, as a consequence, is an honorary lecturer in applied psychology at the University of Leicester.

Gavin de Becker, *Gavin de Becker & Associates, 11684 Ventura Blvd, Suite 440 Studio City, CA 91604, USA*
Gavin de Becker is widely regarded as America's leading expert on the prediction and prevention of violence. His book *The Gift of Fear: Survival Signals that Protect Us from Violence* was on the New York Times bestseller list for 17 weeks, and is published in 14 languages. His book *Protecting the Gift: Keeping Children and Teenagers Safe (and Parents Sane)* was the number one parenting bestseller in America. Mr de Becker is a three-time Presidential appointee, has served on the Governor's Advisory Board at the California Department of Mental

Health, and is a Senior Fellow at UCLA's School of Public Policy and Social Research. He is co-Chair of the Domestic Violence Council Advisory Board.

Paul Fitzgerald, *Dandenong Psychiatry Research Centre, Monash University Dandenong Area Mental Health Service and Research Centre, David Street Dandenong, Victoria 3175, Australia*
Dr Paul Fitzgerald, MBBS (Hons), MPM, FRANZCP is deputy director of Dandenong Psychiatry Research Centre and the Monash University Research Centre for Women's Mental Health. He is a senior lecturer with the Department of Psychological Medicine at Monash University and holds an appointment as a consultant psychiatrist with the Dandenong Area Mental Health Service. Dr Fitzgerald completed psychiatric training at Dandenong and a fellowship in schizophrenia research at the University of Toronto, Addiction and Mental Heath Corporation, Clarke Division in Toronto, Canada. Dr Fitzgerald heads the Transcranial Magnetic Stimulation Program at DPRC, and conducts research into the pathophysiology and treatment of schizophrenia and the affective disorders with a particular interest in gender issues and psychopharmacology.

Stephen D. Hart, *Simon Fraser University, 8888 University Drive, Burnaby, British Columbia, Canada V5A 1S6*
Stephen D. Hart is professor of psychology at Simon Fraser University. He obtained his PhD in clinical-forensic psychology at the University of British Columbia. His major research interests are violence risk assessment, psychopathic personality disorder, and mentally disordered offenders. Dr Hart has conducted training workshops for mental health, law enforcement and correctional professionals throughout North America, Europe and Australasia. He is also Director, Training and Development for Proactive Resolutions Inc., a consulting firm that specialises in the management of workplace change and conflict.

Paul Infield, *5 Paper Buildings, Temple, London EC4Y 7HB, UK*
Paul Infield was called to the Bar in 1980 and practises in civil law from the Chambers of Richard King at 5 Paper Buildings, Temple, London. Between 1992 and 2000 he was a member of the Board of Visitors of HM Prison Wandworth, which he chaired between 1996 and 1998. He is the co-author (with Graham Platford) of *The Law of Harassment and Stalking* (Butterworths, 2000) and has lectured and broadcast widely on stalking and harassment. He is a Trustee of the Suzy Lamplugh Trust and involved with Tracey Morgan's Network for Surviving Stalking. He is married, with two children, and lives in London.

P. Randall Kropp, *Forensic Psychiatric Services, Suite 300, 307 West Broadway, Vancouver, British Columbia, Canada V5Y 1P8*
P. Randall Kropp is a clinical and forensic psychologist specialising in the assessment and management of violent offenders. He works for the

Forensic Psychiatric Services Commission of British Columbia, Canada, is a research consultant with the British Columbia Institute against Family Violence, and is Adjunct Professor of Psychology at Simon Fraser University. He has conducted numerous workshops for mental health professionals, police officers, and corrections staff in North America, Australia and Europe. This training has focused on risk for violence, psycholegal assessments and criminal harassment (stalking). He has frequently consulted with provincial, state and federal government ministries on matters related to violence against women and children, and the assessment and treatment of violent offenders.

Douglas LePard, *Vancouver Police Department, Canada*
Douglas LePard has been a member of the Vancouver Police Department for 20 years and is currently the Inspector in charge of the Planning and Research Section. In 1996, as a Detective in the Major Crime Section, he created the VPD's Criminal Harassment Unit to investigate stalking cases, the first operational anti-stalking unit in Canada. He was promoted to Detective-Sergeant in charge, and personally investigated or supervised the investigation of hundreds of stalking cases until he was promoted out of the unit in 2000. Doug is married with two children, and holds a BA in Criminology from Simon Fraser University.

David R. Lyon, *Doctoral Student in the Law and Forensic Psychology programme, Simon Fraser University, 8888 University Drive, Burnaby, British Columbia, Canada V5A 156*
David R. Lyon is a doctoral student in the Law and Forensic Psychology programme at Simon Fraser University. His primary research interests concern stalking, workplace violence, psychopathy and violence risk assessment. He is a recent graduate of the Faculty of Law at the University of British Columbia and he is currently articling at the Vancouver law office of McCarthy Tetrault while he finishes work on his dissertation.

Marijke Malsch, *NISCALE, PO Box 792, NL-2300 AT Leiden, The Netherlands.*
Marijke Malsch, PhD, is senior researcher at the Netherlands Institute for the Study of Law and Criminality (NISCALE).

Nicola Marshall, *Metropolitan Police, London, UK*
Nicola Marshall after 14 years service as a constable in the Metropolitan Police, she has recently been promoted to the rank of Detective Sergent. She has specialised in the investigation of serious sexual offences and child abuse, and is the author of a police training document, 'The chaperon's guide'. She is currently working on a major complex child abuse investigation in East London.

Joseph T. McCann, *United Health Services Hospitals, 151 Leroy Street, Binghampton, NY 13905, USA*
Joseph T. McCann, PsyD, JD is a clinical psychologist at United Health Services Hospitals in Binghamton, New York and a Clinical Assistant Professor of Psychiatry at the State University of New York Upstate Medical University. He is both a psychologist and a lawyer and serves as a forensic psychological consultant in criminal and civil cases. His research and teaching interests include interpersonal violence, threat assessment and personality disorders. Dr McCann is editor of the *Journal of Threat Assessment* and the author of several scholarly publications, including the books *Stalking in Children and Adolescents: The Primitive Bond* and *Threats in Schools: A Practical Guide for Managing Violence.*

J. Reid Meloy, *Clinical and Forensic Psychology, 964 Fifth Avenue, Suite 409 San Diego, CA 92101, USA*
J. Reid Meloy is a diplomate in forensic psychology of the American Board of Professional Psychology. He is in independent practice, specialising in criminal forensic consultation, research, writing and teaching. He is an associate clinical professor of psychiatry at the University of California, San Diego, and adjunct professor at the University of San Diego School of Law. He is a Fellow of the American Academy of Forensic Sciences, and past President of the American Academy of Forensic Psychology. He is also chairman of Forensis, Inc. (www.forensis.org), a private, nonprofit corporation devoted to forensic psychiatric and psychological research. Dr Meloy's most recent books are *Violence Risk and Threat Assessment* and *The Mark of Cain* (Analytic Press, 2001).

Paul E. Mullen, *Victorian Institute of Forensic Mental Health, Thomas Embling Hospital, Locked Bag 10, Fairfield, Victoria 3078, Australia*
Professor Paul E. Mullen, MB BS, DSc, MPhil (Psych Med), FRANZCP, FRC Psych, is currently Professor of Forensic Psychiatry at Monash University Medical School and is also Clinical Director at the Victorian Institute of Forensic Mental Health. He has over 100 publications in academic journals and with Michele Pathé and Rosemary Purcell is author of *Stalkers and Their Victims* (Cambridge University Press, 2000). His current research interests are stalking, the relationships between mental disorder and criminal behaviour, and the querulous complainant.

Michele Pathé, *Victorian Institute of Forensic Mental Health, Thomas Embling Hospital, Locked Bag 10, Fairfield, Victoria 3078, Australia*
Dr Michele Pathé is a consultant forensic psychiatrist and Assistant Clinical Director at the Victorian Institute of Forensic Mental Health in Melbourne, Victoria, Australia. She is an honorary senior lecturer at Monash University in Melbourne and a Fellow in the Department of Criminology at the University of Melbourne. Her research interests

and publications cover sex offender management, stalkers and stalking victims.

Graham Platford, *5 Paper Buildings, Temple, London, EC4Y 7HB, UK*
Graham Platford was called to the Bar in 1970 and practises in civil law from the Chambers of Richard King at 5 Paper Buildings, Temple, London. He is co-author (with Paul Infield) of *The Law of Harassment and Stalking* (Butterworths, 2000) and has lectured on stalking and harassment. He lives in London with his wife and two daughters.

Mary V. Seeman, *Centre for Addiction and Mental Health, 250 College Street Toronto, Ontario, Canada, M5T 1R8*
Dr Mary V. Seeman, MDCM, FRCPC, FACP, is professor of psychiatry at the University of Toronto and former Tapscott Chair of Schizophrenia Studies. Since the early 1960s, Dr Seeman has been involved in work with schizophrenia patients, especially women. She has published extensively and has done some of the early work in studying De Clerambeault's syndrome. She is currently part of a clinic that assesses and treats women with psychotic disorders. Dr Seeman has edited and co-edited several texts about schizophrenia, among them *Gender and Psychopathology*, (American Psychiatric Association Press, 1995) and *Parental Psychiatric Disorder: Distressed parents and their Families* (Cambridge University Press, 1996).

Dr Lorraine Sheridan (*see* About the Editors)

Frans Willem Winkel, *Victimology Programme, Department of Clinical Psychology, Vrije Universiteit Amsterdam, Van der Boechorststraat 1, 1081 BT Amsterdam, The Netherlands*
Frans Willem Winkel, PhD, is senior lecturer and the coordinator of the Victimology Programme of the Vrije Universiteit Amsterdam. He is the current president of the European Association of Psychology and Law.

Foreword

In July 1999 the Suzy Lamplugh Trust sent out media information warning of the danger of stalking following the publication of research findings. The Trust "welcomed the publication of stalking research of the University of Leicester which shows how devastating stalking and harassment can be for victims". The University had analysed over 80 questionnaires collated by the Suzy Lamplugh Trust over the past few years from stalking victims. The Trust reported that the research "showed that stalking could happen to all sorts of people, both male and female, in all walks of life. It is excellent research which will further our understanding of why stalkers behave in the way they do".

The Trust went on to say that we had campaigned for several years for a change in the law to give the police more powers to combat stalking, and continued to run conferences and seminars on the subject. We believe that the law has already been effective in preventing death and serious injury to stalking victims.

I continued, "Stalking is often committed by someone known to the victim. In most cases the situation gets more dangerous and more violent as the stalker becomes increasingly desperate to be noticed. We urge people to go to the police straight away. Since the introduction of the Protection from Harassment Act, last June, the police have much greater powers to deal with stalkers".

I spoke from the heart. By this time I knew that had I been aware of the potential dangers of a stalker, I might have been able to save my daughter, Suzy. I also knew that I could not help her now. However, I was convinced that action must be taken to help others.

Since that time I have been waiting for this book, which contains the wisdom of everyone one could wish to read. The authors are the world experts on all angles of stalking. No one should miss this splendid, authoritative as well as readable book, which is designed to help those in need, be they potential victims, police, lawyers, academic, journalists and of course those who care.

I had just dismissed the man as yet another suitor chasing a very lovely, lively girl who sat in the window of a Fulham estate agency, a position designed to attract new business and potential male clients. It never occurred to any of us to consider this man to be an active threat to Suzy, even when she suddenly went missing during one beautiful summer working day after showing a client round a house. Even when we were beginning to have to accept that Suzy had been murdered, we never considered that a man who appeared to be chasing her as a potential boyfriend might be the man who could have killed her.

Suzy had such a wide and interesting group of friends who were all not only working hard but also enthusiastically enjoying themselves—windsurfing, ski-ing and tennis all played prominent roles in their daily activities. These young people were streetwise and confident. Danger did not appear to lurk at their heels. It took some time to recall this "outsider" and to tell the police, realising by then that any detail might count.

Even then I was very cautious when encouraged to add a new project to the increasing work being undertaken by the Trust specialising in personal safety which we had set up in Suzy's name. Our aim was to enable everyone to lead safer lives through research and positive informed action, training, education, practical resources, raising awareness of issues and campaigning for changes in the law when necessary. Was this apparently new idea of stalking really a personal safety issue?

From 1995 onwards, the Trust became increasingly aware of the problems suffered by victims of "stalkers" through calls from people desperate for help. There appeared to be no pattern and few answers, and only anecdotal knowledge. Research has always been my baseline. Is the problem real? How many people are affected? There were a few celebrity cases—were ordinary people also at risk?

It was the contact made by two dedicated officers from Hampshire Constabulary who were in charge of the Tracey Morgan case that convinced me that the present law was quite inadequate in many cases to deal with the scale of the problem. It was these two officers and Tracey herself who encouraged the Trust as an "independent body" to launch a campaign to call for specific anti-stalking laws.

I was sceptical. We sat by the Thames and these two police officers, D.S. Linda Dawson and Ian Smith, highlighted the interest in the case. As we talked on that sunny, breezy day and I listened to the harassment which Tracey Morgan had been forced to endure, I suddenly felt icy cold. I remembered that Suzy had referred to her pursuer as "scary" and I realised that she must have been a victim of "stalking", and that this behaviour, this cold, obsessive form of torture, could become deadly. I knew then that I might have been able to save my daughter had I been aware.

In 1995 the Trust led the campaign for a new law. The Association of Chief Police Officers (ACPO) and in particular A.C.C. Maria Wallis were most supportive and undertook a useful survey of each force. The Police Federation confirmed that it was backing the campaign in early 1996.

The result of their debate was 100% unanimity in favour of pushing this policy.

In March 1997 the Trust called a meeting with representatives from prisons, the police, probation, experts on stalking psychology and victims of stalking, to discuss the potential problems which might arise when stalkers were placed in custody, such as stalking from prison by phone or through other prisoners being released.

The Protection from Harassment Act was introduced to the House of Commons on Monday, 16 June 1997. Further sections, dealing with the way in which a civil injunction is dealt with if breached, came into effect in September 1998.

However, the Trust has remained concerned that the Protection from Harassment Act is still not being fully implemented or proving useful enough to those who need it, the victims. We are therefore delighted—and somewhat relieved—that this book has been so well researched and edited by the two people most deeply involved with research in the UK.

We recommend that it is read by everyone who cares. After all, it appears that none of us is immune from this indiscriminate, destructive crime.

DIANA LAMPLUGH, OBE
Director, The Suzy Lamplugh Trust
The National Charity for Personal Safety

Series Preface

The Wiley Series on the Psychology of Crime, Policing and the Law publishes integrative reviews of important emerging areas of contemporary research. The purpose of the series is not merely to present research findings in a clear and readable form, but also to bring out their implications for both practice and policy. In this way, it is hoped that the series will not only be useful to psychologists, but also to all those concerned with crime detection and prevention, policing and the judicial process.

As the editors of the current volume remind us, the legal recognition of stalking—systematic harassment and intimidation directed at one individual by another—has only recently been recognised as a distinct form of criminality. One of the important features of stalking as a crime is that its appearance sometimes presages even more serious criminal acts against the victim, including physical violence and murder. For instance in September 2001, a former British naval officer, Anthony Hurdle, was sentenced to life imprisonment for attempted murder. His partner at the time had broken off her relationship with him after discovering that he had a history of stalking offences against other women. She in turn was then stalked by Hurdle for several months before suffering a horrific attack at his hands in her own home. Predicting when such escalation will occur and how to snuff out the behaviour before it takes place is a challenge to all forensic psychologists and psychiatrists, police officers, lawyers and criminologists who are drawn to this problem.

Stalking and Psychosexual Obsession: Psychological Perspectives for Prevention, Policing and Treatment provides the first comprehensive treatment of the topic, examining not simply the prevalence of stalking and the nature of the stalkers themselves, but also what can be done, through police action and the courts, to combat the activity in its many forms. Sadly, governments have often legislated in haste, without a full appreciation of the range of activities undertaken by stalkers or the scope of the problem. Likewise, beyond sensationalised accounts of individuals who have stalked celebrities, little is known about the personality and background of the men and women who become stalkers. This important book also looks at the victims of stalking and the new phenomenon of cyberstalking: the harassment of victims through the Internet and electronic mail. Its very ubiquity in Western societies (we know little of stalking in other cultures) may owe something to the ease of communication between individuals that we prize today.

The editors, Julian Boon and Lorraine Sheridan, are well placed to collate an authoritative and multifaceted view of research and practice. Julian Boon is an academic and chartered forensic psychologist, and is also one of the handful of Home Office accredited offender profilers in the United Kingdom. His wide-ranging involvement in high-profile cases has given him first-hand experience, both of stalkers and other sexual obsessives and their victims. Lorraine Sheridan has carried out the first systematic studies of the nature and incidence of stalking in the United Kingdom and has published widely on the topic as well as advising government agencies and charities on anti-stalking measures. Their reputations have ensured that this book brings together some of the foremost authorities on stalking and sexual obsession in Europe, Australia and North America to provide an up-to-the-minute and authoritative account of this ubiquitous, malign, but poorly understood activity.

GRAHAM DAVIES
University of Leicester

Preface

Stalking was labelled "the crime of the nineties". Even so, despite international media interest, surprisingly little research was conducted into the phenomenon until the late 1990s. Much of the literature that existed prior to this time took a discursive form, focused on the pursuit of celebrities and other public figures, or attempted to form typologies of stalkers and/or their victims, concentrating on small and possibly unrepresentative clinical and court samples. The media coverage of stalking meant that anecdotal and sensationalist accounts were far more prevalent than were systematic investigations. The words of one British victim, writing in 1996, neatly outlines the situation as it was then: "Stalking is one of the most serious crimes of the 1990s, but no one, apart from the victims, seem to realise it".

As we have moved into the 21st century, increased interest from the media, writers, the public, academics, clinicians and law enforcement agencies has led to the emergence of a more informed picture. Stalking is now rightly recognised as a significant social problem. Still, however, there are a number of areas in which any detailed information is extremely scant. One of the most fundamental unresolved issues associated with stalking concerns definition. That is, there exists no agreed definition of what the phenomenon actually constitutes, nor is it entirely clear who the stalkers or their victims are likely to be.

Throughout the 1990s, much of the developed world introduced anti-stalking legislation, yet in legislative terms, significant international differences in approach to the creation of laws have emerged. For example the Protection from Harassment Act which was introduced in England and Wales in 1997 is broadly drafted without the specification of particular forms of criminal behaviour. By contrast the Australian approach to stalking legislation has been to itemise specific exemplars of behaviour which constitute criminal stalking activity. To complicate matters further, while in England and Wales there is a uniform application of the law, in Australia and the United States there are inter-State differences in application. In many ways that there is such diversity of practice is unsurprising since providing an agreed definition of the stalking phenomenon has proven very difficult.

One thing all attempts at defining stalking must address is that it is an extraordinary type of crime. Often it may consist of no more than the targeted repetition of an ostensibly ordinary or routine behaviour. The major legislative difficulty is that the term "stalking" does not apply to a single action or actions which can easily be defined in legal terms and prohibited: rather, it embraces a *multitude* of activities. For example, stalkers can harass victims using illegal actions, such as making obscene phone calls or committing acts of violence. Frequently, though, stalkers do not overtly threaten, but use behaviour which is ostensibly routine and harmless, and not in itself illegal. Examples of this might include following somebody around a shop, or frequently driving past their house.

As far as the general public is concerned, it may be that stalking is like great art: they cannot define it, but know it when they see it. For the purposes of this preface, however, it is proposed to work with a definition which makes reference to kernel aspects of the phenomenon without being prescriptive as to specific acts which underpin it. It is therefore proposed to define "stalking" activity as being composed of "a set of actions which, taken as a whole, amount to harassment or intimidation directed at one individual by another". From this deliberately flexible perspective, it will be possible then to flag up key issues which are emergent from contemporary lines of groundbreaking thinking and research. The primary objectives of this book are two-fold: first, to explore and clarify previous work, and second, to expand on this and introduce new insights to key aspects of stalking.

Reflecting these objectives, the chapters which follow have been contributed by international figures from a diverse range of backgrounds and expertise. Specifically, the range of issues that have been covered relate to differing facets of victimology, classificatory systems and stalkers, the role of stalker violence, the treatment of offenders, and the global legal context. These are complemented by chapters on aspects of stalking that have been covered less extensively to date, such as stalking from female and young populations, and cyberstalking.

In more detail, four aspects of victimology are explored. In Chapter 1, Michele Pathé and Paul Mullen from Melbourne provide an overview of victim characteristics and experiences. Chapter 2 reports the findings from a Dutch study conducted by Eric Blaauw and colleagues from Amsterdam on the psychological consequences for victims of stalking. Additionally, a world authority in the area, Gavin de Becker, based in California, advises in Chapter 3 on the process of becoming a victim and factors to be aware of in preventing victim status. Finally, of the chapters specifically addressing victims, Gary Copson and Nicola Marshall from the Metropolitan Police in London look at ways of assisting and supporting victims of stalking and psychosexual harassment in Chapter 4.

The editors contribute a chapter which offers a classificatory system of stalkers specifically created to be of practical utility for law enforcement agencies. In this regard it attempts to provide case assessment criteria and explores the implications for case management and victim perspective.

The focus then switches to matters relating to violence. Anna Baldry from Rome in Chapter 6 discusses the link between domestic violence and stalking. J. Reid Meloy from California provides an overview of the course and nature of stalker violence, its assessment and factors associated with risk.

Chapters 8 and 9 provide dual perspectives on the British and Canadian experience of the treatment and supervision of stalkers. The British experience is offered by the consultant forensic psychiatrist Richard Badcock while Randall Kropp, Stephen Hart, David Lyon and Douglas Lepard provide a multidisciplinary Canadian approach.

Additional aspects are developed in Chapters 10–12. First, Paul Fitzgerald of Melbourne and Mary Seeman from Toronto discuss erotomania in women—from its history to its role in modern stalking cases involving female perpetrators. Next, the hitherto neglected subject of children as perpetrators and victims of stalking is explored by Joseph McCann of New York. Ann Burgess and Timothy Baker look at new developments in cyberstalking, with reference to case examples and advice to victims.

Our final contribution comes from London barristers Paul Infield and Graham Platford, who provide a discussion of the development of the first British anti-stalking legislation.

Collectively, the foregoing chapters represent a showcase of that which is currently internationally known about the phenomenon of stalking and psychosexual harassment.

JULIAN BOON
LORRAINE SHERIDAN

CHAPTER 1

The Victim of Stalking

Michele Pathé

and

Paul Mullen

Victorian Institute of Forensic Mental Health, Fairfield

INTRODUCTION

The phenomenon of stalking is of legitimate interest to mental health professionals not only because many stalkers are mentally disordered, but because their activities evoke fear and distress in their victims. The lives of victims are frequently severely disrupted by being stalked, producing psychological, social and vocational dysfunction. The impact of stalking may also be observed in the victim's family members, friends, work colleagues and other significant figures in the victim's world. Mental health professionals have additional cause to heed the emergence of stalking since they are more vulnerable than most other occupational groups to becoming targets of such behaviour.

The victim is central to stalking. Stalking has been criminalised because of its impact upon its victims. In many jurisdictions the crime of stalking is dependent on the behaviour creating fear in the target. The reaction of the victim becomes central to the definition of the crime rather than, as is customary, the criminal intentions of the offender. Thus stalking becomes a victim-defined crime.

The study of victims has significantly contributed to our understanding of the perpetrators of stalking behaviours. It is only through the reports of victims of stalking that we can begin to fully appreciate the contexts

Stalking and Psychosexual Obsession: Psychological Perspectives for Prevention, Policing and Treatment.
Edited by J. Boon and L. Sheridan. © 2002 John Wiley & Sons, Ltd.

in which stalking emerges and the factors that motivate such offending. Ultimately optimal management approaches to control stalking behaviours, be they primarily therapeutic or dependent on judicial sanction, are directed to alleviating the burden of this behaviour on both victim and stalker.

There is still only limited literature pertaining to the victims of stalking. Even more troubling is the paucity of dedicated and coordinated services for victims. One of the factors that has contributed to the invisibility of the majority of victims of stalkers is the popular misperception of stalkers targeting exclusively celebrities or other public figures. Until quite recently there has been little appreciation of the scale of the problem within the general community and the prevalence of this experience among ordinary citizens. Large-scale, representative community studies conducted over the past five years challenge earlier notions that stalking is the exclusive domain of the famous, as do the experiences of law enforcement agencies, victim organisations and health care providers, all of which are confronted with victims of stalking in increasing numbers. While few would argue that public figures attract a disproportionate share of stalkers, this is a crime that selects from a diverse pool of potential victims. Virtually anyone, irrespective of age, gender, social or marital status, cultural background, physical appearance or sexual orientation, can be targeted by a stalker.

STUDIES OF STALKING VICTIMS

In one of the earliest empirical studies of stalking behaviours, Jason and colleagues (1984) interviewed 50 Chicago women who had been subjected to harassment by men after terminating a relationship, or refusing to enter into one. The study was conducted well before the term "stalking" was attached to this type of behaviour. The harassing behaviours reported by all subjects persisted for at least one month and could by most contemporary criteria be labelled stalking. In 92% of the sample, for instance, repeated telephone calls were received, while 48% reported unwanted approaches, 26% following and surveillance, 24% received unwanted letters or other material, and threats and physical assaults were claimed by almost a third of respondents. Upon ending the relationship (for reasons such as their boyfriend becoming too serious, exhibiting strange behaviours, or subjecting them to physical or verbal abuse) or after refusing to date a would-be lover, these victims were harassed for on average 13 months (range 1–120 months).

Jones (1996) analysed data on 7472 Canadians who reported stalking or harassment to police over a two-year period. Eighty per cent of the victims were female, and the majority of reports involved stalking by an ex-spouse (33%) or a person with whom they had shared an intimate relationship

(14%), or a casual acquaintance (28%). Only 8% indicated they were pursued by a stranger, and in 5% of cases the victim was stalked by a family member other than a spouse. This analysis found that women were more likely to report stalking by a former intimate while men more commonly reported stalking by a casual acquaintance or somebody with whom there had been a work or business relationship.

Fremouw and co-workers (1997) surveyed 600 psychology undergraduates, of whom 30% of females and 17% of males fulfilled the study criteria for victims of stalking. The subjects knew their stalker in 80% of cases, and prior romantic involvement was a common finding (43% of females; 24% of males). This study also explored the coping strategies employed by victims. Surprisingly few reported the intrusions to police or sought other legal remedies. Some of the males who were pursued by ex-intimates even tried to reconcile with their stalker in a desperate bid to end the harassment.

A large random, community survey of women's experiences of physical and sexual violence conducted by the Australian Bureau of Statistics (ABS) (1996) included questions on stalking and harassment. As many as 15% of this cohort of 6300 adult women reported being stalked by a man at some time in their lives. It could be argued that this figure is likely to be an underestimate because stalking of male and same gender victims was excluded. However, the definition of stalking was rather less stringent than those adopted today such that it is probable that some instances of isolated, inadvertent behaviours were included as stalking.

Another Australian study (Pathé & Mullen, 1997) surveyed 100 self-selected stalking victims, 83% of whom were female. Twenty-nine per cent of the sample indicted that their stalker was a former intimate, 21% were prior acquaintances and 16% of victims did not know their stalker before the harassment commenced. For a quarter of the victims in this study the stalking arose in a professional context, most often a doctor–patient relationship, while a further 9% of the sample first encountered their stalker in another work-related context. More than a third of victims could be classified as professionally employed, the majority being medical practitioners, lawyers or teachers. The nature and range of harassment methods to which this sample was subjected did not depart significantly from the earlier victim studies, the median duration of stalking being two years (though over half the cohort reported ongoing victimisation). Explicit threats occurred in 58% of cases, directed at the primary victim and at others, such as relatives and friends perceived to be obstructing access to the victim, and 34 of the respondents had been physically and/or sexually assaulted.

A non-random, self-selected sample of 145 stalking victims (Hall 1998) was again predominantly female (83%), with a mean age of 35 years. As noted in earlier studies (Pathé & Mullen, 1997), this cohort had a higher educational background than the general public. The sample was divided into "prior sexual intimates" (57% of respondents), "prior acquaintances"

(35%) and "strangers" (6%). Thirteen per cent of these victims had been stalked for more than five years (with a range of less than a month to 31 years.)

The US National Institute of Justice (NIJ) (Tjaden & Thoennes, 1998) overcame some of the methodological shortcomings of the ABS survey when it commissioned a study to specifically examine the extent of stalking in a large, random community sample of 8000 women and 8000 men. The victim population in this telephone survey was 78% female and the majority of victims fell in the age range 18–29 years. In most cases the stalker was known to his or her victim, 59% of female and 30% of male victims indicating that their stalker was an intimate partner. However, in 23% of female and 36% of male victims the stalker was believed to be a stranger. The lifetime cumulative incidence of stalking in this study was 8% for women and 2% for men, with an annual incidence of 1% and 0.4% respectively. Employing less stringent criteria for stalking victimisation— that is, the reporting of behaviours that evoked only minimal, rather than a significant degree of fear—boosted the lifetime cumulative incidence to 12% for women and 4% for men.

Although the NIJ employed a random digit dialling technique, telephone surveys are problematic in stalking victimisation surveys because it is likely that many of the more severely affected stalking victims cannot or will not answer the phone. In a more recent representative community study in the Australian state of Victoria, 3700 men and women were randomly selected from the electoral roll. In Australia, voting is compulsory so electoral rolls cover over 95% of the adult population (18 years upwards.) Of the 1844 respondents, 75% were female and, although 43% of the cohort was aged between 16 and 30 years at the onset of the harassment, neither children nor the elderly were spared (range 6–76 years.) Overall, this survey suggests that the prevalence of stalking experiences in the community may be substantially higher than that reported in the earlier population-based studies, with 10% of respondents reporting 10 or more intrusions by their stalker that were moderately frightening or worse (Purcell et al., in press).

In the first study to examine stalking in children and adolescents McCann (2000) described 13 stalkers or obsessional followers ranging in age from 9 to 18 years. The relationship between offender and victim included ex-girlfriend, classmates, strangers, teachers and parent. In half the sample these young offenders targeted same-age peers. Victims were most commonly subjected to physical approaches and unwanted sexual advances, and to a lesser extent telephone calls, letters and property damage. This study lent support to earlier work suggesting that stalking may be a subset of sexually harassing behaviour in schools (American Association of University Women, 1993).

THE CLASSIFICATION OF VICTIMS OF STALKING

There have been various attempts to classify victims of stalking, most employing relational typologies (Zona et al., 1993; Harmon et al., 1995; Meloy & Gothard, 1995; Meloy, 1996; Emerson et al., 1998). Mullen and colleagues (2000) developed a classification based on the prior relationship between victim and stalker, the context in which the stalking arose and a typology of stalkers.

Prior Intimates

Random community studies suggest that this is the largest group, comprising former spouses, former co-habitants and former boyfriends or girlfriends but it can include also prior intimate relationships of a non-sexual nature, such as those involving close friends and longstanding business partnerships. Victims in this category may even be pursued by a sibling or parent. In one case known to us a father stalked his adult daughter when she moved away from home. She complained that he was very strict and intrusive and she could no longer abide by his house rules. Her father monitored her new lifestyle by following her on social outings, sitting in his car outside her flat and rummaging through her rubbish bin, and he twice attempted to abduct her.

The vast majority of prior intimate victims are women. Up to half will have been exposed to harassment while the relationship was still intact, in particular following, surveillance, threats and violence. These behaviours effectively control and intimidate the victim, isolating them from their usual supports and hampering their efforts to extricate themselves from the situation. Victims of former intimates are characteristically subjected to a wide range of harassing behaviours, including threats, property damage and assaults. Tjaden & Thoennes (1998) included current intimates in this category of stalking victims, although we would argue that these behaviours cannot constitute stalking unless the victim has left the relationship and unequivocally communicated her wish for no further contact with the ex-intimate. They found that over 80% of women who were stalked by a current or former partner were physically assaulted. They also found that 30% were sexually assaulted prior to leaving their stalker.

The pursuit of former intimates is typically persistent and—in the absence of effective legal sanctions or treatment of any underlying psychopathology such as morbid jealousy—it can also be prolonged (Mullen et al., 1999). The duration of stalking increases with the stalker's emotional investment in the relationship, such that the pursuit is less likely to be relinquished if victim and stalker have had an enduring relationship and particularly where they share children. Conversely, if the romantic liaison has been relatively brief (e.g. "date" stalkers) both violence and persistence are less characteristic.

Friends and Casual Acquaintances

For these victims, stalking commences after a casual social encounter, a dispute with a neighbour or the breakdown of a friendship. The majority of male stalking victims fall into this category (Hall, 1998; Purcell et al., in press). These victims are typically subjected to the repeated approaches of an infatuated acquaintance pursuing a relationship, or an acquaintance reacting to the breakdown of a friendship and the humiliation of persistent rejection, or the vengeful intimidation of a resentful neighbour. They are seldom exposed to violence on a scale experienced by former intimate victims, and they are likely to be stalked for comparatively shorter periods. In some instances of neighbour stalking, however, the victim can only escape persistent persecution by moving out of the neighbourhood.

Professional Contacts

Some professional groups such as psychiatrists, psychologists, primary care physicians, social workers, lawyers and teachers have a heightened risk of being stalked. In essence, almost any profession that comes into contact with the lonely and disordered and in whom sympathy and attention is easily reconstructed as romantic interest are particularly vulnerable (Mullen et al., 2000). Often, the stalker is seeking a relationship, however improbable, or believes, in the case of the erotomanic, that a relationship already exists. Others are reacting to the termination of a therapeutic relationship, with a mix of rage, vengeance and desperation to restore the lost union. Some victims in this category will instead attract more resentful stalking patterns, as in the case of the cosmetic surgeon threatened by a former patient dissatisfied with her rhinoplasty, or the lawyer harangued by a client who held him responsible for an unsuccessful family court appeal.

Although this category of stalking victims is not commonly exposed to violence, most being subject to repeated phone calls, letters and other unsolicited material, it is not unusual for stalkers to launch an attack on their professional reputation. Malicious complaints can be made to professional disciplinary bodies, the police, the media or even other patients or clients. Much time and expense can be wasted defending such cases and many affected professionals report feeling ill-prepared and unsupported by their colleagues. These victims can experience considerable distress and disillusionment with their chosen career (Orion, 1997; Pathé

& Mullen, 1997), such that some abandon their profession in pursuit of less threatening vocations. One such case under our care, a senior social worker, now works in a sandwich bar. She feels far less fulfilled and her wages have plummeted but she refuses to return to a career that almost destroyed her life.

Workplace Contacts

Stalking that arises outside of the workplace will in many cases extend to that setting. This category is instead reserved for instances where the victim is first targeted in a work-related context, most stalker–victim relationships being employer/supervisor–employee, employee–employer or employee–employee in nature, but included also are customer–service provider relationships. While some individuals fall victim to the socially inept approaches of a would-be suitor, others become the focus of another worker's disgruntlement and embitterment. This may be consequent upon organisational changes or disciplinary action against the stalker. He may consider he has been unfairly passed over in favour of the targeted co-worker and he may contest the perceived discrimination before various tribunals and appeal boards, the harassment escalating as the complaints are dismissed. The victim is typically subject to threats, and the aggrieved worker may closely monitor his or her activities.

There are occasional spectacular examples of workplace stalking, such as the case of Californian software engineer Robert Farley who became infatuated with co-worker Laura Black (Simon, 1996). He responded to her repeated rebuttals by stalking her and, four years later, after being sacked by the company where Black still worked, he stormed his former workplace and shot seven innocent employees. Black, though seriously wounded, survived.

Strangers

These victims are not aware of any prior contact with their stalker, who is typically motivated by the desire for an intimate relationship with the victim. Those who stalk as a prelude to a sexual attack are also likely to target strangers, and these victims may be men, women or children. Those targeted by stranger stalkers may be selected on the basis of physical attractiveness or social status but this is by no means always the case. Increasingly in the age of cyber technology stalkers are pursuing individuals whose social standing and physical attributes remain largely unknown quantities unless the stalking extends offline, though that is not to say that the cyberstalker does not form his own fantasised version of the victim, however improbable.

The Famous

Victims in this group are drawn from radio, television and film but not infrequently include sports stars, politicians, writers and royalty. Any public figure is potentially a target, typically attracting stalkers seeking intimacy, the morbidly infatuated and the erotomanics. With the advent of mass media, the famous intrude themselves into our homes, often creating a pseudo-intimacy which, for individuals whose lives are otherwise bereft of intimacy, can fill a void and foster stalking behaviours. It is also not surprising, given that these victims often epitomise success, that they would also become targets of resentful individuals whose stalking is motivated more by revenge.

The famous are also at greater risk of being victimised by *multiple* stalkers. Such is the magnitude of the problem that protecting the stars has become a thriving industry in areas where fame is concentrated, such as Los Angeles (de Becker, 1997).

SECONDARY VICTIMS OF STALKING

Stalkers will not uncommonly harass individuals associated with the primary object of attention. Family and friends particularly, but also work colleagues, flatmates and boarders, may be indirectly or secondarily targeted. Often this is because they are perceived (correctly, in many cases) as protecting the victim or "brainwashing" the victim against the stalker. These individuals are regarded as obstacles and they are typically subjected to threats, property damage and even physical attacks as the stalker strives to subvert them. Ritchie (1995) reports on a case in which an infatuated woman stalked a married man. When she learnt that his wife was pregnant she arranged for her brutal murder and very nearly succeeded in framing her erstwhile love object for the crime.

The romantic partners of victims pursued by ex-intimates and would-be suitors are particularly vulnerable. Dramatic examples abound in which extreme violence is perpetrated against hapless new partners, the stalker reasoning: "If I can't have her, nobody else will". On occasion pathologically jealous stalkers have slain friends of the victim who were mistakenly perceived to be in an intimate relationship with them.

In some instances threats against loved ones are communicated to the victim with the intention of amplifying their distress. They may be told, for instance, that their precious children will be abducted, or that the victim's isolated, elderly mother will be raped and tortured. Some stalkers kill family pets, causing considerable grief to the victim's children and raising concerns for the *children's* physical safety. There may also be threats to disclose sensitive information to family members with the intention of creating anguish, as in the case of the spurned lover of a prominent businessman who threatened to "out" him to his dying father.

Children can suffer considerably as a consequence of a stalker's actions. In addition to being directly threatened or losing pets, they may be subjected to high levels of parental anxiety, depression and dysfunction. Some are exposed to property damage, home invasions and the stalker's more bizarre activities, such as leaving mutilated animals at their victim's front door. A stalked woman under our care was too anxious to drive her eight-year-old son to school or to music classes. Ultimately, she became house-bound and her son increasingly and inappropriately assumed his mother's domestic role. Because the victim felt emotionally numbed she was unable to hug the child and she was uncharacteristically irritable towards him and her spouse. The marital relationship deteriorated, and the child was trapped in an increasingly acrimonious home environment. The victim also became overprotective, refusing to allow her son to venture beyond their letter box, answer the phone or open the mail, conservatism that was understandable and even justified in this case but enormously restrictive for the child nonetheless. One day, the victim looked outside to find her son and his young neighbour playing "stalkers", taking turns to be the victim. Until then, this woman had not fully appreciated the extent to which the stalking had engulfed her entire family's consciousness.

Others at risk of secondary victimisation are the primary target's co-workers. They too may be perceived as thwarting the stalker's access to the victim, by shielding them when the stalker arrives at the workplace or refusing to bring them to the phone. A secretary who responded to repeated harassing calls from her boss's former wife by informing her that he was overseas was confronted at her desk by the enraged woman after she discovered he had been at work all the time. She was removed from the building by security guards, and thereafter stalked the secretary, damaging her vehicle in the office car park, painting "LIAR" over her fence and letter box, filling the locks on her garage door with superglue and phoning the office hundreds of times a day. The repeated intrusions of a stalker at the victim's workplace can be enormously disruptive to any work environment, creating fear, distress and absenteeism. In the current example the secretary took months of stress leave and filed a worker's compensation claim.

Those close to the stalking victim may experience profound misery and upheaval regardless of any direct intimidation from the stalker. Family and friends commonly report feelings of helplessness. They cannot end the victim's purgatory nor are they able to fathom the changes in their loved one consequent upon the stalking. Some victims withdraw from their usual supports while others become more dependent, placing an additional burden on others. One victim became so anxious she returned to the parental home and begged her mother to forfeit her job so she could stay at home with her terrified daughter. Her mother escorted her everywhere and was forced to park her car in illegal bays so that her daughter did not feel intolerably exposed by having to walk long distances in public. Thus, in many instances of stalking there is more than one victim, and a multitude of people who are at risk of suffering its deleterious effects.

THE IMPACT OF STALKING

Unlike most other criminal offences and isolated traumatic events, stalking is characterised by *repeated* and *persistent* intrusions. Its victims are almost always exposed to multiple forms of harassment, including threats that may proceed to assaults upon the victim and/or other parties. Often the stalker strikes unpredictably, casting a menacing shadow over the victim's world, a world that is increasingly viewed as malevolent and untrustworthy. Stalking victims characteristically experience a loss of control over their situation, as appeals to logic fail and rational strategies prove ineffectual. Many drift away from their support networks, often because the victim perceives that these people lack understanding or are critical of them. They seek the help of professionals in law enforcement, legal, medical and mental health fields, but many are confronted by attitudes of indifference, disbelief or ignorance, and often little in the way of constructive advice. One victim was told by a police officer that she should feel "flattered" by the attentions of an infatuated stranger, while a married teacher pursued by an adolescent student, both of them male, was regarded with suspicion by police and was questioned about a possible illicit sexual relationship. A very attractive woman stalked by a socially awkward male acquaintance was flippantly told by a medical practitioner that she should "take the neon sign off on her forehead", and that if she was *really* serious about avoiding unwanted admirers she should "try to look less enticing". This advice was accompanied by a prescription for sleeping tablets.

These are all common experiences reported by victims of stalking. They are also important ingredients in the recipe for chronic stress reactions and related psychological sequelae. Trauma research has found that adverse effects on functioning can occur when an individual remains for an extended period in a situation where he or she feels under threat. Trauma involving loss of control would appear to produce more persistent disquiet in its victims, Baum and co-workers (1993) observing that "events involving loss of control and violation of expectations for control have different effects than do events that remind us of forces over which control was never expected", such as natural disasters. Stress resistance research also highlights a central role for social support in reducing trauma-related morbidity (Holahan & Moos, 1991).

Victims of stalking live in a state of persistent threat, regardless of any explicit threat or actual physical violence. This is aptly reflected in the terms that some stalking victims have used to describe their experience, such as "psychological terrorism" and "emotional rape". The survey of 100 stalking victims (Pathé & Mullen, 1997) found that in most cases stalking was reported to have had a deleterious impact on the victim's psychological, social and occupational functioning. The stalking necessitated major lifestyle changes in 94% of the cohort, such as changing routines, withdrawing from certain activities, installing (often costly) security or changing cars. Social activities were curtailed by 70% of the sample through fear of encountering the stalker, further alienating the victim from valuable supports. More than half either decreased their work hours or ceased their work or school attendance altogether, due to incessant telephone calls or other disruptions at the victim's workplace. Many experienced increasing absenteeism as a consequence of fear of travelling to work, medical appointments or attendance at court or police stations, and/or deteriorating work performance with the onset of stalking-related stress symptoms. Ultimately, more than a third of this cohort failed to return to work or moved to other jobs or schools. The victim felt compelled to move house in 40% of cases, some on two or more occasions, several moving interstate or overseas. The financial cost of these measures was often considerable, and in a few cases the relocations were futile. One stalker learnt his victim's new address from the real estate agent managing the sale of the victim's former home, and another was given the new interstate address by a naïve court official, after indicating he might infringe the 200 metre restriction on the victim's restraining order if he didn't actually know where she *lived*! Some stalking victims changed their names by deed poll and others attempted to alter their appearance by gaining significant amounts of weight, changing their hair colour or discarding their make-up. None of these measures proved effective in deterring the stalker, serving only to exacerbate the victim's plummeting self-esteem and social confidence.

The Pathé & Mullen (1997) sample almost unanimously reported deterioration in mental and physical well-being as a consequence of the harassment. Three quarters said they felt powerless in the face of the stalker's repeated intrusions, 65% admitted to aggressive thoughts toward the perpetrator, and in several cases the desire to retaliate was barely contained. (There are a number of examples of desperate stalking victims who have attacked and even killed their harasser; see Mullen & Pathé, 1994; Lion & Herschler, 1998). Guilt was common, especially where stalker and victim had a prior intimate relationship and there was a perception by the victim—that was often reinforced, with the benefit of hindsight, by the victim's family and friends—that he or she had made a poor choice of partner. Suicidal ideation and attempts were acknowledged by 25% of the sample, some believing this would be their only means of escaping a life sentence of stalking. Increased anxiety was experienced by 80% of respondents, manifesting as hypervigilance, "jumpiness", "shakes" and panic attacks, and 75% reported chronic insomnia, usually a consequence of nightmares or hyperarousal. Some stalking victims lay awake at night listening for nocturnal visitations, one woman parked her car directly underneath her bedroom window to ascertain whether her stalker tampered with it, and a number reported being unable to settle to sleep because their phone rang repeatedly through the night. These victims often described a preoccupation with their stalker, one commenting: "I think I've become as obsessed as the stalker himself".

Almost half the sample claimed significant appetite disturbance and consequent weight changes, while symptoms such as headaches, nausea, altered bowel habit, weakness and excessive tiredness were commonly acknowledged. Alcohol and cigarette consumption increased in a quarter of the sample and pre-existing physical conditions such as hypertension, eczema, asthma, psoriasis and peptic ulcers were reportedly exacerbated in some cases. Some women experienced hair thinning and loss, and miscarriages were attributed in a few cases to the stress of the harassment and/or stalking-induced alcohol misuse.

The constellation of symptoms that comprise a diagnosis of posttraumatic stress disorder (PTSD) according to the fourth edition of the *Diagnostic and Statistical Manual of Mental Disorders* (DSM-IV) (American Psychiatric Association, 1994)—avoidance, intrusive memories, numbing of responses and excessive arousal—well captures the psychological sequelae of stalking. Most victims in the Pathé & Mullen (1997) study endorsed at least one of the symptoms of PTSD, with 55% reporting recurrent intrusive recollections of the stalking and 38% describing avoidance or numbing symptoms, particularly feelings of detachment. The American Psychiatric Association's definition is, however, restrictive in that it only allows for psychological decompensation following a discrete or relatively circumscribed traumatic event that threatens or actually harms one's *physical* integrity. This conceptualisation fails to acknowledge the psychological distress produced by trauma that is protracted and repeated, and which occurs in the absence of any explicit threat or attack upon the victim, a not uncommon scenario in stalking. One third of this cohort met DSM-IV criteria for a diagnosis of PTSD, while a further 20% fulfilled all criteria but for the physical stressor. It was noted that posttraumatic stress symptoms occurred more commonly in female respondents and those subjected to following or violence. Victims who were pursued by a former intimate were also more likely to report posttraumatic stress symptoms, a reflection perhaps of the preponderance of women and of violence in stalking that arises in an "ex-intimate" context.

Westrup and colleagues (1999) examined the psychological impact of stalking on 36 female undergraduates, comparing them with 43 females who had been harassed and 48 controls. They administered standardised measures of psychological distress, including the Posttraumatic Stress Disorder Scale, the Symptom Checklist-90-R and the Self-Report Interpersonal Trust Scale. Relative to the comparison groups, these stalking victims were more likely to be depressed, have heightened interpersonal sensitivity and obsessive–compulsive symptoms, and more frequent and severe posttraumatic stress symptoms.

Participants in Hall's (1998) study of 145 stalking victims reported similar levels of distress and upheaval, with many leaving their jobs, and some changing their names and their appearance, even undergoing breast reductions to disguise their identities. Over 80% felt that their personalities had changed as a consequence of the stalking, with nearly 90% describing themselves as cautious, easily frightened (52%), paranoid (41%) and much more aggressive (27%). This was in stark contrast to the friendly, outgoing personality traits and behaviours that reportedly characterised this group prior to the onset of stalking. Another prominent finding was the increased loneliness, isolation and distrust experienced by these victims, and the fear and apprehension that persisted in those who were no longer being stalked.

Similarly, Purcell and co-workers (in press), in their random survey of 1844 adult men and women, found that the majority altered their lifestyle in response to being stalked. Almost a third increased their home security, 14% changed their telephone number to evade unwanted calls and 7% moved home. Work security was upgraded in 16% of cases and 15% reported absenteeism associated with the harassment (14 of these losing a month or more of work). A third of the sample modified their daily routine to avoid the stalker's intrusions and 16% restricted their social outings. In this study 14% of subjects reported deterioration in intimate partner relationships, and a similar proportion felt that family relationships had suffered. Some of the cohort attributed their increased consumption of alcohol and cigarettes (10% and 13% respectively) to being stalked. Sixty-nine per cent of victims sought assistance, usually from family and friends (51%), then police (35%), and health (13%) and legal (12%) professionals.

The destructive impact of stalkers upon their victims clearly highlights the need for effective and accessible services for both the stalker and those they target. It is also evident that these services cannot be restricted to celebrity victims or to those who suffer physical harm at the hands of their stalker. The distress and upheaval of stalking impact directly or indirectly on the lives of a significant sector of the population, and this can be minimised with appropriate intervention at the earliest juncture. Interventions aimed at curbing the stalker's activities should not ignore the needs of the victim or their role in the stalking dynamic. Indeed, in situations where the stalker is inaccessible or refractory to treatment, managing the victim's responses to their situation may be the most cogent means of discouraging the stalker's advances.

REDUCING THE IMPACT OF STALKING ON VICTIMS

Although specialised services and support organisations for victims of stalking are gradually emerging (Dziegielewski & Roberts, 1995; Orion, 1997; Pathé & Mullen, 1997), in most parts of the world there remains a scarcity of specific services for this group. Stalking victims are presenting to the helping professions in growing numbers. Many of them are subject to ongoing victimisation, some having endured years of harassment, while for others the stalker has left but his legacy continues. Previous efforts to secure help have frequently failed, reinforcing feelings of helplessness and distrust in the helping professions and the justice system. The following approaches are based largely on the authors' clinical experience of treating victims of stalking (Pathé & Mullen, 1997; Mullen et al., 2000). It is recognised that only a small percentage of victims will ever seek treatment at a mental health facility and these are likely to represent the more severely affected end of the stalking victim spectrum.

There are several priorities in the management of stalking victims. Such treatment has as its primary objective the alleviation of the victim's distress and the restoration of interpersonal, social and occupational functioning. It is nevertheless important to recognise that for those victims who continue to be pursued, any treatment endeavours must be accompanied by strategies that promote the safety of the victim and other parties at risk. Whenever stalking victims present it is essential to assess their suicide potential and continue to monitor this. The therapist must also ensure that the stalking victim is properly versed in practical strategies that discourage the perpetrator.

Those who work with stalking victims must adopt a supportive, educational and advocacy role, and possess the requisite therapeutic skills to address the psychological sequelae of stalking. A sound understanding of stalking behaviours is a necessary therapeutic tool, as is a comprehensive knowledge of the resources available to combat them. The therapist must have an encouraging and non-judgmental attitude and be capable of forging a trusting alliance with the victim. Treatment should ideally occur in a setting where all staff, including nonclinical administrative staff, are attuned to issues of safety and confidentiality.

COMBATING STALKING

Since stalking is not a uniform behaviour with any one consistent motive there is no single, effective method for halting it. Any attempt to combat stalking will need to take account of the individual circumstances, including the nature of the prior relationship between the victim and stalker, the stalker's likely motivation and psychopathology, his methods of harassment, and the relevant anti-stalking legislation in that jurisdiction. As a minimum, victims should be encouraged to inform trusted others of the stalking, report the harassment to police, review their home and/or work security practices, protect personal information, document all incidents related to the stalking and retain all evidence. Contact with their local victims of crime support organisation may also be beneficial (for further details see Gross, 1994; Schaum & Parrish, 1995; Mullen et al., 2000).

It is crucial to establish early in treatment that the victim has actually conveyed, in unambiguous terms, that they do not want the stalker's attentions. Victims may not understand that many stalkers are socially incompetent and will fail to grasp obvious, let alone subtle, social cues. Words to the effect of: "I do not want a relationship with you" require no additional explanation, and any attempts to elaborate will only give the stalker the opportunity to challenge the victim's decision. Victims are discouraged from making statements like: "I'm not interested in/too busy for a relationship right now" (stalker reads "but she will be later"), or "I already have a boyfriend" (stalker reads "She'd have me if *he* wasn't in the way"). Victims should be encouraged to be assertive and not to "let the stalker down gently" by delivering their message in instalments, as this is frequently perceived by the would-be suitor as indecision. Where appropriate these words should be delivered directly and in person, and in a public or other safe venue (Dziegielewski & Roberts, 1995). Delivering the message by phone or letter allows the stalker to protest that they didn't understand or receive it. Delivering it via friends may be interpreted as the *friend's* wishes, not those of the victim.

Once a victim has appropriately communicated to the stalker their need to be left in peace all further contact with the stalker should be avoided. The victim must understand that continuing appeals to logic or angry confrontations will only aggravate the situation. Each answered phone call (even the victim's voice on her answering machine), and each letter or gift returned to its sender only acknowledges and rewards the stalker's efforts. He has heard the message but chooses not to respect it, or he is prevented from doing so by virtue of major psychopathology that is amenable only to psychiatric intervention, not negotiation. There may be an initial escalation in the stalker's intrusions as a consequence of the thwarted contact so it is necessary to reinforce the perils of giving in to frustration. Victims must be warned that if a stalker phones them 100 times and the victim finally loses her resolve and responds, the stalker has learnt that persistence (indeed, *101 phone calls*) pays off.

Stalking laws are finding greater utility as a first-line approach to deterring stalkers. Criminal prosecution has a number of advantages, not the least of which is the capacity to ensure perpetrators are brought to psychiatric attention, by placing appropriate conditions on any custodial or noncustodial disposition. Civil remedies remain a popular initial approach, however. It is wise for victims to initiate protective injunctions (known variously as restraining orders, non-molestation orders or intervention orders) as early as possible in the course of the harassment. This will convey unequivocally to most stalkers that their behaviour is unwanted and distressing; the greater the delay the more intense will be the stalker's emotional investment in their victim and consequently the more unreasonable their response to the order is likely to be. There is no universal recommendation about the use of protective orders, and victims should be advised to consult with police, their legal adviser, victims of crime support services and/or mental health specialists to determine whether such an order would be of benefit given their individual circumstances. The overriding message to anyone seeking a protective injunction, especially if the stalker is an ex-intimate, is that the period immediately following the issuance of the order is an emotionally charged time and often one of heightened risk of physical harm. These orders should never bring with them expectations, at least in the immediate term, of protection and resolution of stalking.

Victims of cyberstalking may be subjected to repeated threats or harassing behaviour over the Internet, via email, chat rooms, newsgroups or other electronic communications (Deirmenjian, 1999). Online stalking can be especially problematic (and potentially endanger the victim) when the perpetrator, armed with their victim's naively imparted personal details, extends the pursuit offline. Victims are advised to tell the offending party that his communications are unwanted and to insist that he stop. They should not respond further nor should they return the harassment or respond to flaming (provocation online). It is best to leave a hostile situation by logging off or surfing elsewhere. They should log all evidence at first notice and download and retain all relevant email for any subsequent police investigation. If the cyberstalking continues the victim should contact the site administrator of the stalker's Internet Service Provider or, in the case of email, of the system from which the stalker is mailing the victim. If the stalking persists, the police should be notified and provided with all tangible evidence (for example, downloaded messages, chat room transcripts or web page URLs). Useful organisations for victims of cyberstalking include CyberAngels, a network of volunteers that monitors the Internet and investigates harassment complaints in addition to offering information and moral support to victims, and working to Halt Online Abuse (see reference list for the URLs of these organisations).

Victims who are impelled to confront their stalker in court will need support. Some stalkers deliberately initiate legal action—typically by appealing against protective injunctions or by making spurious allegations against the victim—to provoke courtroom contact or to exact revenge. The victim should be accompanied by a reliable friend or family member and, wherever possible, should contact in advance a court support worker who familiarises witnesses with court protocol as well as providing practical and emotional support. In many jurisdictions it is now possible to minimise face-to-face contact with the stalker by giving evidence from a place other than the courtroom using closed-circuit television or by employing screens to remove the stalker from the victim's direct line of vision. The presiding magistrate or judge, police prosecutor, court support services, security staff and the victim's lawyer should be alerted if there is any threat to the victim's safety.

CLINICAL APPROACHES TO STALKING VICTIMS

The clinical management of stalking victims is a complex undertaking and in some cases a protracted one. This is because the course of the stalking may be variable and chronic, but also some victims will require professional intervention long after the stalking has been brought under control.

Psychological Therapies

Victims of stalking often respond to cognitive-orientated psychological therapies because stalking breaches previously held assumptions about their safety. The belief of victims in their strength and resilience and their confidence in the reasonable and predictable nature of the world are frequently shattered, to be replaced with feelings of extreme vulnerability and an expectation of pervasive danger and unpredictable harm. Cognitive therapies attempt to restructure these morbid perceptions of the world that threaten the victim's adaptation and functioning. Of course, such assumptions and evaluations may be valid in cases of ongoing victimisation, and in these circumstances psychological therapies must focus on rebuilding a realistic and viable sense of safety for the victim, in conjunction with measures that optimise the victim's safety and seek to discourage the stalker's continued intrusions.

Avoidance symptoms may also need to be addressed. Although the avoidance of threatening situations or cues, such as the ringing of the telephone, is entirely reasonable and even adaptive in some cases, avoidance can extend to other areas of the victim's life, such that the victim can no longer drive, go to work or even leave home. This can have a devastating impact on the victim's recovery. Avoidance can respond to behavioural therapies such as prolonged exposure and stress inoculation, which aim to assist victims to gradually resume abandoned activities and manage the associated anxiety (Foa & Meadows, 1997).

Biological therapies

Pharmacotherapy is an important adjunct to cognitive–behavioural and supportive approaches in those victims who develop comorbid psychiatric disorders, or for whom anxiety symptoms are severe and disabling. In prescribing medication the treating clinician should remember that for some stalking victims the harassment and its psychological sequelae may have a chronic course, with the potential requirement for long-term chemical treatment. Moreover, because the majority of stalking victims have had no previous exposure to psychotropic agents, clinicians should be judicious in their choice and dose of drug in order to avoid unpleasant side effects that compound the victim's distress and dysfunction.

Selective serotonin reuptake inhibitor (SSRI) antidepressants have demonstrated efficacy in the treatment of stress-related symptoms. A recent randomised, double-blind, placebo-controlled trial of sertraline (50–200 mg/day) in 187 outpatients with PTSD (mostly secondary to physical or sexual assault) offered further support for this. Sertraline treatment produced greater improvement compared to the placebo group in a number of areas including avoidance/numbing experiences, social and occupational functioning and overall quality of life scores (Brady et al., 2000). SSRIs are an appealing choice in the pharmacotherapy of stress-related syndromes because of their proven efficacy in comorbid conditions such as alcohol abuse, depression and panic disorder (Brady et al., 1995).

The use of benzodiazepine anxiolytics such as Valium (diazepam) and hypnotics such as Rohypnol (flunitrazepam) should be minimised in this patient population, largely because of the potential for long-term use of these agents and resultant problems of tolerance and dependence. Also, the effects of this class of drugs on cognitive functioning may exacerbate the victim's social and vocational impairment and their potential disinhibiting properties limits their use in patients who may be experiencing suicidal or homicidal ideation. They are best reserved for bringing extreme distress under rapid control, but always in conjunction with the aforementioned psychological therapies that emphasise control over negative emotional states and long-term self-efficacy.

Tricyclic antidepressants have a role in the treatment of stalking victims, especially in those with high levels of arousal, severe insomnia and comorbid depression, but in contemporary practice they are usually reserved for patients who are unable to tolerate the newer SSRI antidepressants (Mullen et al., 2000). Appropriate caution must be exercised in prescribing these agents to potentially suicidal individuals given their substantially greater toxicity in overdose. Moclobemide, a reversible MAO-A inhibitor antidepressant, has been used with some success in stalking victims, producing a marked reduction in depressive and anxiety symptoms and, to a lesser extent, avoidance/numbing episodes (Mullen et al., 2000).

Finally, attention should be paid to the victim's general health, which may be compromised by the effects of chronic stress, poor sleep and inadequate diet, self-neglect, the abuse of alcohol, painkillers or tranquillisers, and increased cigarette consumption. One hypertensive stalking victim under our psychiatric care suffered a mild stroke, possibly as a consequence of preoccupation with his stalker to the extent that he forgot to take vital blood pressure medication. Another developed severe gastritis after taking arthritis medication without food, drinking excessive quantities of alcohol and doubling her one-pack a day cigarette habit. In some cases it may be necessary to refer the victim for further medical assessment or to an alcohol/drug rehabilitation programme.

Partner and Family Therapies

It is often appropriate and indeed beneficial to involve the victim's partner and other family members in therapeutic interventions. These people can provide valuable collateral information that assists in devising optimal strategies to counter the stalking. Many are likely to be suffering the indirect effects of stalking, such as lifestyle disruptions and altered relationship dynamics, and some will be secondary targets of the stalker's threats and violence. Again, personal safety issues are paramount. It is necessary to provide education about stalking and its impact, since informed loved ones are better equipped to address security needs and offer constructive support to the primary victim. Working with partners and families often facilitates the victim's recovery as they will be less inclined to criticise or judge the victim. Some family members may ultimately require referral for individual counselling or a support group.

Group Therapies

Self-help groups for victims of stalking can play a significant role in their rehabilitation by diminishing feelings of isolation and alienation. In the supportive environment they afford, participants experience mutual understanding, validation and trust. Victims regard these groups as safe venues for sharing feelings of anger, frustration and loss. Groups can also function as a useful resource for stalking victims in the absence of any other dedicated service, as participants can exchange helpful tips, reading matter, security equipment and useful contacts. Therapeutic support groups should ideally be facilitated by a clinician who is familiar with the issues confronting stalking victims and the complex psychological sequelae associated with being stalked. The role of these therapists is to enhance and maintain mutual support in the group as well as focusing on the reduction of psychological distress by instructing group members in realistic techniques to manage anxiety symptoms, anger and/or depression.

Support Organisations for Victims of Stalking

Several prominent support organisations have been established for victims of stalking in recent years. They generally provide educational and safety information together with practical advice and emotional support for victims and their families. Most, such as Survivors of Stalking (SOS) in the USA and the National Anti-Stalking and Harassment Campaign and Support Association (NASH) in the UK, were founded by stalking victims disillusioned with existing services (Orion, 1997; Mullen et al., 2000).

The stalking victim should be encouraged to be an active participant in the quest to eradicate stalking from their life. Activities such as reviewing the anti-stalking legislation in their jurisdiction or writing to local politicians reinforces the message that victims are ultimately responsible for their own safety and protection (a function that no one else can provide on a daily basis) and fosters independence and enhanced self-efficacy. There will, however, be some victims who have become so disabled by their ordeal that the therapist may need to assume a more active role, advocating on the victim's behalf and galvanising other services to intervene as appropriate.

It behoves all who work with stalkers and stalking victims to educate others about the issues, not only to facilitate appropriate intervention for stalkers and optimise support for victims but also to prevent future victims. Such education should not be confined to the family and friends of victims of stalking but encompass also police, lawyers, the judiciary and the public at large. Indeed, given the prevalence of stalking behaviours in our community and the extent of the damage they inflict it is crucial that the plight of the stalking victim be recognised as a legitimate concern for society as a whole. This is not only because of the considerable cost of supporting victims who can no longer work and who may have long-term health care needs but because virtually every one of us has the potential to become the victim of another's unwanted attentions. The effective management of this crime requires the education, cooperation and coordination of legislators, law enforcement, the judiciary, treatment services and—importantly—stalking victims themselves.

REFERENCES

American Association of University Women (1993). *Hostile Hallways: The AAUW Survey on Sexual Harassment in American Schools*. Washington, DC: American Association of University Women.

American Psychiatric Association (1994). *Diagnostic and Statistical Manual of Mental Disorders*, 4th edition. Washington, DC: APA.

Australian Bureau of Statistics (1996). *Women's Safety, Australia, 1996*. Canberra: Commonwealth of Australia.

Baum A., Cohen L. & Hall M. (1993). Control and intrusive memories as possible determinants of chronic stress. *Psychosomatic Medicine*, **55**, 274–86.

Brady K.T., Sonne S.C. & Roberts J.M. (1995). Sertraline treatment of comorbid posttraumatic stress disorder and alcohol dependence. *Journal of Clinical Psychiatry*, **56**, 502–5.

Brady K, Pearlstein T. & Farfel, G.M. (2000). Efficacy and safety of sertraline treatment of posttraumatic stress disorder: a randomized controlled trial. *JAMA*, **283**, 1837–44.

de Becker G. (1997). *The Gift of Fear: Survival Signals that Protect us from Violence*. London: Bloomsbury.

Deirmenjian J.M. (1999). Stalking in cyberspace. *Journal of the American Academy of Psychiatry and Law*, **27**(3), 407–13.

Dziegielewski S.F. & Roberts A.R. (1995). Stalking victims and survivors: identification, legal remedies, and crisis treatment. In A.R. Roberts (ed.) *Crisis Intervention and Time-Limited Cognitive Treatment* (pp. 73–90). Thousand Oaks, CA: Sage Publications.

Emerson R.M., Ferris K.O. & Gardner C.B. (1998). On being stalked. *Social Problems*, **45**, 289–314.

Foa E. & Meadows E. (1997). Psychosocial treatments for posttraumatic stress disorder: a critical review. *Annual Review of Psychology*, **48**, 449–80.

Fremouw W.J., Westrup D. & Pennypacker J. (1997). Stalking on campus: the prevalence and strategies for coping with stalking. *Journal of Forensic Sciences*, **42**, 666–69.

Gross L. (1994). *To Have or to Harm: True Stories of Stalkers and their Victims*. New York: Warner Books.

Hall D.M. (1998). The victims of stalking. In J. Reid Meloy (ed.) *The Psychology of Stalking: Clinical and Forensic Perspectives* (pp. 113–37). San Diego, CA: Academic Press.

Harmon R.B., Rosner R. & Owens H. (1995) Obsessional harassment and erotomania in a criminal court population. *Journal of Forensic Sciences*, **40**, 188–96.

Holahan C.J. & Moos R.H. (1991) Life stressors, personal and social resources, and depression: a 4-year structural model. *Journal of Abnormal Psychology*, **100**, 31–8.

Jason L.A., Reichler A., Easton J., Neal A. & Wilson M. (1984) Female harassment after ending a relationship: a preliminary study. *Alternative Lifestyles*, **6**, 259–69.

Jones C. (1996) Criminal harassment (or stalking). *Juristat*, **16**(12) (see: *www.chass.utoronto.ca:8080/~cjones/pub/stalking*).

Lion J.R. & Herschler J.A. (1998). The stalking of clinicians by their patients. In J. Reid Meloy (ed.) *The Psychology of Stalking: Clinical and Forensic Perspectives* (pp. 163–73). San Diego, CA: Academic Press.

McCann T. (2000). A descriptive study of child and adolescent obsessional followers. *Journal of Forensic Sciences*, **45**(1), 195–9.

Meloy J.R. (1996). Stalking (obsessional following): a review of some preliminary studies. *Aggression and Violent Behaviour*, **1**, 147–62.

Meloy J.R. & Gothard S. (1995). A demographic and clinical comparison of obsessional followers and offenders with mental disorders. *American Journal of Psychiatry*, **152**, 258–63.

Mullen P.E. & Pathé M. (1994). Stalking and the pathologies of love. *Australian and New Zealand Journal of Psychiatry*, **28**, 469–77.

Mullen P.E., Pathé M., Purcell R. & Stuart G.W. (1999). Study of stalkers. *American Journal of Psychiatry*, **156**, 1244–9.

Mullen P.E., Pathé M. & Purcell R. (2000). *Stalkers and their Victims*. Cambridge: Cambridge University Press.

Orion D. (1997). *I Know You Really Love Me: A Psychiatrist's Journal of Erotomania, Stalking, and Obsessive Love*. New York: Macmillan.

Pathé M. & Mullen P.E. (1997). The impact of stalkers on their victims. *British Journal of Psychiatry*, **170**, 12–17.

Purcell R., Pathé M. & Mullen P.E. (in press). The incidence and nature of stalking in the Australian community. *Australian and New Zealand Journal of Psychiatry*.

Ritchie J. (1995). *Stalkers*. London: HarperCollins.

Schaum M. & Parrish K. (1995). *Stalked: Breaking the Silence on the Crime of Stalking in America*. New York: Pocket Books.

Simon R.I. (1996). Workplace violence. In Simon R.I. (ed.) *Bad Men do What Good Men Dream* (pp. 237–77). Washington, DC: American Psychiatric Press.

Tjaden P. & Thoennes N. (1998). *Stalking in America: Findings from the National Violence against Women Survey*. Washington, DC: National Institute of Justice and Center for Disease Control and Prevention.

Westrup D., Fremouw W.J., Thompson R.N. & Lewis S.F. (1999) The psychological impact of stalking on female undergraduates. *Journal of Forensic Sciences*, **44**(3), 554–7.

Zona M.A., Sharma K.K. & Lane J. (1993) A comparative study of erotomanic and obsessional subjects in a forensic sample. *Journal of Forensic Sciences*, **38**, 894–903.

Internet Addresses

CyberAngels: http://www.cyberangels.org

Working to Halt Online Abuse: www.haltabuse.org

CHAPTER 2

The Psychological Consequences of Stalking Victimisation

ERIC BLAAUW, FRANS WILLEM WINKEL
Vrije Universiteit Amsterdam

LORRAINE SHERIDAN
University of Leicester

MARIJKE MALSCH
Netherlands Institute for the Study of Law and Criminality, Leiden

and

ELLA ARENSMAN
Leiden University

INTRODUCTION

There is very little information on the impact that stalking has on victims (Meloy, 1996; Pathé & Mullen, 1997), despite an ever increasing awareness that this crime does constitute a noteworthy public health issue. In particular, very few studies have considered the economic and social effect on victims of being stalked and even less attention has been paid to the psychological or psychiatric consequences of stalking. In Australia, Pathé & Mullen (1997) distributed questionnaires among 100 stalking victims who contacted the authors or were referred to the authors' clinic. Three studies carried out in the USA took a similar approach. In Chicago, Jason and colleagues (1984) interviewed 50 women who had been subjected to

Stalking and Psychosexual Obsession: Psychological Perspectives for Prevention, Policing and Treatment.
Edited by J. Boon and L. Sheridan. © 2002 John Wiley & Sons, Ltd.

persistent harassment for at least one month. Brewster (1997) used victim service agencies and law enforcement agencies to identify 187 Pennsylvanian women who were recent former intimate stalking victims. In yet another study in the United States, Hall (1998) identified 145 self-defined stalking victims by using regional voicemail boxes that had been set up in seven target cities.

These studies have invariably shown that stalking results in serious economic and social difficulties for victims. In particular, in many cases the victims suffer direct financial loss (Brewster, 1997), are forced to leave their job or place of education, "go underground" (i.e. temporarily living and working elsewhere) or move permanently to a new area of the country, change their appearance in a variety of ways, change their name, take greater security precautions both in the home and while away from home, and generally avoid social contact etc. (Brewster, 1997; Hall, 1998; Jason et al., 1984; Pathé & Mullen, 1997; Tjaden & Thoennes, 1997). This research also shows unsurprisingly that stalking results in negative psychological effects for almost all its victims, eliciting a greater degree of distrust, suspicion, caution, fear, nervousness, anger, paranoia, depression and introversion. This manifests itself through many of the stereotypical physical symptoms of stress, such as chronic sleep disturbance, excessive tiredness and weakness, tension, headaches, appetite disturbance and persistent nausea (Brewster, 1997; Pathé & Mullen, 1997). Furthermore, many stalking victims report that stalking results in personality change (Hall, 1998) and a propensity to seriously consider or attempt suicide (Pathé & Mullen, 1997). Specifically, 37% of the victims fulfil the DSM-IV criteria for a diagnosis of posttraumatic stress disorder (PTSD). Furthermore, an additional 18% would have fulfilled all the criteria if they had also been exposed to a stressor that involved actual or threatened physical harm or a threat to one's physical integrity (Pathé & Mullen, 1997).

Unfortunately, only two of the aforementioned studies included data from the victims concerning standardised measures of psychopathology (Brewster, 1997; Pathé & Mullen, 1997) and none of the studies compared the levels of psychopathology experienced by stalking victims and by individuals from community samples. Therefore, from a scientific point of view there is little firm evidence that stalking is associated with a *heightened* prevalence of psychopathology among victims. Nevertheless, given the high levels of consistency in findings about the economical, social, psychological and psychiatric problems experienced by stalking victims, it seems reasonable to conclude that stalking poses a serious mental health threat to victims.

PSYCHOPATHOLOGY AMONG STALKING
VICTIMS IN THE NETHERLANDS

On 12th July 2000 stalking became a punishable offence in the Netherlands. Before that date, it was possible to prosecute only certain stalking behaviours, like trespassing, following and assault, but it was not possible to prosecute the total array of stalking behaviours (Malsch & Blaauw, 2000). The Netherlands has about 16 million inhabitants. The development of the Dutch stalking law was to some extent attributable to a published report containing a description of the experiences of persons who were registered as victims at the Dutch Anti-Stalking Foundation (SAS). SAS strived towards a public recognition of stalking as a public health issue and the criminalisation of stalking behaviours by providing information to the public. SAS was dissolved at the end of 2000 because the founders had achieved their goal.

In 1998 a questionnaire was distributed among the 470 members of SAS. A total of 266 questionnaires were returned by mail, of which 246 were considered suitable for analysis. The questionnaire included a Dutch translation (Koeter & Ormel, 1991) of the 28-item version of the General Health Questionnaire (GHQ-28) (Goldberg & Hillier, 1979). The GHQ-28 is a self-administered questionnaire designed to identify individuals with a diagnosable psychiatric disorder (for further information see Goldberg & Hillier, 1979; Koeter & Ormel, 1991).

The responses to the GHQ-28 revealed strikingly high levels of psychopathology among stalking victims in the Netherlands, even though victims differed markedly in their reports of psychiatric symptoms. Stalking victims' average GHQ-28 total score and the scores on the sub-scales Somatic Symptoms, Anxiety and Insomnia, Social Dysfunction, and Severe Depression were more in line with those of psychiatric outpatients than with those of general practitioner patients or the Dutch general population (see Blaauw et al., 2002). In confirmation of this, 77% of the stalking victims scored six points or higher on the GHQ. This indicates that they were suffering from a diagnosable psychiatric disorder. Thus, not only were the victims' symptom levels found to be more in accordance with those of psychiatric outpatients than with those of general population samples, but also three-quarters of the victims displayed a symptom level that indicated psychiatric disorder. It must be concluded from these findings that stalking is indeed associated with serious mental health problems among victims (see also Brewster, 1997; Hall, 1998; Pathé & Mullen, 1997).

STALKING BEHAVIOURS AND PSYCHOPATHOLOGY AMONG VICTIMS

Little is known about the impact of specific stalking behaviours on victim's psychopathology. Pathé & Mullen (1997) noted that victims were more likely to suffer posttraumatic stress symptoms if they had been followed or exposed to violence, and that "victims indicated that they might have coped better with the more tangible damage of physical assault" than with the "stalker's constant intrusions and menace" (p. 15).

In the Dutch study, the questionnaire contained questions about ten features of stalking behaviour (cf. Pathé & Mullen, 1997; Wright et al., 1996), namely telephone calls, letters, surveillance of victim's home, following, unlawful entry, destruction or theft of property, direct unwanted approach, threats about bodily harm or death, physical assault (including sexual assault) and other behaviours. In Table 2.1 it can be seen that many of these stalking behaviours have fairly equal distributions in the different samples of victims that have been examined by previous research. The stalking behaviours reported most commonly by victims in all the studies were direct unwanted approach, following, surveillance of their homes and receiving harassing telephone calls. Direct unwanted approach and receiving harassing telephone calls were by far the most common stalking behaviours in the Dutch study. More than half of these telephone calls were made at night and included continuous pleas (often for reinstating a former relationship), negative remarks, death threats or continuous silence.

Table 2.1. Features of stalking behaviour (%) in the present study, including a comparison with samples from three other studies

Stalking behaviour	Present study	Brewster (1997)	Hall (1998)	Pathé & Mullen (1997)
Telephone calls	86	90	87	78
Sending letters	41	59	50	62
Surveillance of victim's home	74	54	84	—
Following	74	68	80	71
Unlawful entry into home	41	36	39	—
Destruction of property	65*	44	43	36
Direct unwanted approach	92	—	—	79
Physical assault	56	46	38	34
Threats to harm or kill victim	45	53	41	51
Duration of stalking (months)				
Median duration	33	12	No data	24
Range	2–476	1–456	1–372	1–240

* Including theft of property.

One victim reported receiving approximately 50 telephone calls each day and night.

There were also some minor differences between the Dutch results and those of other studies. Physical assault was more common in the former, while receiving letters was less common. Destruction of property was also more common in the Dutch sample, although this could be because the definition of this particular stalking act also included incidences of theft. Furthermore, approximately half of the Dutch victims spontaneously reported other stalking behaviours, such as rumour spreading, ordering of goods for the victim, false accusations, injuring of pets and abduction. It is unknown how many of these stalking behaviours were also reported in the other studies. Nonetheless, the fairly equal distributions of the other stalking behaviours indicate that to a large extent stalking behaviours are similar in different countries (see also Sheridan & Davies, 2001).

The victims in the Dutch study reported having experienced a median of six stalking behaviours. Most respondents reported having been the victim of several different intrusive behaviours (median $= 3$, $M = 2.6$, $SD = 1.2$) and several violent behaviours (median $= 2$, $M = 1.6$, $SD = 1.0$). These findings indicate that the majority of the victims were exposed to an extensive array of stalking behaviours. Note also, however, that only 7% of victims reported that they were not exposed to intrusive following behaviours (e.g. surveillance of victim's home, following, unlawful entry, unwanted approach) and only 15% reported that they were not exposed to violent behaviours (destruction/theft of property, threats, assaults).

In line with the victims that constituted Pathé & Mullen's (1997) Australian sample, the victims in the Dutch sample reported higher symptom levels when the stalking they experienced included following or theft/destruction of property (for more information about the analyses, see Blaauw et al., 2002). Interestingly though, no relationship was found between exposure to physical assault and symptoms of psychopathology. Furthermore, contrary to the notion of Pathé & Mullen (1997), neither the number of violent behaviours nor the number of intrusive behaviours was significantly associated with the level of psychopathology. Put simply, Dutch victims did not cope better with violent behaviours than with constant intrusive behaviours.

STALKER-VICTIM RELATIONSHIP

Several classifications of stalking victims are used in the literature, all based on the prior relationship between victim and stalker. Usually the largest category consists of ex-intimates, the commonest victim profile being a woman who has previously shared an intimate relationship with her (usually male) stalker (Mullen et al., 2000, p. 45). The second largest category usually consists of casual acquaintances and friends, professional contacts (health care providers, lawyers, teachers) and workplace contacts. The third category consists of strangers, where the victim is not aware of any prior contact with the stalker. In all studies, male stalkers are found to be far more common than female stalkers and female victims are found to be far more common than male victims. The same is true in the Dutch sample, where the majority of victims were ex-intimates (67%), 27% were prior acquaintances and 7% were strangers. In total, 89% of the victims were female and 87% of the stalkers were male. The majority of stalkers and victims (56%) were of about equal age, with an age difference of less than five years. However, there were also some cases where the stalker was several decades older or younger than the victim.

Meloy (1996) noted that stalking behaviours are related to the type of relationship between stalkers and their victims, which raises the question of whether the type of stalker–victim relationship is also related to heightened levels of symptomatology. Pathé & Mullen (1997) found that post-traumatic stress symptoms were more likely to be experienced by those victims reporting a prior relationship with their stalker. In the Dutch sample of victims symptom levels were not found to be associated with the type of stalker–victim relationship (see Blaauw et al., 2002). In addition, the age of the stalker or the victim and the age difference between stalker and victim were not found to have a relationship with the symptom levels. However, female victims were more likely to experience higher levels of symptoms than were male victims, which is not an odd finding because women in all sorts of samples usually score higher on measures of psychopathology than do men.

COUNTERMEASURES

Stalking victims often take many countermeasures to prevent stalking from re-occurring or to cope with their experience, like seeking mental health care assistance, turning to the police, starting a lawsuit, acquiring an unlisted telephone number, relocating residence, going underground, quitting their job or working less, changing jobs, avoiding social outings, taking additional security measures, and assaulting the stalker. In the study in the Netherlands, closed-ended questions explored these eleven countermeasures. The findings showed that all victims had taken one or more countermeasures in attempts to deal with their stalking experience (median $= 6$, $M = 5.8$, $SD = 2.1$). Many had consulted mental health care agencies or professionals (93%) or the police (89%) whereas 45% had started a lawsuit. Consistent with the findings of Brewster (1997) and Pathé & Mullen (1997), the mental health and legal systems were perceived to have let the victims down due to disbelief or powerlessness on the part of the police, insufficient evidence for sentencing, unresponsiveness or incompetence of mental health professionals, or no effects of warnings, arrests, sentences or restraining orders. Indeed, many victims had been forced to take action themselves by acquiring an unlisted telephone number (81%), relocating (44%), going underground (40%), quitting their job or working less (39%), changing jobs (21%), avoiding social outings (63%), and taking additional security measures (65%). Nineteen per cent of the victims went even further and assaulted the stalker or had the stalker assaulted by friends or acquaintances (although a few of these assaults were acts of self-defence). Again, many of these actions did not terminate the stalking, with the perpetrator managing to contact their victim again, leading to the perception that "nothing seems to work". Again, this apparent stress and helplessness seemed to feed through into symptoms of psychopathology: victims who reported having taken six or more measures to stop their stalking reported significantly more symptoms than did victims who had done less. Thus, it is uncertain whether the countermeasures were effective in stopping the stalking experience, and it is equally unclear whether these countermeasures had a *psychological* benefit for the victim.

OTHER STALKING FEATURES

It is well known that stalking experiences may vary in intensity, duration and intrusiveness. This was also found to be true in the Dutch sample of victims. Earlier it was noted that the Dutch sample of victims were exposed to a median number of six stalking behaviours, which indicates a highly intrusive experience. The average duration of exposure was almost five years in the Dutch sample and clearly this was not due to one or two outlying cases of considerable duration: 66% of the Dutch sample reported that their stalking had persisted for at least two years and 13% reported that their stalking had lasted for more than ten years. This experience of stalking was not incessant, of course, since many of our Dutch victims claimed that the frequency of stalking differed from day to day, month to month and year to year, consistent with the findings of Brewster (1997) and Hall (1998). Indeed, in several cases the stalker would disappear for several months only to re-appear and resume their actions. In short, these findings indicate that exposure to stalking was often a long-term experience. Furthermore, the frequency of the stalking behaviour varied over time, occurring on a daily basis for 68% of cases at their onset but only 34% of cases at the end of the stalking episode. In approximately half of the Dutch cases (47%), the frequency of the stalking behaviour had decreased over time. However, in 48% of cases the frequency of stalking remained constant over time, and in a further 4% it had actually increased. Thus, all in all these findings indicate a pattern of prolonged and persistent stalking.

Hardly anything is known about the relationship between the frequency, duration, intensity and intrusiveness of stalking behaviour on the one hand and the seriousness of victims' symptoms on the other. One means of understanding this may lie in Dohrenwend's (1998) adversity–distress model. The model argues that suffering a stressful life event causes a direct increase in psychological distress, such that the more stressful the event(s) so the worse the psychological impact should be. This model might indeed lead us to expect the high psychopathology symptom levels witnessed in stalking victims. Their prolonged, pervasive and intensive stressful experiences would be expected to lead to major psychological distress. Experiences of this nature lead to a higher degree of toxic exposure, which would lead to a higher chance of psychological distress or the possibility of a higher *degree* of psychological distress.

Analyses did indeed show that the Dutch victims reported more symptoms when recent stalking behaviours occurred on a daily basis and when the frequency of stalking had not decreased (see Blaauw et al., 2002). Analyses also showed that victims who reported exposure to six or more stalking behaviours had more symptoms of psychopathology than victims who reported exposure to fewer stalking behaviours. Symptoms were less severe when the victims had been exposed to a prolonged period of stalking, which may be explained by Dohrenwend's (1998, p. 546) claim that chronic stressors can lead to habituation on the part of sufferers. Symptoms of psychopathology were not related to the cessation of stalking, which seems remarkable, or to how recently the stalking experience had started.

INDIVIDUAL DIFFERENCES

Stalking possesses many of the features that may produce symptoms of psychopathology (see also Mullen et al., 2000). Victims are often subjected to many intrusive behaviours and many violent behaviours over which they have no or limited control. In addition, victims often have to endure these behaviours for a long time, often not knowing when and how the stalker will strike again. Over time stalking experiences may vary in intensity, duration and intrusiveness. It was discussed that victims' symptom levels were found to be high in comparison with those of people in the wider community and that these symptom levels were found to be dependent on the type (following, theft/destruction of property) and number of stalking behaviours, the victim's sex, the number of countermeasures taken by the victim, the frequency of stalking, the duration of the experience, whether stalking occurred on a daily basis and whether the frequency of stalking had decreased. As we have also seen, several of these aspects of stalking are interrelated. Consequently, a stepwise regression analysis was used to analyse multivariate relationships between victims' symptoms of psychopathology (as indicated by their GHQ-28 total score) and the different features of stalking (see Blaauw et al., 2002). This showed that two features of the stalking were able to explain 9% of the high levels of symptoms experienced by victims. These two features were a decrease of the frequency of stalking and the number of countermeasures. Other stalking features did not significantly explain any additional variance.

In short, this means that the adversity–distress model leaves unexplained 91% of the variance in victims' symptoms of psychopathology. The model cannot explain the many instances where relatively mild stalking led to major psychological disturbance or where terrible stalking episodes led to relatively few symptoms in their victims. Clearly then, a dose–reponse type approach, such as that proposed by the adversity–distress model, cannot explain a great deal of stalking victims' symptomatology. A better explanation may be provided by Bowman's (1997) vulnerability (resilience)–distress model. Research on the model followed several studies of PTSD that had identified a "disappointingly weak" relationship between mental health outcomes and life events. Bowman (1997) concluded that "People respond to acute events with great individual variability which arises mostly from individual differences in long-standing qualities . . . When both event and pre-event individual difference factors are included in studying post-event responses, individual differences account for more of the variance in response than event features do" (p. 35).

Consistent with this is the finding that victims reported less pathology when the stalking period was relatively prolonged. Perhaps some of these victims had regained the resilience needed to deal with their stalking. This in turn may explain why victims' symptoms were less pronounced when they had taken relatively few countermeasures. Perhaps they still felt that they could deal with their prevailing circumstances. Individual differences such as resilience to stalking may account for the lack of success of the adversity–distress model in explaining the data. It is likely that some of the victims were already vulnerable to psychopathology prior to the onset of their stalking episode. For example, one woman had been raped repeatedly and had been forced by her husband to have sex with strangers, another woman had suffered from PTSD symptoms after a car accident, and a third woman claimed that her husband and a psychiatrist had conspired against her during her treatment for sexual problems. Indeed, previous psychological difficulties were reported by approximately half of the victims (although it remains unclear whether these difficulties were experienced recently or a long time prior to the onset of stalking). Furthermore, a small minority of the Dutch victims reported bizarre or even unlikely stalking behaviours, which suggests that these reports were more likely to be reflections of the personality of the respondents in question rather than descriptions of actual stalking behaviour. One woman claimed to be stalked by her gynaecologist who "wanted to see her naked again". Another woman claimed to be stalked by the police and by two strangers who allegedly spoke to her through the walls of her living room. A third woman claimed to be followed "everywhere, 24 hours per day by people who were never seen". A fourth woman claimed that groups of people were sometimes loitering nearby, which was logical because she was living near to a dancing school. One man even claimed to be stalked by the police because they gave him parking fines too often.

It seems then that the vulnerability (resilience)–distress model may help to explain the level of psychological distress experienced by victims of stalking, perhaps in conjunction with the adversity–distress model. If so, then this has some important therapeutic implications. In particular, better outcomes might be expected when therapists focus on improving victims' general resilience to stalking, improving their coping skills and decreasing their vulnerability. Less attention should be paid to dealing specifically with the stalking episode. In the light of this it is unfortunate that the Dutch research did not directly investigate vulnerability factors, and future research might consider these in more detail. Furthermore, the participants in the present research were all registered with the Dutch Anti-Stalking Foundation. As with other victim studies (Brewster, 1997; Hall, 1998; Pathé & Mullen, 1997) this sample may of course represent the most seriously stalked, those with the poorest coping strategies, or indeed any one of the other numerous characteristics that could set them apart from the population as a whole. Nonetheless, it can be concluded that stalking victims struggle with serious mental health problems that may not necessarily be related to their stalking experience.

REFERENCES

Blaauw, E., Winkel, F.W., Arensman, E., Sheridan, L. & Freeve, A. (2002). The toll of stalking: the relationship between features of stalking and psychopathology of victims. *Journal of Interpersonal Violence*, **17**, 50–63.

Bowman, M. (1997). *Individual Differences in Posttraumatic Response: Problems with the Adversity–Stress Connection*. Majwa, NJ: Lawrence Erlbaum.

Brewster, M. P. (1997). *An Exploration of the Experiences and Needs of Former Intimate Stalking Victims: Final Report Submitted to the National Institute of Justice*. West Chester, PA: West Chester University.

Dohrenwend, B. P. (1998). *Adversity, Distress and Psychopathology*. New York: Oxford University Press.

Goldberg, D. P. & Hillier, V. F. (1979). A scaled version of the General Health Questionnaire. *Psychological Medicine*, **9**, 139–45.

Hall, D. M. (1998). The victims of stalking. In J. Reid Meloy (ed.), *The Psychology of Stalking: Clinical and Forensic Perspectives* (pp. 113–37). San Diego, CA: Academic Press.

Jason, L. A., Reichler, A., Easton, J., Neal, A. & Wilson, M. (1984). Female harassment after ending a relationship: a preliminary study. *Alternative Lifestyles*, **6**, 259–69.

Koeter, M. W. J. & Ormel, J. (1991). *General Health Questionnaire Nederlandse bewerking* (Dutch version). Lisse: Swets & Seitlinger.

Malsch, M. & Blaauw, E. (2000). De nieuwe wet belaging: handhaving en alternatieven. *Nederlands Juristen Blad*, **35**, 1743–7.

Meloy, J. R. (1996). Stalking (obsessional following): a review of some preliminary studies. *Aggression and Violent Behavior*, **1**, 147–62.

Mullen, P. E., Pathé, M. & Purcell, R. (2000). *Stalkers and their Victims*. Cambridge: Cambridge University Press.

Pathé, M. & Mullen, P. E. (1997). The impact of stalkers on their victims. *British Journal of Psychiatry*, **170**, 12–17.

Sheridan, L. & Davies, G.M. (2001). Stalking: the elusive crime. *Legal and Criminological Psychology*, **6**, 133–48.

Tjaden, P. & Thoennes, N. (1997). *Stalking in America: Findings from the National Violence Against Women Survey*. Denver, CO: Center for Policy Research.

Wright, J. A., Burgess, A. G., Burgess, A. W., Laszlo, A. T., McCrary, G. O. & Douglas, J. E. (1996). A typology of interpersonal stalking. *Journal of Interpersonal Violence*, **11**, 487–502.

CHAPTER 3

I Was Trying to Let Him Down Easy

GAVIN de BECKER

Gavin de Becker & Associates, Los Angeles

With these words begins a story my office hears several times each month. Before meeting with me, the intelligent young woman may have told it to friends, a psychologist, a private detective, a lawyer, a police officer, maybe even a judge, but the problem persisted. It is the story of a situation that once seemed innocent, or at least manageable, but is now frightening. It is the story of someone who started as a seemingly normal suitor but was soon revealed to be something else.

There are two broad categories of stalking: unwanted pursuit by a stranger, and unwanted pursuit by someone the victim knows. The cases of total strangers fixating on private citizens are, by comparison to other types of stalking, very rare, and they are also the cases least likely to end in violence. Accordingly, I'll be exploring those cases that affect the largest population of victims: stalking by someone who has romantic aspirations, often someone a woman has met or dated.

Though it is fashionable for the news media to report on stalkers as if they are some unique type of criminal, those who choose regular citizens are not. They're not from Mars—they are from Miami and Boston, San Diego and Brentwood. They are the man our sister dated, the man our company hired, the man our friend married.

Reprinted from *The Gift of Fear: Survival Signals that Protect Us from Violence* by Gavin de Becker. Copyright © 1997 by Gavin de Becker. By permission of Little, Brown and Company (Inc.).

Stalking and Psychosexual Obsession: Psychological Perspectives for Prevention, Policing and Treatment. Edited by J. Boon and L. Sheridan. Published 2002 John Wiley & Sons, Ltd.

Against this background, we men must see in them a part of ourselves in order to better understand the issue. Giving talks around the country, I sometimes ask the audience, "How many of the men here ever found out where a girl lived or worked by means other than asking her?" "How many have driven by a girl's house to see what cars were there, or called just to see who answered the phone and then hung up?"

By the overwhelming show of hands, I've learned that the acceptability of these behaviours is a matter of degree. After one speech, a policeman who'd been in the audience asked to talk with me alone. He told me how he realized just then that he had relentlessly pursued a female student at the police academy when he was on the staff there. She said no to him for eighteen months, all the while concerned that the rejection would have an impact on her career. "She gave me no indication that she wanted a relationship with me, but I never let up, not for a moment," he said. "It paid off, though. We got married."

I suppose you could say it paid off, but the story tells more about how complicated the issue of romantic pursuit is. It is clear that for women in recent decades, the stakes of resisting romantic attention have risen sharply. Some invisible line exists between what is all right and what is too far—and men and women don't always agree on where to place that line. Victims and their unwanted pursuers never agree, and sometimes victims and the police don't either.

Everyone agrees, however, at the point where one of these situations includes violence, but why can we not reach consensus before that? To answer this, I have to recall the images of Dustin Hoffman storming into a church, and Demi Moore showing up uninvited at a business meeting. I have to talk about regular, everyday guys, and about the dictionary. It may seem that these things aren't related to stalking and unwanted pursuit, but—as I'm sure your intuition has already told you—they are.

In the sixties, a movie came out that painted a welcome and lasting picture of how a young man could court a woman. It was *The Graduate*. In it, Dustin Hoffman dates a girl (played by Katherine Ross) and then asks her to marry him. She says no, but he doesn't hear it. He waits outside her classes at school and asks again, and then again. Eventually she writes him a letter saying she's thought it over carefully and decided not to marry him. In fact, she is leaving town and marrying another man. That would seem a pretty clear message—but not in the movies.

Hoffman uses stalking techniques to find her. He pretends to be a friend of the groom, then a family member, then a priest. Ultimately, he finds the church and breaks into it just seconds after Katherine Ross is pronounced the wife of another man. He then beats up the bride's father, hits some other people, and wields a large wooden cross against the wedding guests who try to help the family.

And what happens? He gets the girl. She runs of with Dustin Hoffman, leaving her family and new husband behind. Also left behind is the notion that a woman should be heard, the notion that no means no, and the notion that a woman has a right to decide who will be in her life.

My generation saw in *The Graduate* that there is one romantic strategy to use above all others: persistence. This same strategy is at the core of every stalking case. Men pursuing unlikely or inappropriate relationships with women and getting them is a common theme promoted in our culture. Just recall *Flashdance, Tootsie, The Heartbreak, Kid, 10, Blame it on Rio, Honeymoon in Vegas, Indecent Proposal.*

This Hollywood formula could be called Boy Wants Girl, Girl Doesn't Want Boy, Boy Harasses Girl, Boy Gets Girl. Many movies teach that if you just stay with it, even if you offend her, even if she says she wants nothing to do with you, even if you've treated her like trash (and sometimes because you've treated her like trash), you'll get the girl. Even if she's in another relationship, even if you look like Dustin Hoffman, you'll eventually get Katherine Ross or Jessica Lange. Persistence will win the war *Against All Odds* (another of these movies, by the way). Even the seemingly innocuous TV show *Cheers* touches the topic. Sam's persistent and inappropriate sexual harassment of two female co-workers—eight years of it—doesn't get him fired or sued. It does, however, get him both women.

There's a lesson in real-life stalking cases that young women can benefit from learning: Persistence only proves persistence—it does not prove love. The fact that a romantic pursuer is relentless doesn't mean you are special—it means he is troubled.

It isn't news that men and women often speak different languages, but when the stakes are the highest, it's important to remember that men are nice when they pursue, and women are nice when they reject. Naturally this leads to confusion, and it brings us to the popular practice of letting him down easy.

True to what they are taught, rejecting women often say less than they mean. True to what they are taught, men often hear less than what is said. Nowhere is this problem more alarmingly expressed than by the hundreds of thousands of fathers (and mothers), older brothers (and sisters), movies and television shows that teach most men that when she says no, that's not what she means. Add to this all the women taught to "play hard to get", when that's not what they are really feeling. The result is that "no" can mean many things in this culture. Here's just a small sample:

Maybe	Not yet
Hmm...	Give me time
Not sure	Keep trying
I've found my man!	

There is one book in which the meaning of *no* is always clear. It is the dictionary, but since Hollywood writers don't seem to use that book very often, we have to. We have to teach young people that "No" is a complete sentence. This is not as simple as it may appear, given the deep cultural roots of the no/maybe hybrid. It has become part of the contract between men and women and was even explored by the classic contract theorists, Rousseau and Locke. Rousseau asked: "Why do you consult their words when it is not their mouths that speak?" Locke spoke of a man's winning "silent consent" by reading it in a woman's eyes "in spite of the mouth's denial." Locke even asserted that a man is protecting a woman's honour when he ignores her refusal: "If he then completes his happiness, he is not brutal, he is decent". In Locke's world, date rape wouldn't be a crime at all—it would be a gentleman's act of courtesy.

Even if men and women in America spoke the same language, they would still live by much different standards. For example, if a man in a movie researches a woman's schedule, finds out where she lives and works, even goes to her work uninvited, it shows his commitment, proves his love. When Robert Redford does this to Demi Moore in *Indecent Proposal*, it's adorable. But when she shows up at *his* work unannounced, interrupting a business lunch, it's alarming and disruptive.

If a man in the movies wants a sexual encounter or applies persistence, he's a regular, everyday guy, but if a woman does the same thing, she's a maniac or a killer. Just recall *Fatal Attraction*, *The King of Comedy*, *Single White Female*, *Play Misty for Me*, *The Hand That Rocks the Cradle* and *Basic Instinct*. When the men pursue, they usually get the girl. When the women pursue, they usually get killed.

Popular movies may be reflections of society or designers of society depending on whom you ask, but either way, they model behavior for us. During the early stages of pursuit situations in movies—and too often in life—the woman is watching and waiting, fitting in to the expectations of an overly invested man. She isn't heard or recognized; she is the screen upon which the man projects his needs and his idea of what she should be.

Stalking is how some men raise the stakes when women don't play along. It is a crime of power, control, and intimidation very similar to date rape. In fact, many cases of date stalking could be described as extended rapes; they take away freedom, and they honor the desires of the man and disregard the wishes of the woman. Whether he is an estranged husband, an ex-boyfriend, a one-time date, or an unwanted suitor, the stalker enforces our culture's cruellest rule, which is that women are not allowed to decide who will be in their lives. It quickly becomes clear that we have something worse than just a double standard—we have a dangerous standard.

I've successfully lobbied and testified for stalking laws in several states, but I would trade them all for a high school class that would teach young

men how to hear "no", and teach young women that it's all right to explicitly reject. The curriculum would also include strategies for getting
away. Perhaps needless to say, the class would not be called "Letting Him
Down Easy". If the culture taught and then allowed women to explicitly
reject and to say no, or if more women took that power early in every
relationship, stalking cases would decline dramatically.

Looking for Mr. Right has taken on far greater significance than getting
rid of Mr. Wrong, so women are not taught how to get out of relationships.
That high school class would stress the one rule that applies to all types of
unwanted pursuit: *Do not negotiate*. Once a woman has made the decision
that she doesn't want a relationship with a particular man, it needs to be
said one time, explicitly. Almost any contact after that rejection will be
seen as negotiation. If a woman tells a man over and over again that she
doesn't want to talk to him, that is talking to him, and every time she does
it, she betrays her resolve in the matter.

In Western society, when a man says No, it's usually the end of the
discussion. When a woman says No, it's the beginning of a negotiation.

If you tell someone ten times that you don't want to talk to him, you *are*
talking to him—nine more times than you wanted to.

When a woman gets thirty messages from a pursuer and doesn't call
him back, but then finally gives in and returns his calls, no matter what
she says, he learns that the cost of reaching her is leaving thirty messages.
For this type of man, any contact will be seen as progress. Of course, some
victims are worried that by not responding they'll provoke him, so they try
letting him down easy. Often, the result is that he believes she is conflicted,
uncertain, really likes him but just doesn't know it yet.

When a woman rejects someone who has a crush on her, and she says,
"It's just that I don't want to be in a relationship right now", he hears only
the words "right now". To him, this means she will want to be in a relationship later. The rejection should be "I don't want to be in a relationship
with you". Unless it's just that clear, and sometimes even when it is, he
doesn't hear it.

If she says, "You're a great guy and you have a lot to offer, but I'm not the
one for you; my head's just not in the right place these days", he thinks:
"She really likes me; it's just that she's confused. I've got to prove to her
that she's the one for me".

When a woman explains why she is rejecting, this type of man will challenge each reason she offers. I suggest that women never explain why they
don't want a relationship but simply make clear that they have thought
it over, that this is their decision, and that they expect the man to respect it. Why would a woman explain intimate aspects of her life, plans,
and romantic choices to someone she doesn't want a relationship with? A
rejection based on any condition, say, that she wants to move to another

city, just gives him something to challenge. Conditional rejections are not rejections—they are discussions.

The astute opening scene of the film *Tootsie* illustrates well why conditional rejections don't work. Dustin Hoffman plays an actor; reading lines at an audition. A voice from offstage tells him he isn't getting the part.

Voice: The reading was fine, you're just the wrong height.

Hoffman: Oh, I can be taller.

Voice: No, you don't understand. We're looking for somebody shorter.

Hoffman: Oh, well look, I don't have to be this tall. See, I'm wearing lifts. I can be shorter.

Voice: I know, but really . . . we're looking for somebody different.

Hoffman: I can be different.

Voice: We're looking for somebody else, okay?

This last line offers no reasons and begs no negotiations, but women in this culture are virtually prohibited from speaking it. They are taught that speaking it clearly and early may lead to unpopularity, banishment, anger, and even violence.

Let's imagine a woman has let pass several opportunities to pursue a relationship with a suitor. Every hint, response, action, and inaction has communicated that she is not interested. If the man still pursues at this point, though it will doubtless appear harsh to some, it is time for an unconditional and explicit rejection. Because I know that few American men have heard it, and few women have spoken it, here is what an unconditional and explicit rejection sounds like:

No matter what you may have assumed till now, and no matter for what reason you assumed it, I have no romantic interest in you whatsoever. I am certain I never will. I expect that knowing this, you'll put your attention elsewhere, which I understand, because that's what I intend to do.

There is only one appropriate reaction to this: Acceptance. However the man communicates it, the basic concept would ideally be: "I hear you, I understand, and while I am disappointed, I will certainly respect your decision."

I said there's only one appropriate reaction. Unfortunately, there are hundreds of inappropriate reactions and while they take many forms, their basic message is "I do not accept your decision." If a man aggressively debates, doubts, negotiates, or attempts to change her mind, it should be recognized for what it is. It should be clear that:

1. She made the right decision about this man. Instead of her resolve being challenged by his response, it should be strengthened.
2. She obviously would not want a relationship with someone who does not hear what she says and who does not recognize her feelings.
3. If he failed to understand a message this clear and explicit, his reaction to anything ambiguous, or to being let down easy, can only be imagined.

Unwanted pursuers may escalate their behavior to include such things as persistent phone calls and messages; showing up uninvited at a woman's work, school, or home; following her; and trying to enlist her friends or family in his campaign. If any of these things happens, assuming that the woman has communicated one explicit rejection, it is very important that no further detectable response be given. When a woman communicates again with someone she has explicitly rejected, her actions don't match her words. The man is able to choose which communications (actions versus words) actually represent the woman's feelings. Not surprisingly, he usually chooses the ones that serve him. Often, such a man will leave phone messages that ostensibly offer closure but that are actually crudely concealed efforts to get a response—and remember, he views any response as progress.

Message: Hi, it's Bryan. Listen, I'm moving back to Houston, but I can't leave town without an opportunity to see you again. All I'm asking for is a chance to say good-bye; that's all. Just a fast meeting, and then I'm gone.

Best response: No response.

Message: Listen, it's Bryan, this is the last call you'll ever get from me. (This line, though spoken often by stalkers, is rarely true.) It's urgent I speak with you.

Best response: No response.

When a woman is stalked by a person she dated, she may have to endure some judgment from people who learn about her situation: "You must have encouraged the guy in some way", "You must be the kind of woman who enjoys being pursued" etc. Someone will also doubtless give her the conventional wisdom on stalking, which should be called conventional *un*wisdom. It will include (as if it is some creative plan): Change your phone number. In fact, our office does not recommend this strategy, because as any victim will tell you, the stalker always manages to get the new number. A better plan is for the woman to get a second phone line, give the new number to the people she wants to hear from, and leave the old number with an answering machine or voice mail so that the stalker is not even aware she has another number. She can check her messages, and when she receives calls from people she wants to speak with, she can call them back and give them her new number. Eventually, the only person leaving messages on the old number is the unwanted pursuer. In this way, his calls are documented (keep the messages), and more importantly, each time he leaves a message, he *gets* a message: that she can avoid the temptation to respond to his manipulations.

We also suggest that the outgoing message be recorded by a female friend, because he may be calling just to hear his object's voice. While people believe that an outgoing message with a male voice will lead the pursuer to believe his victim is in a new relationship, more commonly it leads him to investigate further.

Stalkers are by definition people who don't give up easily—they are people who don't let go. More accurately, the vast majority of them are people who don't let go at the point most of us would, but who ultimately do let go—if their victims avoid engaging them. Usually, they have to attach a tentacle to someone else before detaching all the tentacles from their current object.

* * *

An axiom of the stalking dynamic: *Men who cannot let go choose women who cannot say no.* Most victims will concede that even though they wanted to, they were initially reluctant to explicitly reject. Often, the niceness or delicacy of a woman's rejection is taken as affection. Demonstrating this, and proving that nobody is exempt from these situations, is Kathleen Krueger, the wife of United States Senator Bob Krueger. She could not shake the unwanted pursuer who had once piloted her husband's campaign plane. When Mrs. Krueger described her case to me, she eloquently explained it from the stalker's perspective: "We were nice to him, not unusually so, but it was obviously a big deal to him. He took it as love. *I guess when you are starving, even a morsel seems like a feast.*"

In cases in which the pursuer has initially gotten what he perceived as favorable attention, or in which he has actually dated or had a relationship with his victim, he may be so desperate to hold on that he'll settle for any kind of contact. Though he'd rather be her boyfriend, he'll accept being just a friend. Eventually, though he'd rather be a friend, he'll accept being an enemy if that's the only position available. As a stalking ex-boyfriend wrote to a young client of ours: "You'll be thinking of me. You may not be thinking good thoughts, but you'll be thinking of me".

Another rule to be taught in the "Getting Rid of Mr. Wrong" class would be: *The way to stop contact is to stop contact.* As I noted above, I suggest one explicit rejection and after that absolutely no contact. If you call the pursuer back, or agree to meet, or send him a note, or have somebody warn him off, you buy another six weeks of his unwanted pursuit. Some victims think it will help to have a male friend, new boyfriend, or a male family member tell the stalker to stop. Most who try this learn that the stalker takes it as evidence that his love object must be conflicted. Otherwise she'd have told him herself.

Sending the police to warn off a pursuer may seem the obvious thing to do, but it rarely has the desired effect. Though the behavior of pursuers may be alarming, most have not broken the law, so the police have few options. When police visit him and say, in effect, "Cut this out or you'll get into trouble", the pursuer intuitively knows that if they could have arrested him they would have arrested him. So what's the result of the visit? Well, the greatest possible weapon in his victim's arsenal—sending the police after him—came and went without a problem. The cops stopped by, they talked to him, and they left. Who got stronger, the victim or the pursuer?

To be clear, I feel that police should be involved when there is an actionable crime that if prosecuted would result in improving the victim's safety or putting a high cost on the stalker's behavior. But the first time a stalker should see police is when they show up to arrest him, not when they stop by to chat.

Pursuers are, in a very real sense, detoxing from an addiction to the relationship. It is similar to the dynamic in many domestic violence situations in which both partners are addicted to the relationship. In date-stalking cases, however, it is usually one-sided; the stalker is the addict and his object is the drug. Small doses of that drug do not wean him, they engage him. The way to force him out of this addiction, as with most addictions, is abstinence, cold turkey—no contact from her, no contact from her designates, and no contact about her.

As with domestic violence situations, victims will often be advised that they must do something (police intervention, warning) to their stalkers. From the larger social point of view, such advice might be correct. If one thinks of a stalker as a danger to society—a virtual tiger lurking around the corner waiting to victimize someone—then it may be true that somebody should do something about it, but nobody is obligated to volunteer for that fight, particularly if it's avoidable. If one could know and warn a stalking victim that as she rounds the next corner, she'll be attacked, which option makes more sense: Go around the corner, or take another route? If the fight is avoidable, and it's my wife, my daughter, my friend, or my client, I would recommend avoidance first. That's because fighting will always be available, but it isn't always possible to go back to avoidance once a war is under way.

Victims of stalking will also hear the same conventional wisdom that is offered to battered women: Get a restraining order. Here, as with battered wives, it is important to evaluate which cases might be improved by court intervention and which might be worsened. Much depends upon how escalated the case is and how much emotional investment has been made by the stalker. If he has been actively pursuing the same victim for years and has already ignored warnings and interventions, then a restraining order isn't likely to help. Generally speaking, court orders that are introduced early carry less risk than those introduced after the stalker has made a significant emotional investment or introduced threats and other sinister behavior. Restraining orders obtained soon after a pursuer has ignored a single explicit rejection will carry more clout and less risk than those obtained after many months or years of stalking.

There is a category of stalker for which court orders frequently help (or at least aren't dangerous). It is the one we call the naive pursuer. He is a person who simply does not realize the inappropriateness of his behavior. He might think, "I am in love with this person. Accordingly, this is a love relationship, and I am acting the way people in love act".

This type of unwanted pursuer is generally rational, though perhaps a bit thick and unsophisticated. Not all naive pursuers are seeking romantic relationships. Some are persistently seeking to be hired for a job or to learn why they were not hired for a job, why their idea was not accepted, why their manuscript was rejected, etc. The naive pursuer is usually distinguishable from conventional stalkers by his lack of machismo and his lack of anger at being rejected. He just seems to go along, happily believing he is courting someone. He stays with it until someone makes completely clear to him that his approach is inappropriate, unacceptable, and counterproductive. This isn't always easy, but it's usually safe to try.

Because victims are understandably frustrated and angry, they may look to a court order to do any of the following things:

Destroy
Expose
Threaten
Avenge
Change
Humiliate

Note that the acronym for this list is also the only goal that makes sense from a safety point of view, and that is to DETACH, to have the guy out of your life. As with battered women, the restraining order may move you closer to that goal, or it may move you farther away. It is one management plan, but not the only one.

* * *

The type of stalker whom a woman has briefly dated (as opposed to a stranger she's never met) is quite similar to the controlling or battering husband, though he is far less likely to introduce violence. His strategies include acting pathetic to exploit a victim's sympathy or guilt, calling on supposed promises or commitments, annoying a victim so much that she gives in and continues seeing him, and finally the use of fear through intimidating statements and actions (threats, vandalism, slashing tyres, etc.).

To illustrate, let's look at the case of Katherine, who asked me if there was a list of warning signs about men who might later become a problem. Her story follows, with the warning signs pointed out in parentheses:

I dated this guy named Bryan. We met at a party of a friend of mine, and he must have asked somebody there for my number [researching the victim]. Before I even got home, he'd left me three messages [overly invested]. I told him I didn't want to go out with him, but he was so enthusiastic about it that I really didn't have any choice [*Men who cannot let go choose women who cannot say no*]. In the beginning, he was superattentive, always seemed to know what I wanted. He remembered everything I ever said [hyperattentiveness]. It was flattering, but it also made me uncomfortable [victim intuitively feels uncomfortable]. Like when he remembered that I once mentioned needing more space for my books, he just showed up one day with shelves and all the stuff and just put them up [offering unsolicited help; loan sharking]. I couldn't say no. And he read so much into whatever I said. Once he asked if I'd go to a basketball game with him, and I said maybe. He later said, "You promised" [projecting onto others emotions or commitments that are not present]. Also, he talked about serious things so early, like living together and marriage and children [whirlwind pace; placing issues on the agenda prematurely]. He started with jokes about that stuff the first time we went out, and later he wasn't joking. Or when he suggested that I have a phone in my car. I wasn't sure I even wanted a car phone, but he borrowed my car and just had one installed [loan sharking]. It was a gift, so what could I say? And, of course, he called me whenever I was in the car [monitoring activity and whereabouts]. And he was so adamant that I never speak to my ex-boyfriend on that car phone. Later, he got angry if I spoke to my ex at all [jealousy]. There were also a couple of my friends he didn't like me to see [isolating her from friends], and he stopped spending time with any of his own friends [making another person responsible to be one's whole social world]. Finally, when I told him I didn't want to be his girlfriend, he refused to hear it [refusing to hear "no"].

All this is done on autopilot by the stalker, who seeks to control the other person so she can't leave him. Being in control is an alternative to being loved, and since his identity is so precariously dependent on a relationship, he carefully shores up every possible leak. In so doing, he also strangles the life out of the relationship, ensuring that it could never be what he says (and maybe even believes) he wants.

Bryan would not pursue a woman who could really say and mean no, though he is very interested in one who initially says no and then gives in. I assure you that Bryan tested Katherine on this point within minutes of meeting her:

Bryan: can I get you something to drink?

Katherine: No, but thank you.

Bryan: Oh, come on, what'll you have?

Katherine: Well, I could have a soft drink, I guess.

This may appear to be a minor exchange, but it is actually a very significant test. Bryan found something she said no to, tried a light persuasion, and Katherine gave in, perhaps just because she wanted to be nice. He will next try one a notch more significant, then another, then another, and finally he's found someone he can control. The exchange about the drink is the same as the exchange they will later have about dating, and later about breaking up. It becomes an unspoken agreement that he will drive and she will be the passenger. The trouble comes when she tries to renegotiate that agreement.

* * *

Popular news stories would have us believe that stalking is like a virus that strikes its victims without warning, but Katherine, like most victims, got a signal of discomfort from the beginning—and ignored it. Nearly every victim I've ever spoken with stayed in even after she wanted out. It doesn't have to be that way. Women can follow those early signals of intuition right from the start.

Dating carries several risks: the risk of disappointment, the risk of boredom, the risk of rejection, and the risk of letting some troubled, scary man into your life. The whole process is most similar to an audition, except that the stakes are higher. A date might look like the audition in *Tootsie*, in which the man wants the part so badly that he'll do anything to get it, or it can be an opportunity for the woman to evaluate important pre-incident indicators. Doesn't sound romantic? Well, daters are doing an evaluation anyway; they're just doing it badly. I am suggesting only that the evaluation be conscious and informed.

The woman can steer the conversation to the man's last break-up and evaluate how he describes it. Does he accept responsibility for his part? Is he still invested? Was he slow to let go, slow to hear what the woman communicated? Has he let go yet? Who broke up with whom? This last question is an important one, because stalkers are rarely the ones who initiate break-ups. Has he had several "love-at-first sight" relationships?

Falling for people in a big way based on just a little exposure to them, particularly if this is a pattern, is a valuable PIN. A woman can explore a new date's perception of male and female roles as well as his ideas about commitment, obsession, and freedom. A woman can observe if and how the man tries to change her mind, even on little things. I am not proposing a checklist of blunt questions, but I am suggesting that all the information is there to he mined through artful conversation.

The final lesson in that ideal class for young men and women would center on the fact that contrary to the scary and alarming stories shown on the local news, very few date-stalking situations end in violence. The newspeople would have you believe that if you're being stalked, you'd better get your will in order, but this level of alarm is usually inappropriate. Date-stalkers do not jump from non-violent harassment to homicide without escalations along the way, escalations that are almost always apparent or at least detectable.

To avoid these situations, listen to yourself right from the start. To avoid escalation if you are already in a stalking situation, listen to yourself at every step along the way. When it comes to date-stalkers, your intuition is now loaded, so listen.

CHAPTER 4

Police Care and Support for Victims of Stalking

GARY COPSON

and

NICOLA MARSHALL
Metropolitan Police, London

INTRODUCTION

The presentation of this chapter follows the authors' collaboration in 1999 in writing "The chaperon's guide" (Marshall, in press). This was a guide to best practice in taking statements of evidence from, and offering after-care to, victims of serious sexual offences, "chaperon" being the designation of the officer who performs that important role. The authors are both serving officers in the UK's largest force, the Metropolitan Police, but it should be noted that this chapter is not written officially for or on behalf of the Metropolitan Police, nor are the views in it necessarily Metropolitan Police policy.

"The chaperon's guide" was written to distil Nicola Marshall's specialist knowledge and expertise as a very experienced sexual offences chaperon. The object of this was to help inexperienced officers faced with the demands of the role, especially those serving in police areas where no formal chaperon training is given. It was based not just on practical experience gained in the field, but also on academic research into the nature of rape and rape investigations (see for example Adler, 1987; Blair, 1985; Davies, 1992; Hazelwood & Burgess, 1995; Lees, 1996)

Stalking and Psychosexual Obsession: Psychological Perspectives for Prevention, Policing and Treatment.
Edited by J. Boon and L. Sheridan. © 2002 John Wiley & Sons, Ltd.

and numerous unpublished quasi-academic police research reports and reviews.

This guide for care and support of stalking victims is of necessity an adaptation of the earlier one since as yet there is no great depth of experience in the care of stalking victims and a paucity of published literature relating to the investigation of stalking and psychosexual harassment. However, by taking what is available and combining it with field experience, the first part of the chapter aims to uncover what it is that victims want from the police. Thereafter an explanation is offered, of what police can realistically do to offer care and support to stalking victims, leading to a discussion of the barriers that exist to doing more.

For the sake of simplicity in the text, the victim will be assumed to be female and the stalker to be male, though it is readily acknowledged that all four gender permutations are realistic possibilities.

It is necessary before proceeding to acknowledge the fundamental difference between a serious sexual offence, such as rape, and stalking. However awful the rape, by the time the police chaperon becomes involved it is over. Of course, the victim is likely to relive it in her mind—even many times over many years—but the physical attack has ended, there exists the possibility for the recovery process to commence, and the after-care from police can be a significant step towards that recovery. In a stalking case the attack has not ended at all and the threat of renewed attack is very real and potentially constant. When you ask a rape victim what she wants from police, her answer might follow any one of half a dozen common themes. When you ask a stalking victim, there is only one thing she wants. She wants the ordeal to end. She wants not to be stalked any more and that is something the police have very limited ability to deliver.

WHAT STALKING VICTIMS WANT FROM POLICE (APART FROM MAKING IT STOP)

To be believed. It is terribly important for a victim of stalking to be believed and the last thing she needs is for police to question her sanity at a time when she may already be questioning it herself.

Honesty. It is essential for a stalking victim to be able to rely on what she is told by police.

To know whom she is dealing with. It is important that there should be a named officer to contact after the initial report is made.

To know what to do if something further happens. It is important to make readily available to the victim emergency contact numbers together with clear instructions as to what to do if something else happens.

To have an easy reference system for reporting new developments. Often, especially out of core business hours, it may not be possible to reach a nominated contact officer, so it is necessary to speak to an officer unacquainted with the case. This is also likely to happen when a series of incidents restarts after a long break, such as after a prison sentence. It is immensely frustrating for the victim to have to go through the history and the detail all over again each time a new report is made to police. The provision of an efficient and effective reporting system can be very helpful in alleviating such frustration.

To be actively involved in gathering evidence for the investigation. It is important for a victim of stalking to be able to have a sense of doing something positive towards regaining control of her life.

To receive practical help. Being stalked can engender feelings of isolation and helplessness, and concrete assistance can be of great emotional and psychological support as well as practical benefit.

Assistance with court processes. The courts, both civil and criminal, are usually found to be the most threatening and confusing part of the criminal justice system for anyone unfamiliar with them.

To be kept informed of developments in the investigation. A sense of progress is very important. This is so not just for the comfort and reassurance that are so valuable to someone who has been rendered so vulnerable, nor just for the feeling that they are regaining some semblance of control over their own life, but also as evidence that their value system is not completely awry. It is important that the victim should be helped to feel that in a civilised society such awful things are not only not allowed to happen without sanction, but that it is safe to expect police action if they happen again. The feeling of desertion that not being kept informed can create can be acute, and can even add to a stalking victim's sense of vulnerability and isolation.

WHAT POLICE CAN ACTUALLY DELIVER

We acknowledged earlier the fundamental difference between caring for a rape victim and caring for a stalking victim. In principle, however, there are some points of similarity and many things the police can usefully do in support of a stalking victim—even some things they can guarantee. Police officers know that every crime inflicts a cost on its victim, that sometimes the cost is intangible, and sometimes its emotional impact can appear out of all proportion to the outward seriousness of the event that triggered it. This can be true of a simple theft or a minor assault, just as much as a rape or a stalking. Most police officers will not have been raped or stalked but that need not preclude understanding, even empathising, in their dealings with people who have. But while police can ensure that their training includes proper understanding of phenomena like rape trauma, they cannot greatly influence the attitudes of either the newspapers or the courts, nor wider public attitudes to what might be seen crudely as women's issues. That is the context within which police operate.

THE RAPE MYTH AND THE STALKING MYTH

Those who advocate that stalking should be treated more seriously than it is at present face similar challenges to those uncovered by rape research ten to twenty years ago. This is best illustrated by the work of Szuszanna Adler, published in *Rape on Trial* (Adler, 1987). Adler studied a series of rape trials at the Central Criminal Court (the Old Bailey) and analysed them for elements that were significant in dictating conviction or acquittal. Adler's findings retain shock value even now—all the more so as follow-up studies suggest that little, if anything, has changed (Lees, 1996).

For a conviction to be secured, the victim should:

- be sexually inexperienced, and preferably a virgin
- be 'respectable.'—she should neither have dressed nor acted in any way provocatively
- not have gone willingly with the rapist to wherever she was attacked
- have fought, and preferably have been hurt
- have complained at the earliest opportunity
- not have known her attacker, and definitely not have had previous sexual relations with him, to any degree

It is also difficult to secure a conviction if the victim has the particular misfortune to be raped by a man of higher social standing than herself.

It is by no means impossible to counter any, or even all, of the above misfortunes, and achieve a conviction. But it does require a good deal of understanding and a great deal of effort to do so. Drawing on many years of hard work and good practice, "The chaperon's guide" contains advice on how this may be achieved, even including practical suggestions from a detective sergeant with a remarkably impressive record in securing convictions of those who rape prostitutes.

Adler's work, replicated and amplified by that of Sue Lees, illustrates the rape myth: that there is an "ideal" rape victim and that it is wise, or, at least, pragmatic, to disbelieve victims who fail to fit that ideal. Likewise, it seems there is a stalking myth, that its victims:

- Secretly like the attention.
- Must have led him on in some way.
- Must have misread innocent signals of affection or romantic betrothal.
- Must be imagining it.
- Must be hysterical.

The underlying assumptions are that stalking (a) only happens to women, and (b) is not really serious in the vast majority of cases. This contrasts starkly with one of the assertions made in a survey of 95 stalking victims (Sheridan et al., 2001), that "stalking is one of the most serious crimes of the 1990s, but no one apart from the victims seems to realise it".

It is a challenge for police over time to develop tactics to counter the stalking myth in the same way as they have over time developed tactics to counter the rape myth. Meanwhile, the police response to stalking victims must take account of the stalking myth, and draw on conventional sexual offences investigation techniques to offer the best service possible, even if this inevitably falls short of the unattainable result they would most like.

ADAPTING "THE CHAPERON'S GUIDE", THIS IS WHAT CAN BE DONE FOR VICTIMS OF STALKING

Adapting "The chaperon's guide" for stalking cases, the following points indicate that which can be done.

First contact. In a short space of time and under difficult circumstances it is necessary for a chaperon to establish a positive rapport with a victim. The information given here sets out what a police officer might do to achieve that rapport which is essential to the building of a satisfactory working relationship.

Empathy through understanding. When dealing with victims of stalking, police should:

- remember the victim is frightened—frightened of the stalker, frightened of being hurt, frightened of being killed, possibly also frightened of the police.
- remember the victim feels vulnerable and powerless—a perceived lack of support from police will compound this, so there is a need for the chaperon to reassure that he or she will listen and take appropriate and agreed action.
- remember the victim feels isolated and might easily feel that no-one—not even the police—can help, or even that no one wants to help.

- remember the victim will feel angry—at her own fear, at her or some other's inability to prevent the incidents from happening, and at the stalker for doing it to her.
- remember the victim will feel frustated at the lack of decisive legal action and redress, and at the slowness of the criminal justice system.

Reassurance.
- The chaperon should introduce him/herself and explain that they will be the sole person dealing with her at this stage of the investigation (provided they are certain that this will actually be the case). The chaperon's role is to help her through the criminal justice process. It is important to prepare from the outset for closure—she is a client, not a friend, and it is not professionally proper that the relationship should be allowed to develop into either a friendship or a long-term dependency.
- It is important to acknowledge the probability that, if her case continues over months or years, it may have to be transferred to a new chaperon and a new investigator. Reassurance should be given that everything possible will be done to ensure this transition is smooth and to ensure that the new officers are aware of everything they will need to know.
- The victim should be told that additional support is available for her from the Victim Support scheme and, with her agreement, the scheme should be contacted as soon as possible.
- It might help for the chaperon to make her aware that he/she will not be embarrassed or shocked no matter what she has to tell him/her.
- It may not be very reassuring for an officer to reveal (if applicable) that this is their first chaperon role or first stalking case.

Building trust.
- No surprises—the chaperon should let her know at the outset that the process is complex and long-winded, that they will explain the process of investigation as they go along, and that she should ask questions as and when she needs to.
- Don't let the victim down. It is essential for the chaperon not to make promises unless he/she knows they can keep them. Especially in the early stages this can ruin a good police/victim relationship.
- Questions generally need to be open ended and non-leading. It is important for the chaperon to keep questions neutral to avoid any implicit assumptions that she may misinterpret as negative.

Reducing her disorientation and fear of the police investigation.
- The victim should be given clear expectations concerning the role of the chaperon, what they will require of her and the roles of other officers involved in her case.

- It is important for police to be aware of possible problems affecting the victim's ability to assist them. These include such considerations as fear, exhaustion, self-blame, embarrassment and lack of education. Also, it is important to keep in mind that the victim is unlikely to understand police procedures or police jargon.
- The victim should be encouraged to tell everything, as she is unlikely to appreciate the importance of information in an investigative context. It is the chaperon's responsibility to elicit all information that will further a jury's understanding of the victim's experience.

Making her realise that police are taking her allegation seriously.
- Quite simply, she should be told explicitly that her allegation is being taken seriously.
- It should be policy to accept what she says, unless there are very substantial grounds for believing it to be false (and, even then, to proceed very carefully in questioning her to establish exactly what, if anything, did happen to cause her to make the report).
- As soon as possible in suitable cases, the victim should be encouraged to identify the stalker, the scene(s) and potential exhibits. And if there is a senior investigator he or she should be told straight away in order that they can consider forensically significant matters such as scene preservation and suspect detention.
- It is good practice to warn the victim of the need to tell her story several times and to explain the need to take things slowly and in a lot of detail because it is vital not to miss anything that is important. Information missed at this stage could cause problems at court later, for example it might be suggested that "You did not tell the police that, you are making it up now because it sounds better than what actually happened." It is terribly important she should understand that quality information is the key to conviction.

Telling her straight.
- It can be very tempting for chaperons to put a positive gloss on things, but they simply must not. They need to be completely honest about the situation and about what she can expect. However well-intentioned, they should never try to comfort a victim by making hopeful promises about:
  – police action
  – arrest or prosecution
  – remands into custody or bail conditions
  – chances of conviction.

Deciding investigative strategy and tactics.
- As discussed elsewhere in this book, there is a wide range of stalking behaviours and differing motives for various kinds of stalkers. This means

that the most appropriate investigative strategy and the most useful investigative tactics can only sensibly be decided once the chaperon has elicited enough information from the victim to enable a judgement to be made as to motive. Boon & Sheridan's typological model (Chapter 5) offers a potentially valuable means of interpreting different behaviours and tailoring police tactics to deal with them most appropriately.

- Investigative strategy and tactics should be discussed with the victim to secure her agreement to police action—it could have serious implications for her. It is important therefore that she needs to be involved in the decision-making processes. An obvious example is the decision to issue a formal warning, so as to be able to demonstrate for the Protection from Harassment Act that the offender knew the effect of his actions. This could have a range of effects on his attitude and behaviour towards her.
- If notes or diaries are seized from the stalker, carefully judged consideration should be given to showing them to and analysing them with the victim. She is the person most likely to be able to interpret them and to assess the nature and degree of threat that they disclose. For example, they might disclose how much he knows about her movements and her vulnerabilities, but only she may be able to interpret how dangerous that knowledge is to her. However, the potential value of such insights will need to be weighed carefully against the risk of adding to the victim's trauma.

Medical examination.
- If the victim has been physically hurt, and especially if there are likely to be visible signs of injury, it will be necessary for her to be medically examined. It will be the chaperon's responsibility to ensure that she understands exactly what is going to happen in the examination and why, and to supply the sympathetic bedside manner if the doctor fails to.
- The officer might ask if she would prefer a male or a female doctor (but not promise one or the other unless they are sure the choice is actually available).

Assisting with court orders.
- In appropriate cases police should assist the victim to obtain a civil court order to restrain the stalker's behaviour. In the UK restraining orders can also be obtained from criminal courts under the Protection from Harassment Act 1997. Either course will entail not just giving her directions and explaining the procedures of the court, but actually going with her to help her in what should be perfectly straightforward for a police officer, but will most likely be a serious ordeal for her.
- In cases where the stalker is charged with a criminal offence it might be possible to restrict his movements or his access to the victim by persuading the court to impose bail conditions.

Offering practical advice.
- Practical advice on coping strategy and evidence collection can be particularly helpful in stalking cases because it gives the victim a focus and a purpose. Psychologically it gives them a sense of empowerment and they might even feel empowered by the idea of fighting back with the police, and therefore justice, on their side. The following advice has been found to be useful:
  - never react to your stalker
  - never communicate with your stalker, no matter how persistent he is—not on the 10th phone call, not on the 50th—to do so simply sends the message that persistence pays
  - try to ensure that no one communicates with your stalker on your behalf, as even this might encourage him, or else it might complicate the situation further
  - keep a log of events and update it as soon after each event as possible.

Supplying clear written instructions.
- The terror that stalking provokes means that even the strongest and calmest among us will find it difficult to think clearly and act coolly under the stress of a fresh attack. It is therefore very helpful to have a custom-made response card, setting out very clear and simple instructions what to do, which numbers to phone, who to ask for and what to say.
- It is useful if such a card can be provided not only for the victim, but also for a partner, close friend or neighbour, so that they can be briefed on exactly what to do if the victim goes into trauma.

Setting up an easy reference system.
- In gauging the appropriate police response when a stalking victim calls police to report a new attack, it is important to have easy access to a case history summary. There are several ways in which this could be set up, using either a CAD (command and despatch call handling system) special scheme or local systems. Whichever system is devised, it is important for the victim to have a unique reference number or password that will direct the officer taking the call to the relevant details.
- Given the potential for a series of stalking incidents to recommence after a cessation of months, or even years, it would be most useful if the data could remain accessible and the unique reference valid for as long as the threat remains realistic.

Evidence gathering.
- To obtain the best results in civil and criminal courts it is necessary to obtain best evidence, so the chaperon should ensure that the victim knows to preserve everything she receives from her stalker for scientific

examination. Suitable packaging materials might be provided for the purpose, together with adequate instructions on how to use them. Alternatively, simple instructions might be given to avoid unnecessary or clumsy handling while waiting for police to collect, so that physical trace evidence is not lost.

- In appropriate cases police might be able to provide a panic alarm, an audio tape recorder or a video camera. In these cases the victim should be given clear instructions on how and when best to use them.

Lifestyle changes.

- Police should think very carefully before suggesting lifestyle changes to a victim of stalking, as a lifestyle change could be construed as amounting in itself to fundamental damage and police might be vulnerable to the suggestion that they inflicted such damage casually, for want of the serious commitment, support and investigation that would have been required to properly protect her lifestyle.

COMPARING WHAT THE VICTIM WANTS WITH WHAT THE POLICE CAN REALISTICALLY DELIVER

It is not always going to be simple, or even possible, to have an easy reference system for reporting new developments. Some police computerised information systems are just not configured that way. And even where the computer systems are amenable, they are not infallible and, like many commercial networked systems, they occasionally "crash", so that the information held in them is temporarily inaccessible. And even where amenable systems are operating well, it might be asking a lot of an officer to be able instantly to take in the enormity and complexity of a long case history, especially when there might be a large number of other pressing demands for his or her attention at the time the stalking victim makes contact.

Police have no control over other agencies in the criminal justice system. Though they might make every effort to try to ensure that things go smoothly at court, police cannot dictate that the Crown Prosecution Service (CPS)—which presents cases in criminal courts—will agree that applications for remands in custody or bail conditions should be made. Neither can police dictate that judges or magistrates will grant them when applications are made. Furthermore, neither do police have any powers that enable them to make things better for vulnerable victims, such as by reducing waiting times. Police cannot even oblige courts to comply with the expectations of them under *The Victim's Charter* (Home Office, 1996). *The Victim's Charter* sets out "what sort of service victims of crime should expect", and "how the agencies who make up the criminal justice system should improve the treatment of victims".

Because *The Victim's Charter* deals in *expectations* it is aspirational, rather than a manual of rights. It says "you can reserve a seat in court for a relative or friend accompanying you". But sometimes defence lawyers will object to a victim receiving moral support while giving evidence, especially from a police chaperon, and judges can uphold such objections so that the friend or chaperon has to sit out of sight of the victim, or even outside the courtroom altogether. It states "while you are waiting to give evidence a member of the CPS will introduce himself or herself. . . to tell you what to expect". But the CPS are not so well staffed that they have a representative for every courtroom, and in practice they can be so stretched that police in many areas have taken this important role upon themselves to make sure that it happens. It further states "you can ask to wait separately from those involved in the case", but acknowledges in small print that "in some courts a lack of space might mean that you cannot". In fact, this is the case in many courts. Most of our courts were built before *The Victim's Charter* was written, or even thought necessary, so there are no separate waiting areas, there are no discreet side entrances, and there are no separate canteens so that victims and their families and friends can take refreshments separate from defendants and theirs. These are therefore factors about which the police can do little or nothing.

Neither can police make absolutely sure that other agencies keep them fully and promptly informed of case developments. Except in a few experimental instances, there are currently no shared computer systems by which CPS or courts can instantaneously inform police of case results, such as the granting of a bail application. Often police might not even be aware that a bail application is being made, let alone that it has been granted. Similarly, communication systems between police and prisons can be poor, so that police will not receive notice when a prisoner is released, either at the conclusion of his sentence or on some kind of pre-release acclimatisation scheme. And if police do not know a stalker has been released from custody, they cannot warn his victim.

Even when police do know what is happening, it can be an enormous logistical problem to keep victims and witnesses informed. A busy detective in a metropolitan police service can easily be carrying responsibility for fifty court cases. Such a case load could involve well over a hundred key victims and witnesses, and keeping in touch with all of them, as *The Victim's Charter* expects, is a major undertaking. Criminal Justice Units, which deal with a lot of the administrative burden of preparing cases for court and with CPS liaison, can perform this role, but they are often similarly stretched in busy police stations. Vulnerable victims of crime can help to ease the burden of communication by making themselves accessible, such as by carrying a dedicated means of communication, like a pager or mobile telephone, and paying attention to it.

There is also a different kind of potential barrier to police care of stalking victims, and that is the vulnerability of the victims themselves. We have set out above some points of good practice, such as never communicating with the stalker, but we understand that there can be huge psychological pressures that militate against following such advice. Likewise, we have set out the need to keep a log and to preserve best evidence, but we understand that these requirements can be onerous and distressing, and that there can be psychological imperatives to destroy, rather than preserve, anything received from a stalker.

EVEN BEST PRACTICE MIGHT NOT BE ENOUGH

Police and victims each need to understand that even the best police service might not be enough on its own. Although police are the entry point into the criminal justice system, and to a large extent the public face of it, they do not have sole responsibility for making everything better. Nor is "successful" police action always enough. In a survey of 95 stalking victims Lorraine Sheridan (in press) found that even where injunctions had been obtained in the civil courts, 15 out of 19 had been breached. And even where criminal convictions were secured, this did not always end the stalking—indeed one respondent reported "since he has been in prison I have had the same number of letters as when he was stalking me from the outside. [He] is due to be released from prison at the end of August—it's like waiting for a time bomb to go off".

SOME PROMISING DEVELOPMENTS

In recent months there have been two particularly promising developments in support of stalking victims. We would like to think that this chapter amounts to a third.

In August 2000 the Metropolitan Police and the Home Office jointly released *An Investigator's Guide to Stalking and Other Forms of Harassment* (Brown, 2000). This guide, written by Detective Inspector Hamish Brown, offers comprehensive, step-by-step good practice advice for investigators. It also offers a summary of restraining orders and offences under the Protection from Harassment Act 1997, some alternative criminal charges that could be preferred, a list of organisations that exist to offer help and advice, and a section on advice to victims, which covers some of the same ground as this chapter, but from a different perspective, that of an investigating officer rather than that of a dedicated chaperon.

More recently, the Home Office has released proposals for a law to extend "special measures" available to vulnerable and intimidated witnesses (2000). These could greatly reduce for stalking victims the trauma of giving evidence. They include the extension to vulnerable adults of the provisions by which children can already make their statement to police in the form of a video, which can then be used in court as their evidence, and the use of screens or television links in appropriate cases to protect them during cross-examination.

CONCLUSIONS

It is important to reiterate that, however well they do within their own spheres of influence, police do not and cannot hold the key to any kind of magic solution for the problems of stalking victims. Police will, however, most often be the entry point to and the public face of the criminal justice system and, even short of ideal solutions, there is a lot police can do to help stalking victims—especially if they appreciate the particular psychological trauma that stalking creates and do what can be done sympathetically and professionally.

In Sheridan et al.'s (2001) survey of 95 stalking victims police attitudes at initial complaint were described by equal numbers of respondents as positive and negative. In respect of subsequent or further complaint reports of negative police attitudes slightly outnumbered those of positive police attitudes. In a more detailed survey of 29 victims (Sheridan, in press) half of those reporting their stalker to police at an early stage reported the police response as indifferent. Police actions were reported in the 95-victim survey as markedly more negative than positive at first complaint, and even more so in response to subsequent complaint. It is to be hoped that Brown's guide (Brown, 2000) might go towards improving police action in response to allegations of stalking, while this chapter might help to improve perceptions of police attitudes in such cases.

REFERENCES

Adler, Z. (1987). *Rape on Trial*. London: Routledge & Kegan Paul.
Blair, I. (1985). *Investigating Rape*. Kent: Croom Helm.
Brown, H. (2000). *An Investigator's Guide to Stalking and Other Forms of Harassment*. London: Home Office.
Davies, A. (1992). Rapists' behaviour: a three aspect model as a basis for analysis and the identification of serial crime. *Forensic Science International*, **55**, 173–94.
Hazelwood, R.R. & Burgess, A.W. (1995). *Practical Aspects of Rape Investigation*. Boca Raton, FL: CRC Press.
Home Office (1996). *The Victim's Charter*. London: Home Office.
Home Office (2000). *Achieving the Best Evidence in Criminal Proceedings: Guidance for Vulnerable and Intimidated Witnesses, Including Children*. London: Home Office.
Lees, S. (1996). *Carnal Knowledge*. London: Penguin.

Marshall, N. (in press). The chaperon's guide, *Police Review*.

Sheridan, L. (in press). The course and nature of stalking: an in-depth victim survey. *Journal of Threat Assessment*.

Sheridan, L., Davies, G.M. & Boon, J.C.W. (2001). The course and nature of stalking: a victim perspective. *The Howard Journal of Criminal Justice*, **40**(3), 215–34.

CHAPTER 5

Stalker Typologies: Implications for Law Enforcement

LORRAINE SHERIDAN

and

JULIAN BOON
University of Leicester

In Chapter 1, Pathé & Mullen detailed the findings of a number of studies of stalking victims. The results illustrated that many of the victims shared some important features. For instance, the majority were employed females. The data also revealed marked differences between these same victims. For example, some stalkers were previously known to their victims, while others were not.

Differences as well as similarities have also been seen among stalkers. For instance, in Sheridan et al.'s (2001) survey of stalking victims, most of the stalkers described were male, and slightly older than their victims. However, around one third were unemployed when they began their harassment campaigns while an additional third were in professional and clerical occupations. Further differences were seen in the methods employed by the stalkers: almost all regularly watched their victim, while only around half threatened assault, and a minority bugged their victim's home.

Research that has discovered similarities and differences such as these, coupled with the need for society to attempt to control aberrant behaviour, has resulted in the creation of a number of diverse stalker classification systems. These systems have been designed for use in different disciplines

Stalking and Psychosexual Obsession: Psychological Perspectives for Prevention, Policing and Treatment.
Edited by J. Boon and L. Sheridan. © 2002 John Wiley & Sons, Ltd.

and as such vary in their aims and scope. No one classification system has been universally accepted by all professionals in the area of stalking. Instead, various attempts have been made to classify stalkers and their victims, as will be illustrated by the examples detailed below.

The majority of these systems distinguish between subtypes on the basis of particular characteristics of stalkers or their victims, while others have made distinctions according to the nature of the prior relationship between the two. Just one current taxonomy may be described as multi-axial. This chapter discusses the various strengths and weaknesses of these different approaches before presenting a new typology of stalkers—one that has been created specifically for use by law enforcement agencies.

CLASSIFICATIONS BASED ON STALKER OR VICTIM CHARACTERISTICS

Dietz and colleagues (1991a, b) considered the level of attachment the stalker had for the victim in the context of cases where the targets were celebrities and other public figures. The principal motivation for perpetrators in these cases was a wish to become physically closer to, or noticed by, their target: this contrasts to the attachment felt towards celebrities by normal people, which is based instead on motivations more to do with obligation or attraction.

Rather than looking at motivation, Geberth's (1992) typology of stalkers considers their mental states. Within this typology, stalker types are labelled as psychopathic personality stalkers and psychotic personality stalkers. The key feature of the psychotic personality stalker is that he or she is delusional, becoming obsessed with an unobtainable target such as a pop star. In cases such as these, stalking is based on the conviction that the target shares these feelings, such that all the stalker has to do is to make the target aware of their existence. In short, these stalkers suffer from "erotomania" (see Chapter 10) in which sufferers believe there exists a reciprocal attraction between themselves and their targets, who are usually of higher socioeconomic status (American Psychiatric Association, 1994). In contrast, psychopathic personality stalkers tend to be dominant ex-partners—they have lost control of the victim and hope to commit acts of violence towards them.

Holmes' (1993) typology was victim-based, concluding that there are six different types of stalker. These types require little further explanation, and are celebrity, lust, hit, love-scorned, political and domestic stalkers. For instance, the celebrity stalker selects his or her victims from the world of entertainment, whereas the domestic stalker selects a former partner. The lust stalker is motivated by sex, moving from one victim to another in a serial fashion. The hit stalker differs dramatically: rather than being motivated by conventional psychological disorder, he or she is instead motivated by money. Following payment by a third party, these stalkers establish their victims' habits before using this information in murdering them.

A review of the psychological, forensic and psychiatric literature was also the basis of McAnaney et al.'s (1993) typology. This stipulates four categories of stalker, namely erotomanic, borderline erotomanic, former intimate and sociopathic. The latter develop criteria for the "ideal victim", and are typically serial murderers and serial rapists. Three of these four stalker types were said to have a delusional mental illness or to be personality disordered. Finally, Kienlen et al. (1997) divided stalkers into two groups simply according to whether they were or were not judged to be psychotic. This is interesting since, unlike Geberth's, the typology does not assume mental illness or personality disorder to underlie *all* cases of stalking.

PROBLEMS WITH EXISTING CLASSIFICATIONS

Although the various classifications described above do much to advance our theoretical knowledge of stalking and our practical understanding of how to deal with it, they are also subject to a number of limitations. First, some fail to account sufficiently for the heterogeneity of the population, which includes some individuals who are "normal" and others who are mentally ill or personality disordered. Second, some typologies contain an element of ambiguity that makes it difficult to classify any given stalker as clearly belonging to *one particular type alone*. Third, the reliability of such typologies may be questioned also, given that the number of cases on which they are based is not always clear, and that some are of a rather arbitrary and impressionistic nature. Fourth, the number of the stalker types defined ranges between two and more than seven: some of the classifications (e.g. Geberth's) may be criticised as too finite, while others (e.g. Dietz's) deal with the stalking of public figures only. Finally, and perhaps most importantly of all, most typologies fail to provide guidance for case management. It is important to remember, however, that any classification of stalkers will likely vary in accordance with the goals of the group who develop it (Mullen et al., 2000).

CLASSIFICATIONS BASED ON THE
STALKER–VICTIM RELATIONSHIP

Zona et al. (1998), drawing on a decade of practical research, posited that the relationship (real or imagined) between stalker and victim best informs an understanding of the psychology of stalkers. Probably the first study that attempted to classify the victim–stalker prior relationship was conducted in 1993 by Zona and colleagues, who categorised the police case files of 74 "obsessional harassers". Victims were divided into two categories, "prior relationship" and "no prior relationship". The former grouping was further subdivided into "acquaintance", "customer", "neighbour", "professional relationship", "dating" and "sexual intimates". Harmon, et al. (1995) classified the "type of prior interaction" between 48 individuals who had been charged with harassment and their victims into: "personal", "professional", "employment", "media" (where the target is a celebrity with no connection to the stalker), "acquaintance", "none" or "unknown".

Fremouw et al. (1997) examined the harassment experiences of 593 US college students, producing four victim–stalker categorisations: "friend", "casual date", "serious date" and "stranger". Wright et al. (1996) suggested that stalking occurs on a continuum from non-delusional to delusional, and argued that what most readily distinguishes stalking behaviour is the type of prior relationship that the stalker has had with his or her victim. That is, on the extreme delusional end of the spectrum no actual prior relationship need exist between stalker and victim, while at the other end of the continuum are actual prior relationships. Finally, Emerson et al. (1998) collected opportunistic victim and archive data from a variety of sources, and produced the following relational categories: "unacquainted stalking", "pseudoacquainted stalking", where the pursuer feels that they have a special bond with a celebrity, and "semi-acquainted stalking", where there has been historical contact, or where there exists a minimal amount of present contact.

Meloy (1997) posited that future studies should utilise a system based on acquaintanceship: those who were prior acquaintances, those who were prior sexual intimates and those who were strangers. He regrouped Harmon et al.'s (1995) data according to this classification and found that 58% were prior acquaintances, 21% were strangers and 12% were prior intimates (8% were unknown). Similarly, Mullen & Pathé (1994) wrote that "the majority of objects of affection had had some contact with the patient, albeit fleeting" (p. 471). Meloy (1997) concluded from his review that the majority of obsessional followers will pursue prior acquaintances, and that the rest will be divided, in some unpredictable proportion, between prior sexual intimates and complete strangers. However, Meloy also pointed out that possibly the most important caveat in the application of early taxonomies was the likely under-representation of spouses or ex-spouses. This is probably because early studies focused almost exclusively on erotomanic disorders, which, by definition, would rule out most spouses and ex-spouses from the stalking population. It may also reflect a selection bias on the part of law enforcement officers, who arrest and prosecute the more "high profile" or "stranger" obsessional followers. Similar trends in prosecution have been observed in child sexual abuse cases (Davies & Noon, 1991).

Wallis (1996) conducted a study of Chief Constables in the United Kingdom, asking them to provide details of stalking cases in their force area. This was the first investigation in the UK that attempted to provide data on the victim–stalker prior relationship. Five broad relational categories were produced. These were: ex-domestic partner (spouse, common law partner, accounting for 16.1% of the total sample of 151), ex-intimate relationship (boyfriend/girlfriend, 21.9% of the sample), casual relationship (e.g. friend, neighbour, 25.8% of the sample), work colleague (15.5%), and finally, in 20.6% of cases the stalker was previously unknown to the victim.

These results seem to correspond with Meloy's prediction, in that the largest proportion of stalkers were said to have been casually acquainted with their victims. Similarly, Pathé & Mullen (1997) found that, of their 100 stalking victims, 29 were ex-partners of the stalker, 25 had first encountered the stalker through a professional relationship, 9 had first encountered him or her in other work-related contexts, 21 had had casual social encounters with or were neighbours of the stalker, and 16 had no knowledge of any prior contact with their stalker.

More systematic recent investigations, however, have confirmed that it is ex-intimates who form the largest category of stalking victims. Hall (1998) found that of 145 victims of stalking who responded to a series of advertisements across the USA, 57% had had an intimate relationship with the person who became their stalker. Mullen et al. (2000) stated in a review that ex-intimate stalkers are "the largest category, the commonest victim profile being a woman who has previously shared an intimate relationship with her (usually male) stalker" (p. 44). In the United Kingdom, 48% of the 95 stalking victims discussed by Sheridan et al. (2001) had been pursued by an ex-partner. It is also now generally accepted that ex-intimate stalkers are the relational grouping most likely to present a danger to their victims (e.g. Harmon et al., 1995; Walker & Meloy, 1998; Mullen et al., 1999; Palarea et al., 1999; Farnham et al., 2000).

A MULTI-AXIAL APPROACH TO STALKER CLASSIFICATION

Although classifying stalkers and their victims in terms of their prior relationship may be useful, it is perhaps simplistic and represents only part of the classification process. As we have already seen with typologies of the stalkers themselves, victim–stalker typologies fail to take sufficient account of the absence or presence of mental illness in the stalker—an important factor considering that, as a group, stalkers are likely to be comorbid for a range of disorders (e.g. Farnham et al., 2000; Kamphuis & Emmelkamp, 2000; Mullen et al., 2000). It may be that the personality-disordered stalker targets ex-partners, strangers or both. Actual stalker behaviour is also an important consideration as distinct stalker types may present different levels of risk to their victims and to third parties. Further, what are the motivations that drive the behaviour of different stalkers? Can different types of stalkers be associated with distinct antecedent, alleviating and exacerbating factors?

Mullen et al. (2000) produced a detailed classification of five stalker types: rejected, intimacy seeking, resentful, predatory and incompetent. The classification was developed using data obtained from stalkers whom the authors had assessed at their specialist clinic in Australia. The classification represented an advance over previous typologies as it took a multi-axial approach, incorporating the context for the stalking and stalker motivations, the stalker's psychiatric status *and* the prior stalker–victim relationship. The need for an examination of what the stalker had to gain personally from their pursuit was recognised, as this would aid an understanding of motivation, goals and the factors that may serve to reinforce the individual stalker's aberrant behaviour. Mullen et al. posited that the context in which the stalking arose is also of importance, as it will be intrinsically related to the stalker's aims. These issues make up the first of the three axes that form the taxonomy.

The second axis involves the prior relationship between stalker and victim. These relational categories were separated into ex-intimate partners, professional contacts, work-related contacts, casual acquaintances and friends, the famous, and strangers. The final axis was related to the stalker's psychiatric status, and all of the 168 stalkers on which this classification was based were diagnosed with at least one psychiatric disorder.

Mullen et al. state that this typology aided decisions on the clinical management strategy that was adopted. For instance, it was discovered that many "intimacy seekers" had psychotic disorders, and while legal measures had little effect, mental health treatment was effective in ending their campaigns. Conversely, "rejected" stalkers (the majority of whom were ex-intimates) were more likely to react to legal interventions.

This taxonomy would appear to be a definite advance on those outlined earlier, and this is primarily for four reasons. First, it is based on sound clinical data and on a relatively large sample (168). Second, it incorporates all the major variables (such as the psychiatric status of the perpetrator and the nature of the prior victim–stalker relationship) that were included piecemeal in the previous typologies. Third, the taxonomy includes details of the context in which the stalking began and the motivations that drive the stalking, features absent from most other classifications. Finally, this multi-axial approach has a clear practical applicability in that it has provided unambiguous guidelines for the treatment of stalkers. If the taxonomy has one major caveat, this would concern its applicability to the policing of stalkers. As the authors themselves note: "Our system of classification . . . works for us but this is in the context of mental health professionals who . . . have no role in law enforcement" (p. 78).

A TAXONOMY FOR LAW ENFORCEMENT

This chapter will now advance a new taxonomy of stalkers that departs from the typologies discussed above in two major ways. First, it is based directly on data obtained from British victims of stalking. Second, it is aimed explicitly at law enforcement practitioners with a view to assessing and managing individual real-world stalking cases. Mullen et al. (2000) have suggested that the most valuable stalker taxonomy is the one that best serves the needs of the user group. While many of the classifications outlined earlier have their origins in the mental health field, the system that is advanced in this chapter is geared to being of greatest use to those in the law enforcement professions—that is, people who require guidance as to patterns in offender motivation and the contingent course of best practice for case management.

It is worth stating the rationale behind creating a stalker classificatory system that is specifically geared toward law enforcement. Such a system should be of use in that it can help investigators to prioritise among the large number of potentially important factors present in any given case. Further, the system should enable its users to better understand the motivations behind various stalking activities. This is especially important given that the same behaviours may present different levels of danger when perpetrated by different stalker types. For example, an "infatuation harasser" and a "sadistic stalker" may both send unwanted flowers and letters, follow their victim, and attempt to glean information from the victim's friends and relatives. However, the motivations for these acts differ markedly. Once law enforcement officers are aware of these differing motivations, they will be equipped with relevant information pertaining to the context for the behaviour, the degree and nature of the threat (if any) faced by the victim, and the criteria for selecting and adopting case management strategies.

Previous work (e.g. Pathé & Mullen, 1997; Hall, 1998) has demonstrated that a wealth of data may be obtained from the victims of stalking themselves. It is perhaps surprising, then, that the majority of the stalker classifications outlined above were based on literature reviews or on case files held by the police and mental health services. There are two main problems associated with building an offender taxonomy from these types of case files. First, the sample on which the taxonomy is based will not be representative of the entire population of stalkers. Rather, it will only represent stalkers who have actually been charged with or convicted of stalking and harassment-related offences, and stalkers who suffer from serious certifiable mental illnesses. Second, such a classification would be forced to rely on archival data, which may be scanty, incorrect or incomplete. Although the current technique of basing a typology of stalkers on the accounts of victims also has associated pitfalls, the victims did provide abundant data pertaining to their experiences. Also, the majority of respondents supplied contact details so that their accounts could be followed up and additional information obtained.

CONSTRUCTION OF THE TAXONOMY

One of the authors is an Association of Chief Police Officers (ACPO) accredited psychological profiler working in the United Kingdom. The profiling work has involved cases of relatively minor stalking through to homicide. The authors also had access to a database of 124 stalking cases, pertinent information on these cases being detailed on questionnaires. The areas explored by these concerned several diverse facets of stalking, including basic demographic information concerning the stalker and his or her victim, full details of the stalking (such as how it began, and which aspects of it changed or remained the same throughout the stalking episode), how the stalking had ended (if it had ended), those factors that the victim thought had exacerbated and alleviated the stalking behaviour, how the emotions experienced by the victim evolved over time, and the responses of both professional agencies and significant others. The data had originally been collected from members of two prominent UK self-help groups which had been set up specifically to aid victims and ex-victims of stalking.

The authors each reviewed the entire 124-case data set with a view to producing a system of classification that would be most applicable to law enforcement practitioners. Because the authors reviewed the data set separately, it was necessary to agree two primary "rules" on which they would base their judgements. The first was that the resulting classifications should maximally facilitate investigations by law enforcement agencies. Specifically, classification should be (i) jargon-free and easily comprehensible, (ii) applicable in the field throughout the course of a case, from its genesis through to its development and conclusion, and (iii) capable of generating specific guidelines for good practice in the management of individual and unique cases. The second "rule" was that the taxonomy should relate to the 124 cases in as simple a manner as possible. It may be argued that the closer the taxonomy related to the 124 stalking cases, then the greater its accuracy and goodness of fit to real-life stalking investigation.

In addition to these guidelines for developing the classification system, two further principles were adopted in constructing these initial classifications. The first of these was that there should be no preset number of stalker categories. In principle, then, there could be just one category that contained all 124 stalking cases, or alternatively, 124 distinct categories each containing one case that was regarded as completely distinct from all others. Second, there was no pre-agreement on the relative proportions of the data that would go to form each category. In other words, some forms of stalking may be far more prevalent than other forms.

THE CLASSIFICATION

On the basis of the 124 stalking cases, the raters produced a stalker classification system. Four major stalker typologies were revealed, two of which are comprised of two further subsections. In addition to this, the raters used victims' reports in generating associated case management interventions. Specifically, these interventions related to the context of and motivations for the level of threat represented in any given typology.

The extent to which each category was represented in the sample of 124 cases is shown in parentheses following their respective titles.

Type 1: Ex-Partner Harassment/Stalking (50%)

Characteristics

- Bitterness and hate, linked to the relationship's history (past orientation).
- Hot-headed anger and hostility (compare with the "sadistic" stalker's cold need for control).
- The prior relationship is likely to have involved domestic violence which has developed into more public violence and verbal abuse.
- Overt threats, particularly where placed in conjunction with recrimination and reference to perceived issues of contention.
- Recruitment of friends and family to perpetuate a campaign of hate toward the target.
- Motivating issues for the stalker relate to custody, property or finance (associated issues of power, control and freedom).
- New relationships engender jealousy and aggressive behaviour.
- Third-party abuse (verbal and physical), e.g. family members and known supporters of the victim.
- Partisanship on both sides.
- The harassment is characterised by high levels of physical violence, high levels of verbal threat, and property damage.
- Triggers for harassment both spontaneous (e.g. following a chance encounter) and premeditated (e.g. sitting in a car outside the victim's home).
- Activity tending towards being anger driven, and impulsivity with corresponding lack of concern about coming to police attention.
- Perpetrator age diverse and reflective of time of onset of strife in relationship.

Case Management Implications

- High risk of violence.
- High risk of property damage.
- Generalised anger, but there is a need to take seriously any specific threats made.
- Any unnecessary retaliation—financial, legal, physical or verbal— should be curbed to an absolute minimum.
- The victim should avoid wherever possible frequenting the same venues as offender.
- In extremis consider relocation with physical distance being even more important than secrecy.

Case Example

A 28-year-old woman left her husband after five years of marriage. Although the husband had always been verbally abusive towards her, he had recently begun to act out violently. After she had left, his first tactic was to attempt to convince their families and friends that she was to blame, and that she was a bad wife and mother. He was more successful in this with his rather than her family. Verbal and physical acrimony and violence ensued. This escalated as a direct function of legal arrangements and chance meetings at locations they had previously both shared (for instance, the marital home). Their respective family and friends separated into two "camps"—each supporting either the husband or his estranged wife—and secondary aggravation between these groups also escalated. Attenuating factors were associated with minimising physical, verbal, written and legal contact, and with maximising efforts to neutralise and avoid any confrontation.

Type 2: Infatuation Harassment (18.5%)

This grouping is divided into two subtypes—young love and midlife love— the case management implications of which are discussed separately below.

Characteristics

- The target is "beloved" rather than "victim".
- Beloved is all pervasive in thoughts.
- The world and events are interpreted in relation to beloved.
- Beloved is focus of fantasy.
- The focus of fantasy is and remains romantic and positive.

- Intense yearning (cf. anger).
- Particular emphasis on hope of what might be (future orientation).
- Beloved is sought out with *non-malicious* ruses, e.g. billet-doux under windscreen wipers, hanging around and pretending any meeting is a chance encounter, quizzing friends and associates regarding any aspects of the beloved.
- Low levels of danger.
- The harassment is *not* characterised by threats, macabre gifts and negative intervention (cf. sinister intrusion of the sadistic stalker as outlined below).
- Perpetrator's age is typically teenage or midlife.

Case Management Implications

In the case of "young love":

- Elevation of the cognitive perspective; that is, a careful and thorough explanation regarding the law and how upsetting the whole thing is to the victim, and the adoption of a sympathetic stance in explaining how the relationship has been misconstrued by the "perpetrator".

In the case of "midlife love":

- Again, a reasoned approach but with the possible exploration of placing physical distance between parties (for instance, a work transfer). Also, possible difficulties resulting from boredom or discord in existing relationship may be addressed via counselling.

Case Example

Mr J, a 53-year-old office manager with grown-up children, had been experiencing marital difficulties for some years. He described himself as "depressed". When he appointed a new secretary, however, he felt that he had been "given a new lease of life". He lost weight, traded in his estate car for a convertible and began to take a renewed interest in his appearance. Eventually he asked his secretary for a dinner date, which was politely refused. Mr J continued to press his attentions on his secretary—regularly buying her flowers, taking an unsolicited interest in all aspects of her life, appearing at her favourite pubs and nightclubs, even suggesting that they take a two-week holiday to the Maldives. The company Personnel Department cautioned him after the secretary complained that she felt intimidated. The secretary found a new job and Mr J attended marriage guidance counselling.

Type 3: Delusional Fixation Stalking (15.3%)—Dangerous

Characteristics

- The stalker tends to be incoherent yet victim fixated (orientation toward the present).
- The victim tends to be at high risk of physical violence and sexual assault.
- Perpetrator likely to have come to the notice of police and mental health professionals and be suffering from, for instance, borderline personality disorder, episodic schizophrenia.
- Perpetrator likely to have a history of sexual problems and offences, including stalking.
- Activities are characterised by the incessant bombarding of the target with telephone calls, letters, visits to workplace.
- Behavioural patterns lacking in coherence, with the stalker likely to appear in diverse places, at irregular times.
- Content of material sent by and conversation of perpetrator likely to be unsubtle, sexual/obscene, and disjointed semantically.
- Delusional fixation stalkers tend to couch their statements of love in terms of sexual intent towards victim (cf. romantic stance of infatuated harasser).
- Stalkers hold a firm belief in a relationship between themselves and the target even though there has been no prior contact.
- Victims are male or female and tend to have some form of elevated/noteworthy status:
  - professionals (e.g. GPs, university lecturers)
  - celebrities
  - non-famous but local and attractive figures.

Case Management Implications

- Not responsive to reason or rejection.
- Refer to a forensic psychiatrist for assessment (although likely to have been assessed already).

Case Example

A 25-year-old woman, Ms G, was approached outside her workplace by an unkempt individual who was blatantly suggestive, asking her for sexual favours. She initially ignored him, but this came to be a daily event. Ms G reported that he was regularly following her home, where he would stand in her garden and howl. The stalker was preoccupied with a belief that the world would soon end and that his only hope of salvation was to be with Ms G when Armageddon came. His topic of speech would veer markedly, however, between this subject and his sexual fantasies involving Ms G.

The case culminated when Ms G tried to reason with him one night in her garden. He was completely impervious to reason and neighbours called police when he moved from verbal suggestions to an attempted sexual assault on Ms G. This led to the stalker being placed in a psychiatric secure unit where he was diagnosed as schizophrenic. He is currently on medication to control his condition and the authorities' efforts are targeted towards maintaining his medication regime.

Type 3: Delusional Fixation Stalking (15.3%)—Less Dangerous

Characteristics

- Stalkers hold the delusional conviction that there is an extant, idealised relationship (present and future orientation).
- Stalker scarcely knows their victim.
- Activity not characterised by threats—just the stated belief that the victim wants to be with him or her (cf. sadistic stalkers' similar statements but with sinister twists such as "in heaven" or simply as a means of accentuating the victim's feelings of despair that nothing works).
- Stalker not amenable to reason from the victim (cf. (i) infatuation harassment, where clarity can attenuate the behaviour, and (ii) sadistic stalking, where the perpetrator consciously exploits their non-response to victims' appeals as a means of demonstrating helplessness in the victim).
- Stalker capable of a complete construction of a fantasy of an extant, reciprocated relationship as though victim were in accord and consensual.
- In the event of an eventual submerged perception that the "relationship" is not fitting with the perpetrator's deluded perception, this is likely to occur with rationalisation that it is someone else's fault (e.g. victim's husband putting demons into her head).
- In the event of a particular individual being identified as thwarting the relationship, there is a contingent element of danger—particularly where that individual is perceived by the stalker as being dangerous to the victim.
- Victims tend to be female professionals.

Case Management Implications

- Victim should seek a legal remedy.
- Victim should be advised not to respond as far as possible.
- If absolutely necessary to respond to the offender, the victim should be advised to do so with a clear negation of the situation and non-angry requests for him or her to go away.
- Again, if absolutely necessary to respond to the offender, the victim should never argue and should keep the encounter down to a minimum.

• Legal agencies should be aware that the stalker is not responsive to reason or rejection.

Case Example

A married male formed a delusional fixation for a married female bank clerk whom he barely knew. His delusional orientation moved over time through three phases. Initially he behaved as if she would immediately leave her husband for him. After several weeks he came to believe that she refused to leave the family home as she did not want to cause her husband to be upset. Several months later, the stalker's orientation changed again in his explanation for her refusal to leave her husband. Specifically he reasoned that the target's husband must be putting voices into her head to prevent her from having a relationship with the offender. The stalker did not threaten his victim or her husband at any point, but the fixation has continued for many more months and the offender's own working and family life have been in effect destroyed.

Type 4: Sadistic Stalking (12.9%)

Characteristics

• The victim is an obsessive target of the offender, and their life is seen as quarry and prey (incremental orientation).
• Victim selection criteria is primarily rooted in the victim being: (i) someone worthy of spoiling, i.e. someone who is perceived by the stalker at the commencement as being happy, "good", stable and content, and (ii) lacking in the victim's perception any just rationale as to why she was targeted.
• Initial low-level acquaintance.
• Apparently benign initially but unlike infatuation harassment the methods of the perpetrator tend to have a negative orientation designed to disconcert, unnerve, and thus take power away from the victim. For instance:
  – notes left *in* the victim's locked car in order to unsettle the target (cf. billet-doux of infatuated harassment)
  – subtle evidence being left of having been in contact with the victim's personal items, e.g. a rifled underwear drawer, reordering/removal of private papers, cigarette ends left in ash trays, toilet having been used
  – "helping" mend victim's car that stalker had previously disabled.
• Thereafter progressive escalation of control over *all* aspects (i.e. social, historical, professional, financial, physical) of the victim's life.
• The offender's gratification is rooted in the desire to extract evidence of the victim's powerlessness with inverse implications for his power, implying sadism.

- Additional implication is the self-perpetuating desire to hone down relentlessly on individual victim(s).
- Emotional coldness, deliberateness and psychopathy (cf. the heated nature of ex-partner harassment).
- Sadistic stalkers tend to have a history of stalking behaviour and the controlling of others.
- Stalkers tend to broaden out targets to family and friends of the target in a bid to isolate the victim and further enhance their control.
- Communications tend to be a blend of loving and threatening (not hate) designed to destabilise and confuse the victim.
- Threats are either overt ("We're going to die together") or subtle (the delivery of dead roses).
- Sadistic stalkers can be highly dangerous—in particular with psychological violence geared to the controlling of the victim with fear, loss of privacy and the curtailment of her social world.
- Physical violence is also entirely possible—especially by means which undermine the victim's confidence in matters normally taken for granted, e.g. disabling brake cables, disarming safety equipment, cutting power off.
- Sexual content of communications is aimed primarily to intimidate through the victim's humiliation, disgust and general undermining of self-esteem.
- The older the offender, the more likely he is to have enacted sadistic stalking before, and he will not be likely to offend after 40 years of age if not engaged in such stalking before.
- Victims are likely to be revisited after a seeming hiatus.

Case Management Implications

- Should be taken very seriously.
- Acknowledge from outset that the stalker's activity will be very difficult to eradicate.
- Acknowledge that there is no point whatsoever in appealing to the offender—indeed, this will exacerbate the problem.
- Never believe any assurances, alternative versions of events etc. which are given by the offender.
- However, record them for use in legal action later.
- The victim should be given as much understanding and support as can be made available.
- The victim should not be given false or unrealistic assurance or guarantees that he or she will be protected.
- The victim should carefully consider relocation. The geographical emphasis should be less on distance per se, and more on where the offender is least able to find the victim.

- The police should have in mind that the sadistic stalker will be likely to (i) carefully construct and calculate their activity to simultaneously minimise the risk of intervention by authorities while retaining the maximum impact on the victim, (ii) be almost impervious to intervention since the overcoming of obstacles provides new and potent means of demonstrating the victim's powerlessness (and thus is self-perpetuating), and (iii) if jailed continue both personally and vicariously through the use of a network.

Case Example

Shortly after the death of her husband, a middle-aged woman, Mrs T, formed an acquaintanceship with Mr H, a local man. Her reliance on this man increased when she began to believe that someone was visiting her home while she was out. She would regularly find that, for example, toothbrushes had been used or that personal letters had been reordered. She was also upset that dead birds were frequently found on her doorstep. Mrs T was finally admitted to hospital when she awoke to find the unearthed remains of her husband deposited on her doorstep. Throughout this time, she described Mr H as "a tower of strength". Three months later, police evidence linked Mr H to the desecration of the grave. During questioning, Mr H revealed that this had been his method of asking Mrs T "What it is that her husband has got that I haven't?".

OVERVIEW OF THE NEW SYSTEM

An overview of the entire system as listed above is provided in Table 5.1.

SUMMARY

This chapter has presented a classificatory system of stalkers that aims to best serve the needs of law enforcement agencies. A particular objective of the taxonomy was to provide a system that could aid the comprehension of the offender behaviour of stalkers and to use this understanding to provide clear strategies for the management of individual cases. It is important to note that the current taxonomy is not being put forward as in any sense "superior" to the classification systems detailed earlier in this chapter. Rather, its distinction is that it has been developed specifically to suit the needs of law enforcement officers who are tasked with investigating stalking crimes.

As described earlier, one potentially attractive feature of a typology like that set out here is that a given individual stalking act can, in isolation,

Table 5.1. Overview of classification system

Attribute	Category (status)			
	Ex-partner (harassment/ stalking)	Infatuation (harassment)	Delusional fixated (stalking)	Sadistic (stalking)
Duration	Long term	Short term (if addressed)	Long term (while in vicinity)	Long term
Victim perception	Anger, fear, hate	Nuisance, embarrassment	Fear, bewilderment	Fear, helplessness
Victim risk	Proximity/ personal circumstance dependent	Low	High	High
Ability to intervene	Potential	High	Low	Very low
Techniques to minimise threat (e.g.)	relocation (distance criterion) reasonable settlements	Sensitive explanation (young)/job relocation (adult)	Perpetrator referred to forensic psychiatrist	Secret relocation/ maximum support
Motive	Hate, resentment	Love	Fixation	Control
Victim selection criteria	Hate, resentment, resources	Object of desire	Proximity, physical attraction	Lack of apparent obvious reason
Probability of victim revisit	Geography/ circumstance specific	Low	Opportunity related	Very high

correspond with more than one type of stalker. However, viewing that act as part of the more general framework of a "type" of stalker has important case management implications. To illustrate this, a more detailed example will now be provided concerning how one particular stalking behaviour can be interpreted differently according to stalker category.

Previous work (e.g. Zona et al., 1993; Meloy & Gothard, 1995; Pathé & Mullen, 1997; Hall, 1998) has shown that it is common for stalkers and harassers to send letters and notes to their victims. The nature of this type of communication, however, will differ, depending on which category of stalker wrote the letters or notes. An ex-partner stalker/harasser would be most likely to send a communication that was volatile in tone and which referred to the ownership of property, possessions, parental access and rights, and past grievances such as extra-marital affairs. In contrast, written communications sent by an infatuated harasser would tend to be of a "harmless" and romantic nature. Letters sent by a delusional fixated stalker to their victim would differ again in that the content would likely be incoherent with a strongly sexual element. Finally, a sadistic stalker's written communications may on the face of it appear to be relatively innocuous. When taken in context, however, with other reports and evidence from the case, it is likely that these letters would actually be threatening. Unlike letters sent by the other stalker types, those written by a sadistic stalker would be carefully couched so as to contain no direct threat that could later be used as evidence against the stalker.

What this example illustrates is that it is not sufficient just to examine the actual behaviour of a stalker. Rather, any stalking investigation should aim to look beyond the physical evidence and into the context for the individual offender's behaviour. What may at first seem to be innocuous may actually represent a threat to the victim, while a barrage of "romantic" material may be no more than harmless longings in written form.

The typology would indicate that all of the stalker types, with the exception of the infatuation harasser, have the potential to be a danger to their victim. The nature of the danger and factors that are likely to trigger it, however, differ across the categories. Ease of prediction of the level and the likelihood of danger presented by the three "dangerous" stalker types will also differ. The most predictable of the three is the ex-partner stalker/harasser. Examination of the 124 stalking cases revealed that physical proximity between stalker and victim, legal disputes and chance meetings all emerged as triggers for both verbal and physical abuse. Ex-partner stalkers also emerged as the group for which means of avoiding stalker danger were easiest to implement. Included among effective case management strategies were measures that limited any chance of grievances being aired and re-aired (such as the victim removing further items of furniture from the former marital home) and placing increased geographical distance between the stalker/harasser and their target.

In those cases classified as sadistic stalking, however, putting geographical distance between stalker and victim was not usually seen to have any beneficial effect. Instead, attempts made by the victim to hide from a sadistic stalker tended to cause an intensification of the stalker's activities and a more determined effort to impact upon all aspects of the victim's life. Only two victims in this group were actually seen to "escape", and in both cases this was due to the victim relocating to secret addresses over 300 miles away, with the help of the police. Both of these victims still expressed the belief that their stalker would eventually track them down. The main factor that distinguished the sadistic stalker from the other three stalker groups was the planned, calculated, meticulous aspect to their approach.

As outlined above, the delusional fixated stalker is, in contrast to the sadistic stalker, more likely to have committed and continue committing criminal offences. Although the delusional fixated stalkers did not emerge as having the meticulous and planned approach of the sadistic stalker, they still demonstrated that they posed a definite risk to their victims. Those intervention techniques that did appear to alleviate the activities of the delusional fixated perpetrator tended to come from a mental health management approach, such as ensuring that the offender was taking their prescribed medication. In the "less dangerous" sub-group of delusional fixated stalkers there was little evidence that any intervention was effective in eradicating the offender's fixation on the victim. As in other studies relating to erotomania there was, however, some evidence that over lengthy time periods the offender eventually can change his or her perspective regarding the victim's motivation. This latter point can be illustrated by the case example given on p. 71.

In conclusion, this chapter has demonstrated that there is no one classification of stalkers or their victims that is favoured by all professionals interested in stalking phenomena. The taxonomy presented here is targeted toward those tasked with policing stalkers, and, as such, it offers clear implications for case management. However, even with the help of the legal authorities, the most dangerous and violent stalkers are difficult to identify within the criminal justice system as they may have been charged with crimes other than stalking or harassment, such as rape or murder. Sadistic stalkers can be particularly adept at avoiding police capture, and often cloud investigations for considerable periods of time, for instance by initiating counter-allegations of stalking. It is hoped that typologies such as this one may help introduce police officers who are unacquainted with the area to the various methods employed by stalkers, and in turn encourage recognition that stalkers are not a homogenous group. Rather, they are complex individuals whose needs and motivations will differ, and who offer various levels of danger, even when their activities, at face value, appear to be very similar.

REFERENCES

American Psychiatric Association (1994). *Diagnostic and Statistical Manual of Mental Disorders*, 4th edn. Washington, DC: APA.

Davies, G.M. & Noon, E. (1991). *An Evaluation of the Live Link for Child Witnesses*. London: Home Office.

Dietz, P.E., Matthews, D.B., Martell, D.A., Stewart, T.M., Hrouda, D.R. & Warren, J. (1991a). Threatening and otherwise inappropriate letters to members of the United States Congress. *Journal of Forensic Sciences*, **36**, 1445–68.

Dietz, P.E., Matthews, D.B., Van Duyne, C., Martell, D.A., Parry, C.D.H., Stewart, T., Warren, J. & Crowder, J.D. (1991b). Threatening and otherwise inappropriate letters to Hollywood celebrities. *Journal of Forensic Sciences*, **36**, 185–209.

Emerson, R.M., Ferris, K.O. & Brooks Gardner, C. (1998). On being stalked. *Social Problems*, **45**, 289–314.

Farnham, F.R., James, D.V. & Cantrell, P. (2000). Association between violence, psychosis, and relationship to victim in stalkers. *The Lancet*, **355**, 199.

Fremouw, W.J., Westrup, D. & Pennypacker, J. (1997). Stalking on campus: the prevalence and strategies for coping with stalking. *Journal of Forensic Sciences*, **42**, 666–9.

Geberth, V.J. (1992). Stalkers. *Law and Order*, **10**, 1–6.

Hall, D.M. (1998). The victims of stalking. In J. Reid Meloy (ed.) *The Psychology of Stalking: Clinical and Forensic Perspectives* (pp. 113–37). San Diego, CA: Academic Press.

Harmon, R.B., Rosner, R. & Owens, H. (1995). Obsessional harassment and erotomania in a criminal court population. *Journal of Forensic Sciences*, **40**, 88–196.

Holmes, R.H. (1993). Stalking in America: types and methods of criminal stalkers. *Journal of Contemporary Criminal Justice*, **9**, 317–27.

Kamphuis, J.H. & Emmelkamp, P.M.G. (2000). Stalking—a contemporary challenge for forensic and clinical psychiatry. *British Journal of Psychiatry*, **176**, 206–9.

Kienlen, K.K., Birmingham, D.L., Solberg, K.B, O'Regan, J.T. & Meloy, J.R. (1997). A comparative study of psychotic and nonpsychotic stalking. *Journal of the American Academy of Psychiatry and the Law*, **25**, 317–34.

McAnaney, K., Curliss, L. & Abeyta-Price, C.E. (1993). From imprudence to crime: anti-stalking laws. *Notre Dame Law Review*, **68**, 819–909.

Meloy, J.R. (1997). A clinical investigation of the obsessional follower: "she loves me, she loves me not…". In L. Schlesinger (ed.), *Explorations in Criminal Psychopathology* (pp. 9–32). Springfield, IL: Charles C. Thomas.

Meloy, J.R. & Gothard, S. (1995). Demographic and clinical comparison of obsessional followers and offenders with mental disorders. *American Journal of Psychiatry*, **152**, 258–63.

Mullen, P. & Pathé, M. (1994). Stalking and the pathologies of love. *Australian and New Zealand Journal of Psychiatry*, **28**, 469–77.

Mullen, P.E., Pathé, M. & Purcell, R. (2000). *Stalkers and their Victims*. Cambridge: Cambridge University Press.

Mullen, P.E., Pathé, M., Purcell, R. & Stewart, G.W. (1999). A study of stalkers. *American Journal of Psychiatry*, **156**, 1244–9.

Palarea, R.E., Zona, M.A., Lane, J.C. and Langhinrichsen-Rohling, J. (1999). The dangerous nature of intimate relationship stalking: threats, violence and associated risk factors. *Behavioral Sciences and the Law*, **17**, 269–83.

Pathé, M. & Mullen, P.E. (1997). The impact of stalkers on their victims. *British Journal of Psychiatry*, **170**, 12–17.

Sheridan, L., Davies, G.M. & Boon, J.C.W. (2001). The course and nature of stalking: a victim perspective. *The Howard Journal of Criminal Justice*, **40**, 215–34.

Walker, L.E. & Meloy, J.R. (1998). Stalking and domestic violence. In J. Reid Meloy (ed.) *The Psychology of Stalking: Clinical and Forensic Perspectives* (pp. 139–61). San Diego, CA: Academic Press.

Wallis, M. (1996). Outlawing stalkers. *Policing Today*, **2**, 25–9.

Wright, J.A., Burgess, A.G., Burgess, A.W., Laszlo, A.T., McCrary, G.O. & Douglas, J.E. (1996). A typology of interpersonal stalking. *Journal of Interpersonal Violence*, **11**, 487–502.

Zona, M.A., Palarea, R.E. & Lane, J.C. Jr. (1998). Psychiatric diagnosis and the offender–victim typology of stalking. In J. Reid Meloy (ed.) *The Psychology of Stalking: Clinical and Forensic Perspectives* (pp. 70–83). San Diego, CA: Academic Press.

Zona, M.A., Sharma, K.K. & Lane, J. (1993). A comparative study of erotomanic and obsessional subjects in a forensic sample. *Journal of Forensic Sciences*, **38**, 894–903.

CHAPTER 6

From Domestic Violence to Stalking: The Infinite Cycle of Violence

ANNA C. BALDRY

University of Rome

I was married to my ex-husband for 11 years. I met him when I was 14 and we soon started going out together. At the beginning he made me feel like a princess. He used to say "you belong to me" and I felt exclusive. When we were dating he was very jealous and possessive. How stupid I was! I used to like that a lot because I thought it meant that he really cared about me. He used to tell me what to do, what to wear and what to say. I was "his girl" and had to keep my mouth shut because what I said was rubbish. I could not go out with my friends because he told me that I had to wait in for his phone calls . . . I used to think I was very lucky because he really cared about me, sending me letters and even flowers. When I was 21 he asked me to marry him. My parents didn't like him and told me that I was too young, that I should wait and look around. I think they understood what type of man he was, but I did not want to listen to them . . .

After the marriage he was kind of nice but kind of obsessive and controlling. He was constantly checking my mail, my phone calls. Each time I wanted to go out he would keep me indoors for hours asking me where I was going, who I was seeing, . . . soon I gave up and stayed at home. I also had to give up my job, you know . . . I had two children, I was made to cope with all of it. He would never help me in anything.

The first time I really got scared was soon after the birth of my first child. We were in a restaurant. When we finished eating I went to the toilet and when I came out he told me that I had taken too long and he shoved me down the stairs, like that, for no reason. This was back in

1985 and I immediately went to a lawyer, I was so scared. The lawyer was very nice and she told me that I had all the rights to ask for a divorce. But I started crying saying that I loved him and that I could not give up my marriage and I started finding excuses for his behaviour saying that it was my fault and that we should try to work things out.

After he hit me he used to say he was sorry and told me that I provoked him and this made me feel guilty. I didn't go back to the lawyer till nine years later when I finally found the strength and courage to leave him, with the help of my sons and a shelter for battered women. I was confused, scared, but determined not to go back. I had had too much and feared that he would kill me and my children. So I did it. "I am free", I thought. Soon after I had to realise that things seemed to get even worse. He started looking for me, following me. He used to check my mileage and leave harassing notes on the windscreen asking me where I had been.

After the divorce he claimed custody of the children! Although this was granted to me he had access every week, with no supervision. The social worker told me that I had to give him my address so that he could come and collect the children. But that allowed the end of my second life or else you could say the beginning of my second end! He would arrive at any time of the day and the night, constantly phoning me telling me that I was a whore, insinuating that I had another relationship and that he would kill me and my "boyfriend". He would constantly phone me using the excuse of speaking with the children. We had arranged that he would come and pick up the children at 3.00 p.m. but he would arrive at 4.00 or even at 5.00. Sometimes he never turned up at all. The children were nervous. He just did it to keep me on the edge to prevent me from doing anything or having my own life. He always told me: "you are mine, nothing can separate us". I called the police several times, filed a compliant, but they often told me that they could not do much because even if I was scared and feared for my life and that of my children, all things he used to do and tell me were not crimes... I did not know what to do.

Now I have my children, my friends, my work, my new boyfriend, my house, my car; yes, you would say, I have my life, but I feel I still miss my freedom—the freedom of leaving the house without the constant need to check who is following me, who is phoning me, who is sitting in the car next to mine. I am not obsessional or a maniac, I am simply scared but I do not want to give up, it would mean letting him have his way, but now it is enough, he had too much of my life. We are tired and exhausted, he took everything from our lives and still tries to do so, but he does not realise that I am not alone any more. People now are helping me, they believe me and support me. My isolation is what allowed his behaviour to go on undisturbed in the past. He would count on that and would do everything to destroy every friendship, relationship or hobby that I had. He knew that nobody would do anything: "you and me alone, no one else can interfere between us!". This is what has changed today and what gives me hope... I too am helping other women to step out of the cycle of violence.

* * *

The above is from an interview conducted by the author with E.P. aged 39, a friend who lives in a constant state of fear but who has the strength and courage to walk with her head held high and to help other women in the Shelters for Battered women run by the NGO "Differenza Donna", an association of women against violence against women based in Rome. This chapter is dedicated to her and to all other women who suffer from domestic violence and stalking.

* * *

It is estimated that in the United States a woman gets beaten every 18 seconds. While you are reading this chapter, approximately 200 women will be assaulted by their partner or ex-partner in the United States, and a further 41 in Italy and in the UK. Every hour, almost 6000 women worldwide will be physically, psychologically or sexually abused, stalked or killed. Each year 2 million women in the US are seriously physically abused or killed by their partner or former partner. According to UNICEF's Annual Report (2000a), "up to half of all women and girls in some countries have experienced physical violence at the hands of an intimate partner or family member. More than 60 million females are missing from population statistics—killed by their own families deliberately or through neglect, because of their gender". Only 44 countries have adopted specific legislation to address domestic violence (including Peru, Chile and Equador); in all other countries there is still no specific legal sanction against rape, battering, stalking, or even the killing of a woman in the domestic setting (UNICEF, 2000b). The Federal Bureau of Investigation, in 1992, reported that 29% of all women murdered in the United States were killed by husbands, boyfriends or ex-partners, and the Bureau of Statistics reported similar figures for 1998 (Rennison & Welchans, 2000).

Domestic violence is considered to be any form of actual or threatened psychological, physical or sexual violence perpetrated within the family. Distinct from family violence, domestic violence is defined as any violence perpetrated in personal relationships, including married and de facto relationships, divorced, separated, past de facto relationships, and dating ones. Domestic violence is often accompanied by another form of violence—stalking—which may be defined as a "course of conduct directed at a specific person that involves repeated visual or physical proximity, non-consensual communication, verbal, written or implied threats, or a combination thereof that requires victims to feel a high level of fear of bodily harm" (National Criminal Justice Association, 1993). Women are at higher risk of domestic violence and stalking than are men (Tjaden & Thoennes, 2000a; Walker & Meloy, 1998). Even if men do report violence perpetrated by an intimate partner, there exist substantial gender differences in terms of the severity of the violence and its consequences, the number of repeated victimisations, the feelings of fear in the victim, and death threats made by the perpetrator. Moreover, some women who use violence against their partner may do so for self-defence purposes (Mirrlees-Black, 1999) and a few men might be beaten by a same gender partner, not by a woman.

Clearly domestic violence and stalking in intimate relationships are gender-based crimes and even if some studies have reported that they are per se gender neutral crimes (Pottie-Bunge & Locke, 2000), the same studies indicated that women are more at risk of being the victims, and men are more likely to be the perpetrators when referring to intimate violence. For the purpose of the present chapter we will refer to domestic violence and stalking perpetrated by men against female partners or former partners, not just limited to married couples but also to de facto relationships.

FACTS AND MYTHS

Domestic violence and violence against women in general are still highly under-reported and under-recorded crimes. It is estimated that fewer than half of all battered, raped or stalked women will report their experiences to the police. These figures vary from country to country and from state to state according to differing laws and attitudes towards these social problems. International and national crime surveys have provided different answers when asking victims for reasons for not reporting such crimes to the police. Victims may think that their situation is not a police but a private matter, or that the police would be unable or unwilling to help (Alvazzi Del Frate et al., 1993). Victims may also not trust the police, fear the aggressor's reprisal and prefer to handle the situation themselves or simply do nothing and comply (Rennison & Welchans, 2000). The proportion of victims of rape and stalking not reporting to the police have been found to be even higher when their aggressor is an ex-intimate (Tjaden & Thoennes, 2000b). The closer the relationship, the less likely it is for women to seek police involvement, and it is even less likely that ex-intimate perpetrators will be convicted when they are reported. In some countries, including Canada, Australia and several federal states, the police have mandatory charging policies for domestic violence cases. In Italy, violence within the family is acknowledged as a serious crime from a legal viewpoint and there is a mandatory charging policy (Baldry, 2001), but most domestic violence cases are not prosecuted because they are not perceived as serious enough or there is not sufficient evidence. Cases are frequently dropped when victims or witnesses are too fearful to provide oral evidence. To overcome this problem, prosecutors in England and Wales can refer to Section 23 (3)(b) of the Criminal Justice Act 1998, which provides for the submission of a written statement in the absence of oral testimony. Research conducted by the Home Office, however, reports that this Section is not often used because of the unwillingness of the Crown Prosecution Service to prosecute such cases (Edwards, 2000a).

In Canada, according to the 1993 Violence Against Women Survey, 29% of assaults on women were reported to the police in the 5 years preceding the survey (Pottie-Bunge & Locke, 2000); in Italy the percentage is even lower (17.3%; Baldry, 2001). Most domestic violence cases go undetected. Regarding stalking, the percentages for cases reported are higher (54.6%) and have increased dramatically since the implementation of new laws in all federal states (Tjaden, & Thoennes, 2000a). This increase is related to the higher proportion of women reporting to the police rather than to an increase in the number of cases overall. Reporting to the police, however, often fails to result in prosecution (Edwards, 2000a), thus implementation of laws is not sufficient if social and individual attitudes fail to recognise these crimes as serious. Official statistics cannot provide a full description of the prevalence and nature of these crimes. More reliable data on the prevalence and incidence of domestic violence and stalking are collected via national and international surveys, conducted with representative samples of the population (Mirrlees-Black, 1999; Pottie-Bunge & Lock 2000; Tjaden & Thoennes, 2000a, b). Other data are provided by victims support agencies and clinical samples.

The Federal Bureau of Investigation reported that domestic violence directed towards women is one of the most frequently occurring crime in the United States. The National Violence Against Women (NVAW) survey conducted in the United States with a sample of 8,000 women and 8,000 men revealed that 64% of all women who were raped, physically assaulted and/or stalked since the age of 18 were victimised by a current or former husband, cohabiting partner, boyfriend or date (Tjaden & Thoennes, 2000b, p. 46). In particular, 7.7% of all interviewed women over 18 were raped by a current or former husband, cohabiting partner, boyfriend or date, compared to 0.3% of all surveyed men. Almost a quarter (22.1%) of surveyed women were physically assaulted and 4.8% were stalked by a current or former husband, cohabiting partner, boyfriend or date.

The British Crime Survey, conducted with a representative sample of 6,000 women and 5,000 men aged 16–59, found that 22.7% of all women interviewed had been a victim of domestic assaults durings her lifetime by hands of a partner or former partner (compared to 15% of all men). Further, 4.2% of the female sample was assaulted in the last year. Women were more likely to report serious consequences from the assault such as injury (47% of women compared with 31% of men) and feeling very upset (90% of women compared with 75% of men) (Mirrlees-Black, 1999).

Stalking can be considered a core element of the cycle of domestic violence (Coleman, 1997). Although the best known cases of stalking involve celebrities or other well-known people stalked by "crazed fans", studies based on national surveys revealed that most stalking cases involve people who know each other (Lowney & Best, 1995). Stalking has gradually been acknowledged as interconnected with domestic violence, and in many cases the two crimes are almost inseparable.

The NVAW survey confirms that most stalked victims knew their stalker (corresponding to 78% of all female victims of stalking). In particular, in 38% of all cases female victims were stalked by their spouse or ex-spouse, in 10% of cases by their cohabiting partner or ex-partner, and in 14% of all cases, female victims were stalked by a current or former boyfriend, a total that amounts to 62%. The English and Welsh study conducted by Sheridan and colleagues (2001) also found that 22.2% of interviewed women reported that their ex-partners refused to accept that the relationship was over, and this is clearly one pattern of stalking.

Of offenders charged with domestic violence in Colorado, some had already stalked during the violent relationship, while others began stalking after the separation (cited in US Department of Justice, Office of Justice Programs, 1998). Intimate stalking therefore does not occur only after the break-up of the relationship (corresponding to 43% of all intimate stalking cases) but it can even start before (21%), and in 36% of cases it takes place before the end of the relationship as well as afterwards (Tjaden & Thoennes, 1998). What these data fail to show, however, is whether the type of stalking behaviour, prior and following the end of the relationship, varies. Women's perception of stalking before and after the end of the relationship might also vary.

Stalking during the relationship is characterised by controlling behaviour, threats, and coercion—all behaviours that can be considered part of the cycle of domestic violence. These behaviours can continue long after the relationship is terminated. When a woman separates from her abusive partner, she will hope to be finally free from violence, but it is often the case that she is still at risk of being followed, threatened or attacked. In most cases women who are stalked by a current or former partner have also been physically and psychologically victimised by the same man. According to Tjaden & Thoennes (1998), 81% of women stalked by a current or former partner were also physically assaulted, and 31% were sexually abused. This led the authors to estimate that, by comparison, an intimate partner or ex-partner has assaulted 20% of married or cohabiting women, and sexually assaulted 5%.

The US estimates of the proportion of murdered women by an intimate violent partner vary from 25% to 59%. Exact data are obviously impossible to obtain because the victim cannot be asked; moreover, not all cases of domestic violence are recorded by the police and therefore cannot be tracked. An evaluation study by Edwards (2000a) for the Home Office in the UK, however, provided interesting data. Results on the assessment of the reduction of domestic violence cases according to the type and speed of the police intervention were examined. These indicated that early intervention by the police on the site of the domestic attack ("First Contact" scheme) significantly reduced the aggravation of cases or even decreased the homicide rate of female intimates.

ANTI-STALKING LEGISLATION IN DOMESTIC VIOLENCE CASES

In the past, stalking was mainly considered a crime occurring between people previously unknown to each other. For this reason it is generally considered that the implementation of the first statute law in 1990 in the State of California was the consequence of the killing of the actress Rebecca Shaeffer by an obsessed fan in 1989. On the contrary, the Californian stalking statute has its roots in domestic violence cases. Judges were constantly frustrated by the law's inability to protect battered women who were eventually killed by their abusive ex-partner, despite the protective orders that prohibited the man from getting physically close to the woman (Lemon, 1994). Subsequent to California, all the other states of North America and the District of Columbia passed anti-stalking laws. In 1992, the US Congress passed a Federal legislation for the development of an anti-stalking law to serve as a model for the states. The Model Code aimed to assist states to develop their own statute laws in the best interest of protecting the victim and close relatives, and it is specially addressing domestic violence cases (National Criminal Justice Association, 1993). Stalking laws therefore were also implemented to respond to domestic violence cases where all other legal actions (e.g. restraining orders) had been implemented but failed.

Other countries such as Canada, England and Wales, Australian States and Territories, Ireland and the Netherlands developed their own harassment or anti-stalking laws (Australian Bureau of Statistics, 1996; Mullen et al., 1999; Sheridan et al., 2001). The United States implemented the Interstate Stalking Punishment and Prevention Act of 1996, making it a Federal offence to stalk across state lines. As in the case of domestic violence, the offender who travels across a state line with the intent to injure, harass or intimidate his partner or violating any protecting order, commits a crime punishable by the Federal law.

In England and Wales, the Protection from Harassment Act 1997 was passed, following great public and political awareness about numerous cases of stalking, because the existing civil and criminal law did not deal with the problem of stalking appropriately. The Act creates two new criminal offences and allows civil courts to make injunctions and award damages, although there is no clear legal definition of what constitutes stalking (Sheridan et al., 2001). The 1997 Act deals not only with stalking cases (Section 4, "either-way offence") but with all types of harassment (Section 2, "summary offence"). It is the stalking background to the Act, however, which explains why the Act requires two incidents of harassment, not one, to prosecute the case. On this basis it is estimated that one in three women in Great Britain "will theoretically be able to prosecute a stalker at least once during her life time" (Sheridan et al., 2001, p. 164). According to the Act there has to be consideration as to whether the act would be committed by "a reasonable person", unlike most criminal offences, which require some degree of intent before an offence is committed. Many stalkers claim that they have no intention of harassing their victims and indeed many believe or pretend to believe that they are in love with their victims, even if that love is unwelcome and unreciprocated. As with most cases of stalking among ex-partners, this is used as an excuse by the violent partner to explain his (violent) behaviour ("woman killed by her ex boyfriend because he could not stand living without her", we often read in newspaper reports).

Many other countries do not have any specific legislation against harassment or stalking, as in the case of Italy, where other statutes criminalising other types of offences have to be relied upon. Laws vary from state to state and from country to country when defining conduct that can be considered stalking; the fear and threat requirement also varies. As in England and Wales, laws usually require two or more unwanted acts that the victim believes are undertaken with the intent to frighten or harm her or a close relative. The "intent to harm" has to be made by the offender through a "credible threat of violence" (either written or verbal) against the victim. In other cases, the threat can be implied and perceived by the victim as such.

In stalking cases among intimate partners where the victim has suffered from domestic violence prior to the stalking behaviour, her fear of bodily harm should be directly implied because of what she had already gone through; stalking in these cases should be easier to accept and notify. When filing a complaint for stalking, police officers and prosecutors should acknowledge whether the stalker has already been charged for domestic violence. Many police districts have now developed "stalking guidelines" for providing practical advice on how to prosecute these cases and provide help and advice to victims. All these guidelines should incorporate a special screening procedure for domestic violence cases. In domestic violence cases the risk of extreme or even lethal violence is very high. Anti-stalking laws have proved to be very effective when the abusive partner has breached any civil restraining order intended to prevent the violent partner from coming close to the victim's house, place of work or relatives. Before the implementation of anti-stalking laws, as long as the man did not violate the order, nothing could be done by the police to protect the victim—even if she feared he could kill her. New legislations can help protect the woman who has been threatened or who fears for her life, and early appropriate intervention can alleviate the chance of the victim being killed.

Stalking can be considered a core ingredient of the cycle of violence, that takes place after the relationship has ended, becoming a further stage of the cycle, or even before, becoming closely connected with the other types of emotional and psychological abuse. In this regard, Tjaden & Thoennes (1998) report that partners or ex-partners who stalked were more likely than non-stalking partners or ex-partners to exercise emotionally abusive and controlling behaviour. In particular, around 80–90% of ex-husbands who stalked (either before or after the relationship ended) made the woman feel inadequate, shouted at her, were jealous or possessive, or tried to provoke arguments. Stalking abusive partners are therefore even more dangerous and emotionally abusive than non-stalking ones.

THE CYCLE OF VIOLENCE

Domestic violence is characterised by a series of actions intended to inflict harm or threat of harm to the victim. We often pose the question: "why doesn't she leave him?". Some women will never manage to step out of these violent relationships because they are too scared or, more often, because nobody really believes them and supports them. The aim of the aggressor is to exercise power and control over the woman to keep her in a submissive role, thereby maintaining a status quo that enables men to perceive themselves as stronger and entitled to dominate women (Crowell & Burgess, 1996; Yllö & Bograd, 1988). Attitudes towards women, gender role stereotypes and perceptions of family violence as a private matter prevent relevant agencies such as the police and social services to take serious legal and social actions to help women and children in danger.

Domestic violence is a complex phenomenon characterised by several consecutive phases. Leonore Walker was one of the first authors to describe the so-called "wheel of violence", characterised by a three-stage process: the "tension build stage", where conflicts increase in tension, the "explosion stage", when the actual incidence of violence takes place in the form of verbal and physical violence, and subsequent to this stage, the "honeymoon stage", where the violent man tries to regain the faith of the victim and reassert his control over her (Walker, 1979, 1984).

This model has been subsequently identified as the "cycle of violence", and the three stages of domestic violence have been extended. Domestic violence is characterised by a sequence of actions and crimes that follow each other in a cycle that increases in severity and frequency each time it concludes and then starts again. At the beginning, women are not always

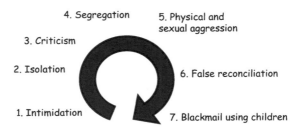

4. Segregation   5. Physical and
                        sexual aggression

3. Criticism

2. Isolation   6. False reconciliation

1. Intimidation   7. Blackmail using children

Figure 6.1.   The cycle of domestic violence

aware of the violence they suffer from; the sequences of the stages of the cycle of violence are often imperceptible and by the time they become aware of it, women are not able to escape from the violent partner (Straus & Gelles, 1990; Walker, 1979).

The violent partner does not commit physical violence from the beginning of the violent relationship; he starts by constantly emotionally and psychologically abusing the woman, undermining her self-esteem, sense of worth and self-confidence. Aggressors, through their perverted actions, render their victims powerless day after day by constantly conditioning them through a moral and intellectual dominance. Victims get immobilised as if in a "spider's web", psychologically, or even physically, entrapped and anaesthetised. According to Hirigoyen (2000), this constant state of psychological dependence implies a gradual erosion; victims are unable to put up any resistance. Women at this stage become fearful but unable to react; they lose their capacity to think and reason with their own mind, and start looking and feeling through the eyes and the body of their aggressor. This state of captivity makes women endure without consenting (Herman, 1992). The cycle of violence can be described through seven stages (see Figure 6.1).

With *intimidation* the man aims to put the woman in a constant state of fear; this is done via coercion, economic control, threats, gestures, use of loud voice and moral blackmail. The man controls what she does, who she sees and talks to, and where she goes. All these behaviours are often confused with jealousy, and men tend to justify their behaviour as an extreme form of expression of love. Men constantly ask their partners to demonstrate their love by giving up their friendships, their interests and often even their job. This leads to the next stage—*isolation*—when a woman is often kept away from any contact with other people, and is unable to understand what is happening. The man often uses his power by treating the woman like a servant, taking decisions on her behalf and abusing her emotionally and verbally, by calling her names and denigrating her. Anything the woman says or does is considered wrong in the man's view;

the woman develops a sense of *worthlessness* and "learned helplessness" that prevents her from reacting. If a woman tries to make things stop or asks for help, or tries to gain respect and speak up for herself, the man will start being *physically violent*, first by damaging objects and property, then by molesting, hitting or even killing pets or other animals, and finally by shoving, pushing, kicking, hitting, slapping, punching, spitting or even attempting to or actually killing the woman. In most domestic violence cases women are also forced to engage in *non-consensual sex*, either because they are afraid of any retaliation or they hope that he will calm down, or because women are culturally conditioned and feel guilty if they do not comply with their partner's requests (Bergen, 1995, 1996). Violence is always accompanied by the so-called *false reconciliation*, a phase when the man pretends that he is sorry, expresses remorse and promises he will change his behaviour. During this stage the violent partner engages in behaviours intended to win back the woman's faith. He gives her presents and flowers, he behaves "normally", he helps to take care of the children and assists the woman in domestic tasks. This only confuses the woman, who wants to believe in his apparent change, not least because it is very hard for a woman to give up her marriage or relationship and "destroy" the family, especially if there are children (Sipe & Hall, 1996). What is difficult for many women in this situation to acknowledge is that the family is already destroyed by a man who is violent.

Soon after, when the woman is again under the man's control, the cycle of violence will resume, and psychological and emotional abuse will further trap the woman. In all these cases the man blames the victim and makes her believe she is to blame for what she had "made him do", either because she did not obey or because she "provoked" him. At other times the abuser uses excuses such as stress or frustration to justify the violence. To the outside world these men deny their behaviour and say that the woman invents everything because she is mentally disturbed or revengeful, either because she wants to have custody of the children or because she has a new partner. In other cases, the abusers claim that their violence is beyond rational control. Studies, however, contradict this myth and illustrate the pattern of premeditation of violence: abusers often limit their beatings to places that will not show (stomach or head), and violent episodes occur almost exclusively in the home where they will not be detected (Walker, 1984).

Another stage in the cycle is the *blackmail of children*, used by the abuser when his partner finds the courage and strength to leave him, especially when the violence is also directed toward the children. At this stage the abuser threatens to report the woman to the relevant welfare services and deprive her of custody of her children. Women, who are not always aware of their rights, often stop struggling and give in to what they perceive as their "destiny".

INTERVENTION POLICIES

Since the late 1970s, the levels of available support have gradually changed thanks to the women's movement, which has pressed public opinion, politicians and legislators to intervene to aid abused women by implementing laws, and increasing public awareness. This has produced a plethora of research, which has been able to explain the complexities of domestic violence and its impact on those directly involved and their children, as well as on society in general. More and more women found the strength and the courage to ask for and to obtain help, to walk away from violent relationships.

As discussed above, however, domestic violence does not necessarily stop with the end of a relationship, and in some cases it can even get worse; this is why it is important that women and their children are believed, helped and supported, and that laws are enforced.

Women leaving the violent partner are most at risk of increased or extreme forms of violence, including rape, attempted murder or murder. The batterer realises that the spouse who was under his control and power is now trying to seek her independence together with their children (Coleman, 1997). During separation and divorce, ex-partners engage in a series of repeated unwanted harassing behaviours, starting with apparently innocuous acts such as phone calls, approaching the victim at work, leaving messages on her answering machine, making hang-up phone calls, claming child custody or modifying child visiting arrangements. Once the man realises that his ex-partner is not giving in to his constant requests and harassing behaviour, he will engage in more serious actions, such as intimidation and coercion, escalating into threats, attempts to cause harm or actually doing so, breaking into her home, damaging belongings, and threats or actual assaults on new partners, relatives or friends (Walker & Meloy, 1998). The abusive partner now becomes a stalker; intimate stalkers not only commit abusive behaviour prior to the break-up, but also engage in hostile and aggressive acts after it. Men who are verbally and physically abusive during the relationship are more likely to pursue their partners in a harassing or violent manner after the relationship has ended (Coleman, 1997, p. 430).

It is essential to understand the strong relation between stalking and domestic violence in intimate relationships. Most female victims of domestic violence, once they leave their violent partner, will suffer some forms of ongoing violence that might assume the pattern of stalking. It is very unlikely that the violent partner will stop his violence once the relationship has ended. In fact, it often gets worse, and the danger presented to the victim grows. The level of violence and degree of stalking behaviour after the relationship ends depends on several variables, such as the type of prior relationship, the presence of children, the number of years into the relationship, the type and duration of domestic violence, whether it has been reported to the police, and the intervention of the police and justice agencies. Garrity & Baris (1995) showed that domestic violence that continues over a long period of time would continue after separation, whereas violence that begins at the end of a marriage may not. This is because the underlying dynamic in most long-term battering is a need for power and control. In addition, abusive former husbands are more likely to engage in more serious and continued forms of violence, compared with former de facto partners. When there has been a marriage, violent men feel they have the right of possession authorised by the marriage bond: "to have and to hold, till death us do part".

The need for possession and control over the former partner is often exhibited via issues of child custody. Child custody and access to visitation also plays a fundamental role when considering intervention and protection in cases of domestic violence and stalking.

CHILD CUSTODY: VISIT ACCESS, JOINT CUSTODY AND FAMILY MEDIATION IN CASES OF DOMESTIC VIOLENCE AND STALKING

A very controversial issue in the field of domestic violence and stalking in intimate relationship is the custody of children after separation and divorce, and arrangements for visits or access by the non-custodial (violent) parent.

Most countries do not prohibit child visitation or access to violent partners, and indeed usually focus on the right of the other parent to have access to the child even by way of unsupervised visiting rights. It is not sufficiently acknowledged, however, that even if children are not directly abused, they are likely to be negatively affected. Fathers who are violent to their partners, especially if they do not fit the stereotype of the "violent man" who is also violent toward the children, are often not perceived as dangerous or harmful to them.

Countries have differing regulations with regard to arrangements for children after divorce or separation. Even if in most countries there is a presumption *against* giving custody to batterers, this still remains an unsolved problem. In England and Wales, the Children Act implemented in 1989 and the subsequent Child Support Act in 1991 have been publicised as being based on the child's interests. In fact, what the Act does is to re-establish a status quo where fathers can again exercise their patriarchal roles and control over the family (Harne & Radford, 1994). One issue brought about by the Act is the elimination of the concept of sole "custody" to one parent and "access" to the other; both parents now had common (legal and/or physical) custody, in the "best interests of the child", which is often equated with "*contact* with the absent parent at all costs" (Hester et al., 1994, p. 105, italics in original). The Act included the possibility of issuing "exclusion orders", but these were rarely applied (Edwards, 2000b). The Act ignored domestic violence issues, and stalking behaviour that might derive from joint custody arrangements or full access for the abusive partner. In this way the Act gave to the abusive partner the full power and authority to retain his presumed rights over the child (Hester et al., 1994).

The Family Law Act 1996 provided special amendments to the Child Act 1989 to protect a child "who is believed to suffer significant harm". The Family Law Act introduced the "non-molestation injunction" to include "exclusion" requirements in interim care orders, enabling the protection of the child from any abusive parent. Already introduced under the Children Act 1989, emergency protection orders or interim care orders could be granted, and in some cases even an exclusion order where the abuser may be removed from the house. According to research conducted by Edwards (2000b), although 2232 emergency protection orders and 58 907 interim care orders were issued in 1998, there was no indication of the number of domestic violence cases. In fact, contact order applications were refused by the court in only 4% of cases. The underlying presumption is that "contact is best", but this may imply danger and underestimation of the safety needs of abused woman (see also Hester & Radford, 1996). The law does not always guarantee its application and intervention for the protection of women and their children.

Court advocates, social and welfare workers, and lawyers have largely ignored the risks associated with the issuing of joint custody in domestic violence cases, and rarely brought the problem into question. The research conducted by Hester et al., (1994) showed how child custody issues were putting the woman and her children at a greater risk of repeated direct or indirect emotional or even physical victimisation. The abusive partner often claimed for joint *physical* custody (arrangements where the child lives for periods of time with both parents) or full visitation access, as a way to gain back control over the former partner. Access per se can constitute a risk in domestic violence cases and may seem like legitimating it. A father's right to know about the child's habits and residence implies that the woman has to reveal her residence address, telephone number and place where the child goes to school. This gives the abusive partner the opportunity to find her, wait for her, constantly phone her with the excuse of wanting to speak to the child, send her threatening messages directly or through the child, or even to assault her. In domestic violence cases, fathers often claim their rights to have access to the child and pretend to demonstrate a "fatherliness" that they had never shown previously. It is a common experience for battered women to describe the father's behaviour toward the child when living together as absent, hostile, non-supportive or even threatening. Fathers who often spent very little time with their children or who never showed any interest suddenly, after divorce or separation, realise their "full devotion" to their children and pretend to be or become excellent fathers (Hester & Radford, 1996). They start a battle (against the mother) to have their rights granted; in most cases the real reason is to demonstrate to the woman their power and control. This pattern is very frequent in domestic violence cases and it should be seriously taken into account as a trigger factor for screening stalking behaviour and preventing future violence (Hooper, 1994; Wolak & Finkelhor, 1998).

In Italy, custody is given to one parent only with regulation of visits provided for the other parent. No special initiatives are taken in cases of domestic violence and stalking because matters of relationships between parents are rarely seen as affecting the child, unless he or she has been a direct target of violence or abuse. In controversial cases such as those where domestic violence is implied, the child's judge (for de facto couples) or the family civil judge (in the case of married couples) delegates an expert witness to assess the parental capacities and personalities, and determine the best custody arrangements in the child's interest. These professionals, although psychologists or psychiatrists, are seldom specifically trained in domestic violence and stalking issues and are unaware of all associated risks. Therefore, they often tend to separate parents' issues from those of custody and rights (of the father), and establish unsupervised visitation by the violent partner even in those cases where the child explicitly expresses his or her fear of seeing or even hearing the voice of the (violent) father. The Family law establishes that a parent's authority can be suspended in serious cases where violence is implicated, and then a decision can be taken whether such parental rights will be limited or terminated. In most cases where there is a risk to the safety of the child, visitations can take place in supervised settings. Recently in Italy, there has been a movement towards granting joint custody with no screening for domestic violence cases.

Courts, when deciding on child custody and visiting arrangements, are often biased in their judgements. Research conducted by the Gender Bias Study Committee of the Supreme Judicial Court of Massachusetts reported by the Women's Rights Network found that "mothers are held to a higher standard than fathers and interests of fathers are given more weight than the interests of mothers and children" (Wellesley Centres for Women, 2000, p. 6). To overcome this problem and others connected to custody and visitation faced by battered women, the Women's Rights Network (WRN) has launched a new project that aims to determine whether the Massachusetts family court system violated the human rights of battered mothers and their children. It will examine such issues as integrity, security of the person, adequate standards of living, equal protection of the law, non-discrimination, and all rights guaranteed under international human rights laws, which are often violated in cases of custody and visitation arrangements involving domestic violence and stalking cases (Pagelow, 1990; Wellesley Centres for Women, 2000).

Recent years have seen the rise of "Fathers' Rights" movements, aimed at claiming fathers' rights over their children. These movements are based on a conservative political ideal aimed at returning families to a traditional gender role structure and reducing divorce rates. This has led to the mushrooming of family mediation services in the UK as well as in other European countries such as Italy.

Family mediation can be a very important tool in helping resolve marital conflicts (Ellis & Stuckless, 1996), but in cases of domestic violence it has proved to be very dangerous unless several precautions regarding safety issues and imbalance of power within the abusive relationship are taken into account (Astor, 1992). For families that have experienced domestic violence, mediation can enhance the batterer's power to intimidate his victim or compel an involuntary agreement. Abusive partners might use mediation meetings as an excuse to harass or even attack the woman. For stalkers, mediation meetings can become an unwitting method to go on undertaking their behaviour undisturbed. To prevent this, the American Law Institute's (ALI) statute on family dissolution, which addresses child custody and visitation access in cases of domestic violence, recommends that if "mediation is suggested by any party, the mediator must conduct a screening for domestic violence before the mediation sessions" (Reihing, 1999). The same applies in Australia (Astor, 1992), and in England and Wales, where Victim Support has developed specific screening guidelines for mediation in cases of domestic violence (Victim Support, 1995).

Some states in the USA and Australia have acknowledged the risks associated with post-divorce visitation and access to children in cases of domestic violence and stalking, and have adopted special regulations for the protection of women and children, especially by recognising that the post-divorce period carries a high risk of enhanced violence for female victims of domestic violence (Reihing, 1999). Violent men and stalkers often use custody as an underhand way of obtaining access to their former partner, and thereby harassing and intimidating her. The stalking behaviour may also be directed at children, who are constantly asked about their mother's life: who she sees, where she goes, what she does. Many separated violent partners appeal for child custody or claim joint custody as a means to constantly molest their former partner, or to financially and economically destroy her. These men are not actually interested in the children as such, but make use of them to assert control over the mother's life. Welfare, social services and family courts often fail to recognise this aspect of stalking behaviour in domestic settings, but focus only on the rights of fathers to have access to their children. Research conducted with a sample of women residing in shelters outlined the risk of visitation access for the woman as well as for the child. The study reported by Reihing (1999) showed that 35% of batterers threatened to take the children in a custody action, 25% used visitation as an occasion to verbally abuse the victim, 10% used visitation to physically abuse the battered woman, and 25% of the batterers kidnapped their children. The author concludes, "the more contact an abuser has with his children, the greater the risk that he will continue to abuse the battered mother or abduct the children. Thus, granting unsupervised visitation to a batterer is often highly unsafe" (Reihing, 1999, p. 394).

Child welfare issues and domestic violence policies have too often been kept on separate agendas, presuming that a violent partner does not imply a violent father (Mullender & Morley, 1994). Children who have witnessed violence between their parents or felt the brunt of that violence themselves, however, may experience emotional and psychological turmoil provoked by the anxiety of living in such a household.

THE CONSEQUENCES OF EXPOSURE OF CHILDREN TO DOMESTIC VIOLENCE AND STALKING BEHAVIOUR

Several studies conducted so far agree that in domestic violence cases women are not the only ones to be affected; children are at risk too, even if the child was not a direct target of the violence. According to the American Psychological Association (1996, p. 57): "Children who witness parental violence have reactions similar to those of children who are direct victims of abuse". Short- and long-term negative consequences show the importance of an early intervention also to stop the intra- and intergeneration cycle of violence. "A child's exposure to the father abusing the mother is the strongest risk factor for transmitting violent behaviour from one generation to the next" (American Psychological Association, 1996, p. 53). According to the review conducted by Widom (1989), up to 70% of violent adults have had a history of child abuse (either as direct victims or as witnesses of violence). Retrospective studies with samples of adult offenders have indicated that around 30% of them had been living in violent families; prospective studies indicate that around 15% of children who witness violence or are directly abused become delinquents. Violence produces violence: children living with domestic violence or those who have been abused are at a higher risk of developing aggressive and violent behaviour than those who have not. Fortunately, several "protective" factors might reduce the risk that these children will become violent. The reduction of exposure to domestic violence, the nurturing presence and support of another significant adult (mother), high levels of self-esteem, therapy and intervention, are all protective factors (O'Keefe, 1994). Intervention strategies for the prevention of violence should focus on these protective factors and implement policies in this direction.

Short- and long-term negative consequences of domestic violence on children include the development of aggressive behaviour or withdrawal, maladaptation, depression, anxiety, psychosomatic symptoms, or even suicide attempts (Kolbo et al., 1996; Barnett et al., 1997). Kolbo et al. (1996) and subsequently Edleson (1999) reviewed studies on how domestic violence affects children exposed to it. They found that boys exposed to domestic violence are more likely to be aggressive and exhibit antisocial behaviour with their peers in school than non-abused children (the so-called "externalised behaviours"), whereas girls are more likely to become submissive and possible targets of bullying or other forms of violence compared to those not exposed ("internalised" behaviours; see also Mullender & Morley, 1994). According to Lane (1989), children living in violent families feel that they do not have any control and power in their own home, and feel isolated and rejected. At school, they look for someone perceived as weaker to pick on and to control. The need for affiliation at school is more a characteristic of girls; the need to exercise power and control is more a characteristic of boys.

Very little is known about the effects of stalking on these children. Stalking in domestic violence cases occurs before and after the women has left her former violent partner. These children, therefore, like their mothers, suffer from a double victimisation. When violence goes on, in the form of stalking, then the child will continue to be affected by the violence even when the abuser not longer resides with them. The climate of fear, intimidation, threat and assault to the mother also has profound and lasting negative effects on her children.

CONCLUSIONS

Clearly, domestic violence is a serious problem that requires intervention of all forces for the protection of the victims and their children. Unfortunately, domestic violence does not always end with the conclusion of the relationship; it can escalate and even become lethal. Domestic violence is strongly associated with stalking behaviour, a combination of actions that even if per se they do not constitute a crime, represent a constant threat to the victim's life and that of her children, of other relatives or close friends. This does not imply that women should not leave their abusive partners, because if they remain the problem will also remain, or escalate. On the contrary, acknowledgement of this link should on one hand help lead to better understanding of why so many victims do not leave the violent partner earlier, often because they are scared, afraid, threatened, as well as psychologically and sometimes economically dependent on abusers. On the other hand, it implies that early intervention policies can be life saving. Law enforcement agencies should not wait for an actual assault to occur before they intervene, but should develop a database to gather evidence such as records of household telephone calls to help keep track of domestic incidents, and intervene at, for example, the third call at the latest. In England and Wales and in the United States, there are already several projects demonstrating that this intervention strategy is effective in reducing the risk of further victimisation and for issuing safety plans (Edwards, 2000b).

What is still lacking, however, is effective coordination between all services and agencies to implement plans of action for the protection of the victim and her family on one hand, and prosecution of the offender on the other.

Several questions are still lacking answers, and further studies should investigate the relationship between family characteristics and the development of stalking behaviour after separation in domestic violence settings. Does the presence of children enhance or aggravate stalking behaviour in former married or cohabitant couples? Is there any difference in the severity and duration of the stalking of ex-partners according to the type of visitation access granted to the former abusive partner? Studies in this regard should compare short- and long-term effects on children exposed to domestic violence where fathers did not stalk the mother after separation with those where stalking took place to check which precipitating factors may be identified.

In terms of prevention strategies, intervention should focus on protective factors that enhance resilience in children. However, if even after separation the abuser continues to stalk then recovery in the child will almost certainly be retarded. Legal intervention in intimate stalking should also address child-related issues and examine any arrangements for custody and visits that put the woman and the children at risk.

These questions are still sorely in need of clear answers, for policy makers and for child protection agencies, as well as for the protection of the lives of millions of women and the well-being of their children.

REFERENCES

Alvazzi Del Frate, A., Zvekic, U. & Dijk van, J. J. M. (1993). *Understanding Crime: Experiences of Crime and Crime Control*. Roma: Unicri Publication.
American Psychological Association (1996). *Violence in the Family: A Report of the American Psychological Association*. Washington, DC: Presidential Task Force on Violence and the Family.
Astor, H. (1992). *Guidelines for Use if Mediating in Cases Involving Violence Against Women*. National Committee on Violence Against Women, Australia.

Australian Bureau of Statistics. (1996). *Women's Safety, Australia, 1996*. Canberra: Commonwealth of Australia.

Baldry, A. C. (2001). Domestic violence in Italy. In R. Summers & A. Hoffman (eds) *Domestic Violence: Global Perspective*. (pp. 55–68). Westport, CT: Greenwood Publishing.

Barnett, O. W. Miller-Perrin, C. L. & Perrin, R. D. (1997). *Family Violence Across the Lifespan*. London: Sage.

Bergen, R. K. (1995). Surviving wife rape. How women define and cope with the violence. *Violence Against Women*, **2**, 117–38.

Bergen, R. K. (1996). *Wife Rape*. London: Sage.

Coleman, F. L. (1997). Stalking behavior and the cycle of domestic violence. *Journal of Interpersonal Violence*, **12**, 420–30.

Crowell, N. A. & Burgess, A. W. (eds) (1996). *Understanding Violence Against Women*. Washington, DC: National Academy Press.

Edleson, J. L. (1999). Children's witnessing of adult domestic violence. *Journal of Interpersonal Violence*, **14**, 839–70.

Edwards, S. (2000a). *Reducing Domestic Violence, What Works? Use of Criminal Law*. London: Home Office, Policing and Reducing Crimes Unit.

Edwards, S. (2000b). *Reducing Domestic Violence, What Works? Civil Law Remedies*. London: Home Office, Policing and Reducing Crimes Unit.

Ellis, D. & Stuckless, N. (1996). *Mediating and Negotiating Marital Conflicts*. London: Sage.

Garrity, C. & Baris, M. A. (1995). Custody and visitation: is it safe? *Family Advocacy*, **40**, 43.

Harne, L. & Radford, L. (1994). Restraining patriarchy. In A. Mullender & R. Morley (eds) *Children Living with Domestic Violence. Putting Men's Abuse of Women on Child Care Agenda* (pp. 68–85). London: Whiting & Rirch.

Herman J. L. (1992). *Trauma and Recovery*, London: HarperCollins.

Hester, M., Humphries, J., Pearson, C., Qaiser, K., Radford, L. & Woodfield, K.S. (1994). Domestic violence and child contact. In A. Mullender & R. Morley (eds) *Children Living with Domestic Violence. Putting Men's Abuse of Women on Child Care Agenda* (pp. 102–21). London: Whiting & Rirch.

Hester, M & Radford, L. (1996). *Domestic Violence and Child Contact Arrangements*. Bristol: Policy Press.

Hirigoyen, M. C. (2000). *Stalking the Soul: Emotional Abuse and the Erosion of Identity*. Gebundene Ausgabe: Helen Marx Books.

Hooper, C. A (1994). Do families need fathers? The impact of divorce on children. In A. Mullender & R. Morley (eds) *Children Living with Domestic Violence. Putting Men's Abuse of Women on Child Care Agenda* (pp. 86–101). London: Whiting & Rirch.

Kolbo, J. R., Blakely, E. H. & Engleman, D. (1996). Children who witness domestic violence: a review of empirical literature. *Journal of Interpersonal Violence*, **11**, 281–93.

Lemon, N. K. D. (1994). Domestic violence and stalking: a comment on the model antistalking code proposed by the National Institute of Justice. Violence Against Women Online Resources: http://www.vaw.umn.edu/BWJP/stalking.htm

Lane, D. A. (1989). Violent histories: bullying and criminality. In D. P. Tattum & D. L. Lane (eds) *Bullying in Schools* (pp. 95–104). Staffordshire: Trentham Books.

Lowney, K. S. & Best, J. (1995). Stalking strangers and lovers: changing media typifications of a new crime problem. In J. Best (ed.) *Images of Issues: Typifying Contemporary Social Problems* (pp. 33–57). New York: Aldine De Gruyter.

Meloy, J. R. (ed.) (1998). *The Psychology of Stalking: Clinical and Forensic Perspectives*. San Diego, CA: Academic Press.

Mirrlees-Black, C. (1999). *Domestic Violence: Findings from a New British Crime Survey Self-Completition Questionnaire*. London: Home Office.

Mullen, P. E., Pathé, M., Purcell, R. & Stuart, G. W. (1999). Study of stalkers. *American Journal of Psychiatry*, **156**, 1244–9.

Mullender, A. & Morley, R. (eds) (1994). *Children Living with Domestic Violence. Putting Men's Abuse of Women on Child Care Agenda*. London: Whiting & Rirch.

National Criminal Justice Association (1993). *Project to Develop a Model Anti-Stalking Code for States*. Washington, DC: US Department of Justice, National Institute of Justice.

O'Keefe, M. (1994). Adjustment of children from maritally violent homes. *Families in Society*, **75**, 403–15.

Pagelow, M. D. (1990). Effects of domestic violence in children and the consequences for custody and visitation agreements. *Mediation Quarterly*, **7**, 347–63.

Pottie-Bunge, V. & Locke, D. (eds) (2000). *Family Violence in Canada. A Statistical Profile*. Canadian Centre for Justice Statistics, Statistics Canada.

Reihing, K. M. (1999). Protecting victims of domestic violence and their children after divorce: The American Law Institute's model. *Family and Conciliation Courts Review*, **37**, 393–410.

Rennison, C. M. & Welchans, S. (2000). *Intimate Partner Violence*. Washington, DC: Bureau of Justice Statistics, US Department of Justice.

Sheridan, L., Davies, G. M. & Boon, J. C. W. (2001). Stalking. Perceptions and prevalence. *Journal of Interpersonal Violence*, **16**, 161–7.

Sipe, B. & Hall, E. J. (1996). *I am Not your Victim. Anatomy of Domestic Violence*. London: Sage.

Straus, M. A. & Gelles, R. J. (1990). *Physical Violence in American Families*. New Brunswick, NJ: Transaction.

Tjaden, P. & Thoennes, N. (1998). *Stalking in America: Findings from the National Violence Against Women Survey*. Washington, DC: National Institute of Justice and Centers for Disease Control and Prevention.

Tjaden, P. & Thoennes, N. (2000a). Prevalence and consequences of male-to-female and female-to-male partner violence as measured by the National Violence Against Women Survey. *Violence Against Women*, **6**, 142–62.

Tjaden, P. & Thoennes, N. (2000b). *Full Report of the Prevalence, Incidence and Consequences of Violence Against Women. Findings from the National Violence Against Women Survey*. Washington, DC: National Institute of Justice and Centers for Disease Control and Prevention.

UNICEF (2000a). *Annual Report*. New York: UNICEF.

UNICEF (2000b). Domestic violence against women and girls. *Innocenti Digest*, no. 6, June.

US Department of Justice, Office of Justice Programs (1998). *Stalking and Domestic Violence: The Third Annual Report to Congress under the Violence Against Women Act*. Washington, DC: US Department of Justice.

Victim Support (1995). *The Rights of Victims of Crime. Victim Support Policy Paper.*, London: Victim Support.

Walker, L. (1979). *The Battered Women*. New York: Harper & Row.

Walker, L. (1984). *The Battered Women Syndrome*. New York: Springer.

Walker, L. & Meloy, J. R. (1998). Domestic violence and stalking. In J. Reid Meloy (ed.) *The Psychology of Stalking: Clinical and Forensic Perspectives*. San Diego, CA: Academic Press.

Wellesley Centres for Women (2000). Advocating for the human rights of battered women and their children. Center for Research on Women, *Research Report*, **22**, 5–7.

Widom, C. (1989). The cycle of violence. *Science*, **244**, 160–6.

Wolak, J. & Finkelhor, D. (1998). Children exposed to partner violence. In J. L. Jasinski & L. M. Williams (eds) *Partner Violence* (pp. 73–112). London: Sage.

Yllö, K & Bograd, M. (1988). *Feminist Perspectives on Wife Abuse*. London: Sage.

CHAPTER 7

Stalking and Violence

J. Reid Meloy

Forensis, Inc., San Diego

The perverse beauty of the crime of stalking is that it provides a fertile Petri dish for the study of interpersonal violence. Stalking per se does not include any violent behaviour, if we understand violence to be an intentional act of aggression against another human being that results in, or is likely to result in, physical injury. Stalking, instead, has historically been defined as a pattern of threat or harassment that induces fear of harm in the victim (Meloy, 1999a). There is a logical relationship between the two—why would someone be fearful of a pattern of threat or harassment if he or she didn't think there might be an attack? But violence does not have to be an aspect of stalking behaviour, and is not an element of the crime of stalking in most jurisdictions. In fact, the crime itself was codified to prevent acts of violence that were, in retrospect, sadly predictable (Saunders, 1998). Therefore, we have two independent variables—stalking and violence—that can be empirically measured to see if there is, in fact, a relationship between them. The independence of variables in research is important, but in all violence research, the frequency of acts of violence is also critical to study. For example, the United States is a well-chosen geographical area in which to study violence because of its high base rate, especially in southern and coastal cities. Taiwan, on the other hand, would not be a good place to study violence because of its very low frequency. Canada is even better, not because its rate exceeds that of the US, but because there is one federal database of violent crime and criminals, making the task of longitudinal research not only possible, but also quite productive (Quinsey et al., 1998). People research when they

Stalking and Psychosexual Obsession: Psychological Perspectives for Prevention, Policing and Treatment. Edited by J. Boon and L. Sheridan. © 2002 John Wiley & Sons, Ltd.

observe phenomena that interest them, and the more observations, the better the research. Unfortunately for victims, individuals who stalk are often violent, a finding which paradoxically bodes well for research.

FREQUENCY OF STALKING VIOLENCE

There has been a substantial amount of research on stalking violence during the past decade. Table 7.1 summarises much of the data, with frequencies of interpersonal violence listed in the far right column.

What is most striking about these data is the large proportion of individuals who stalk who are violent, usually toward the object of pursuit, at some point during their stalking crime. In most studies of violence, on the other hand, base rates[1] usually do not exceed 30% per year, even in the most violent groups (Meloy, 2000). For example, if we had the power to pardon 100 men from death row at San Quentin State Prison in California, and released them to the community, at least 70 of those men would not be physically violent during the subsequent year. Another pattern that emerges from this table is the increase in frequency of violence across samples of stalkers as more recent studies are cited. This may be an artefact of data gathering, or it may be a true finding. What is most disconcerting is the rate of violence when stalkers who are prior sexual intimates of the victim are extracted from the overall samples—violence among prior sexually intimate stalkers usually exceeds 50%. This means that it is more likely than not that an ex-girlfriend, boyfriend or estranged spouse of a stalker will be physically assaulted by that stalker at some point during the pursuit.

This startling finding is not from one research group who may have unwittingly reported biased or inaccurate data. In a period of three years, four research groups in four urban areas on two continents (Harmon et al., 1998; Palarea et al., 1999; Meloy et al., 2001; Mullen et al., 1999) reported frequencies of violence among their prior sexual intimate stalking samples which were 67%, 78%, 89% and 59%, respectively. The only other subsample of stalkers in which violence frequencies approach those of prior sexual intimates are the "predator" stalkers, a name given by Mullen et al. (2000) to those individuals who stalk with the intent to sexually assault the victim. The stalking in these cases may be covert, such as observation, surveillance or following from a distance, or deliberate deception, such as a con or a ruse to falsely convince the victim she is desired for something

---

[1] Base rates control for time, frequencies do not. There has yet to be a study of base rates of stalking violence, because data gathering has not controlled for time.

Table 7.1. Frequencies of interpersonal violence among obsessional followers, stalkers and criminal harassers

Study	Sample	Location	Frequency (%)
Meloy & Gothard (1995)	20	California	25
Harmon et al. (1995)	48	New York	21
Garrod et al. (1995)	100	British Columbia	0–42
Kienlen et al. (1997)	25	Missouri	32
Schwartz-Watts et al. (1997)	18	South Carolina	39
Meloy et al. (2000)	65	California	46
Mullen et al. (1999)	145	Australia	36
Harmon et al. (1998)	175	New York	46
Schwartz-Watts & Morgan (1998)	42	South Carolina	48
Palarea et al. (1999)	135	Los Angeles	76

other than sexual assault. This subsample is the smallest of their five types in their published studies to date (Mullen et al., 1999, 2000).

THE NATURE OF STALKING VIOLENCE

There have been a few studies which have attempted to gather data on the actual acts of violence that are perpetrated by stalkers. Meloy (1992b) reported a small sample of violent stalkers (n = 6), of whom two subjects murdered their victims, one a prior boyfriend and one a brief dating companion. The prior girlfriend killed her boyfriend with a .357 magnum revolver. The dating companion, a young Persian woman, was stalked for three years and then murdered through the use of acid, gasoline and fire by a 37-year-old male. In only two of the six cases was the stalker a complete stranger to the victim, and in both cases he did not injure her. Meloy and his colleagues (Meloy, 1992a; Meloy & Gothard, 1995; Meloy et al., 2000) reported in two samples of "obsessional followers" (n = 85) gathered from the same court diagnostic clinic that the violent subjects typically grabbed, choked, hair pulled, threw, shook, hit, slapped, kicked or punched the victim, usually without using a weapon. When a weapon was used, in less than one out of three cases, it was a firearm, knife or automobile, and yet in all cases of weapons use the victim was neither shot, cut, nor run over. Most of the violent stalkers in their studies were prior sexual intimates or acquaintances of the victim. Harmon and colleagues (Harmon et al., 1995, 1998) found in a large sample of 175 "obsessional harassers" a variety of personal and property violence. Unfortunately, they noted the specific nature of the violence only in their first 48 subjects (Harmon et al., 1995). Acts included chasing a taxi and pounding on its hood, throwing bottles, following and grabbing, beating with fists, hitting on the back of the neck, kicking and lunging with a knife, stabbing with a knife, and dragging one young woman whose handbag was subsequently grabbed and masturbated upon.

Mullen and colleagues reported in a series of studies (Mullen & Pathé, 1994a, b; Mullen et al., 1999, 2000) the violent behaviour of several samples of stalkers totalling 168 subjects in their recent publication. In the majority of their cases, "the attacks constituted an impulsive lashing out in response to rejection or perceived insult" (Mullen et al., 2000, p. 212). They reported assaults that caused mostly bruises and abrasions, but also included in their sample individuals who had sexually assaulted, usually stopping short of rape, and in one case, the murder of a 25-year-old female singer who was publicly stabbed to death by a 49-year-old erotomanic stalker (Mullen & Pathé, 1994b). When this research group introduced their typology of stalkers (Mullen et al., 1999, 2000), the rejected group had the highest assault frequency (59%), followed in descending order by the predatory (50%), resentful (29%), intimacy (24%) and incompetent (21%) groups (p = 0.001). Property assaults were also highest in the rejected group (62%), of whom most were ex-partners. In a related study of 100 victims of stalking (Pathé & Mullen, 1997)—it is unclear if any of these subjects were victims of their large sample of stalkers—they reported similar assaults against 31% of the victims: blows to the face, kicks to the groin, attacks with a broken bottle, strangulation, strychnine poisoning, abduction, false imprisonment and rape.

It appears from these studies that most stalking violence is *affective*: a mode of violence which is preceded by autonomic arousal, accompanied by anger or fear, reactive to an imminent threat (usually rejection), and unplanned (Meloy, 1988, 1997a). This mode of violence has been researched in both animals and humans for the past thirty years, is referred to by some researchers as "impulsive" or "reactive" violence (Barratt et al., 1997; Cornell et al., 1996) and appears to be biologically based (Mirsky & Siegel, 1994; Eichelman, 1992; Raine et al., 1998).

There is, however, another mode of violence called *predatory*: it is not preceded by autonomic arousal, and it is unemotional, planned, purposeful and carried out in the absence of an imminent threat. The evolutionary basis of predatory violence is hunting. Predatory violence has also been researched, although not as thoroughly as affective violence, and appears frequently among certain clinical groups, such as psychopaths (Cornell et al., 1996), and in certain kinds of targeted violence, such as mass murder (Hempel et al., 1999) and bombing (Meloy & McEllistrem, 1998). Others refer to this mode of violence as "instrumental" (Cornell et al., 1996). Military training is often an attempt to teach predatory violence where affective violence would normally reign (Grossman, 1995). Forensic criteria for discriminating between affective and predatory modes of violence are listed in Table 7.2.

Table 7.2.   Forensic criteria for differentiating affective and predatory violence

Affective violence	Predatory violence
1. Intense autonomic arousal	Minimal or absent autonomic arousal
2. Subjective experience of emotion	No conscious emotion
3. Reactive and immediate violence	Planned or purposeful violence
4. Internal or external perceived threat	No imminent perceived threat
5. Goal is threat reduction	Variable goals
6. Possible displacement of target	No displacement of target
7. Time-limited behavioural sequence	No time-limited sequence
8. Preceded by public posturing to reduce the threat	Preceded by private ritual to fuel narcissism/reduce paranoia
9. Primarily emotional/defensive	Primarily cognitive/attack
10. Heightened and diffuse awareness	Heightened and focused awareness

Sources: Meloy (1988, 1997a, 2000).

There is one study which suggests that individuals who stalk and attack public figures are likely to engage in a predatory mode of violence. Fein & Vossekuil (1998, 1999) assembled a large sample of 83 individuals who near-lethally approached, attacked or assassinated a public figure during the second half of the twentieth century in the United States. They were able to clinically interview approximately one quarter of their sample who were still living, incarcerated and consented to participate in the research. The pattern of behaviour which preceded the actual attack was very consistent with predatory violence: it was typically planned, purposeful, carried out over the course of weeks or months, and motivated by the idea of assassination which was gradually translated into a behavioural plan. Intense emotion, such as anger, and heightened autonomic arousal in response to an imminent threat, were conspicuously absent at the moment of violence. Weapons use was also common, with the majority using a firearm to carry out their attack.

This study begs an important question: is there a fundamental difference between stalkers who are violent toward a private party, often someone they have intimately known, and a public figure, often a celebrity or political figure who is perceived in the public domain, but actually known only through fantasy? I think there is, although there will always be exceptions to this general supposition. Here is an example of affective violence toward a private party from my case files:

Mr A was a financial advisor in a brokerage firm who developed bipolar disorder in his late 20s. Initially resistant to medication and psychotherapy, he experienced deterioration in his work and marriage to the point where his wife left him and he was terminated from his position. Desperate for contact with his estranged spouse and their two young children, he kept visiting her home despite her protestations to keep his distance. On one occasion, she let him in to discuss their situation in the dining room. He erupted in rage during their conversation concerning visitation and punched a hole in the wall. He then stormed out of the house. Now frightened of his behaviour, the wife obtained a restraining order, and Mr A was confronted by the police that if he continued his attempts to contact her, he would be considered stalking her. He persisted in his pursuit, however, for six months, approaching the house and calling her at all hours. Unwilling to arrest for violation of the restraining order, the police finally caught up with him at her home after a violent encounter in the garage: Mr A accosted his wife as she pulled her car into the garage. The children stayed in the car while she attempted to persuade him to leave. Suddenly he grabbed her by the shoulders and threw her against the wall. She attempted to brace herself, but in the process, fractured a finger. Mr A was arrested and charged with assault and battery with injury. He was subsequently not prosecuted following his compliance with psychiatric treatment, return to his job, and desire of his wife to see him remain as the father of the children and a source of financial support for them. They did not reconcile as husband and wife.

Here is an example of predatory violence in a public stalker:

Mr B idealised a man who was attempting to win his party's candidacy for President of the United States. His idealisation was based upon his Palestinian roots and this public figure's support for his people in the Middle East. One day, however, he was confronted with a horrible reality: his idealised figure had voted for the sale of fighter bombers to Israel. He was furious at this betrayal, and shortly resolved that this public figure must die. Over the course of the next six months, he put his plan into action: he got a .22 calibre pistol from a relative and began practising at a local shooting range. He began to track the appearances of the candidate. He used self-hypnosis to maintain his motivation and the certainty of his goal. In the weeks before the planned assassination, he physically approached the public figure on at least four occasions in several cities. He never communicated a threat directly to his target, but did refer to his desire to kill the target in several conversations with friends. On 8 June 1968, he successfully hid in the pantry of the Ambassador Hotel in Los Angeles, and subsequently shot the public figure in the back of his head while more than 70 people crowded into the small space that had been chosen as his exit path moments before. The public figure died the next day.

Some of you will recognise this case as the assassination of Robert Kennedy by Sirhan Sirhan. This was a politically motivated attack, but there were also many psychiatric and psychological problems on the part of Sirhan which were testified to at trial (Kaiser, 1970; Meloy, 1992b). Nevertheless, the predatory mode of violence in this case should be quite evident, and the stalking behaviour—although there was no such crime at the time—should be equally obvious.

There are other recent cases of the stalking of public figures which culminated in predatory violence: the firearm killing of Rebecca Schaeffer by Robert Bardo, the firearm killing of John Lennon by Mark Chapman, the firearm wounding of President Ronald Reagan by John Hinckley, Jr, and the knife wounding of Teresa Saldana by Richard Jackson. All of these attacks and assassinations were preceded by a thoughtful plan, involved pre-offence stalking behaviour, were carried out in the absence of an imminent threat, and utilised a lethal weapon. Most of these subjects were also diagnosed with a schizophrenic disorder and the plan, although organised, was motivated by a delusion. A fifth case involving a public figure, however, the 1995 stalking of the singer Madonna by Robert Hoskins, culminated in affective violence. Ironically, the victim of the violence was the stalker in this latter case, shot at point blank range by Madonna's security guard during a struggle for his .45 calibre semi-automatic pistol in her backyard. Hoskins physically assaulted the guard, demanding that he be allowed to see his "wife" (Meloy, 1997b; Saunders, 1998).[2]

Predatory violence has also been documented in stalking cases involving private parties (Meloy, 1997a, 1999b), and both modes of violence should be considered in every case. Further research, however, may support the presumption that I am suggesting: if stalkers of public figures attack, it will likely be a predatory mode of violence; if stalkers of private figures (everyone else) attack, it will likely be an affective mode of violence.

STALKING AND HOMICIDE

Meloy estimated in earlier work (Meloy, 1996, 1998, 1999a) that homicide rates among stalkers were less than 2%. Mullen et al. (2000) pointed out that this estimate grossly exaggerates the risk of homicide in stalking cases, and they are correct. In 1998 there were 1830 murders (the wilful killing of one human being by another) in the United States attributable to intimate partners, a category which includes spouses, boyfriends, girlfriends, ex-spouses, and ex-boyfriends or ex-girlfriends (Bureau of Justice Statistics, 2000). A random probability sampling telephone survey of 16 000 adult men and women (Tjaden & Thoennes, 1997) determined that approximately 1 million women and 0.4 million men are stalked each year

---

[2] Although Hoskins purportedly used methamphetamine extensively during his stalking of Madonna in 1995, which may have accounted for his waxing and waning delusional belief that Madonna was his wife, videotaped interviews of him after five years in custody also suggest a chronic schizophrenic or schizoaffective diagnosis. His thought content is still grandiose, delusional and religious, and he evidences a severe formal thought disorder (author's personal viewing and discussions with K. Mohandie, November 2000). He receives no psychotropic medication in prison.

in the US. Fifty-nine per cent of the women (590 000) and 30% of the men (120 000) were stalked by current or former sexual intimates. Even if we assume that all intimate partner homicides were preceded by stalking—a likely exaggeration—then the proportion of prior sexual intimates who were stalked and then killed would be 0.25% of the total number of individuals stalked. In other words, the highest estimation is that one in four hundred individuals who are stalked by prior sexual intimates will be intentionally killed by them.[3]

STALKING AND DOMESTIC VIOLENCE

Although stalking is not limited to prior sexual intimates, a growing body of research suggests that there is a strong empirical relationship between stalking and domestic violence. Tjaden & Thoennes (1997), for example, found that 81% of the women who were stalked by husbands or cohabiting partners were physically assaulted by the same partner, and 31% had been sexually assaulted by the same partner. Twenty-one per cent of these stalking victims said that the stalking occurred *before* the relationship ended, and 36% reported that the stalking occurred both before and after the relationship ended.

Although the association between stalking and domestic violence needs further research, trends in violence toward current or former intimate partners may be useful data for suggesting risk of violence during stalking. Between 1993 and 1998, women experienced intimate partner violence at five times the rate of men. For the women, being black, young, divorced or separated, earning lower incomes, living in rental housing, and living in an urban area were all associated with higher rates of victimisation. Among men, being young, black, divorced or separated, or living in rented housing increased the risk of intimate partner victimisation. Violence was most likely to occur in the victim's home between 6 p.m. and 6 a.m. Although physical attacks occurred a majority of the time when the victim was female, most injuries were minor, involving cuts or bruises (simple assault). Only 8% of the female victims required emergency care at a hospital. Half of the intimate partner violence was reported to the police; the most likely reason for non-reporting was characterisation of the incident as a "private or personal matter" (Bureau of Justice Statistics, 2000). An adult woman in the US was slightly more likely to be victimised by a simple assault than by stalking when the perpetrator was a current or former sexual intimate.

---

[3] In this computation I have limited my inquiry to the stalking group with the highest rates of violence toward their victims.

MOTIVATIONS FOR VIOLENCE

The reasons for violence during stalking are as complex and multi-determined as the reasons for all violence: they likely encompass social, psychological and biological factors, and are much more confidently dissected after the violent act than before. Notwithstanding the empirical problems of postdiction and prediction of any violence, it is important not to be simplistic in considering this question, and also to appreciate that both unconscious and conscious motivations likely determine whether or not the stalker will be violent.

Affective violence among those who stalk private parties is typically triggered by an imminent threat, usually an actual or perceived rejection by the object of pursuit or a third party who is communicating the wishes of the object. Rejection is a threat because there is an emotional investment in the object, and abandonment inflicts a wound that cuts deeply, often into the feelings about the self, which may be defensively inflated and thus vulnerable to such attacks. A metaphor often used to describe the self-esteem of such pathologically narcissistic individuals, which includes many stalkers, is an inflated balloon which can be easily pricked by the tiniest needle. This sudden deflation is often accompanied by acute feelings of shame or humiliation—the public exposure of the self as bad—which envelops the body like porcupine quills and must be quickly eradicated. The emotion which defends against this acute sense of deflation and vulnerability is anger, or more precisely rage, which often fuels a sudden, physical lashing out toward the object interfering with the pursuit and instils a momentary sense of omnipotence.

The generic purpose of all affective violence is to reduce the threat and return to homeostasis, or optimal physiological arousal. From an evolutionary perspective it ensures the survival of the organism, and is often referred to as defensive violence. Although it may appear as if the affectively violent stalker initiated the physical attack, there is usually an environmental stimulus that triggered the emotions I have described in the seconds before the attack. This is not an excuse for the violence, but the behavioural–emotional–cognitive sequences are important in understanding the internal thoughts and feelings that result in violent behaviour.

Borderline personality organisation (Kernberg, 1984) is often present among stalkers in the manifest form of various diagnosable personality disorders, with narcissistic, histrionic, borderline, antisocial, paranoid, dependent and compulsive traits. In one study the modal Axis II personality disorder diagnosis among 65 stalkers was Personality Disorder NOS with narcissistic, paranoid and compulsive features (American Psychiatric Association, 1994; Meloy et al., 2000). The majority of this sample had a personality disorder diagnosis. Borderline personality organisation is characterised by part-object representations, impaired reality testing, and developmentally less mature psychological defences. All three aspects facilitate affective violence. Part-object representations suggest that the working models (Bowlby, 1969) of self and others are defined in relatively simple and polarised ways: the stalker may conceive of his object as a classic beauty, a quintessential goddess deserving only of his attention. (In a non-romantic context he might idealise a work promotion that he has been denied.) The self may likewise be partially conceived as the perfect intimate, the partner of destiny. When rejection occurs, devalued representations of the self and the object may be activated, and suddenly neither the object of his pursuit, nor himself, deserves to live. What is missing in this representational world are whole conceptions of the self and other which are anchored in the various shades of reality, thus supporting the toleration of ambiguity, or simply put, mixed feelings.

Impaired reality testing—the inability to clearly demarcate between internal and external stimuli—likewise muddies the stalker's perceptual world and facilitates affective violence (Meloy, 1992a). In borderline personality organisation this can mean that the origin of emotional stimuli is misperceived. For example, rage may be sensed as coming from the object of pursuit, when in fact she is feeling and communicating intense fear. Instead of accurately perceiving the fear in her, and the rage in himself, and thus restraining his behaviour, the stalker suddenly feels threatened and escalates his attack. Likewise his propensity to be jealous of her behaviour with other men—despite, for example, a divorce that was finalised two years ago—leads to surveillance of her home and accusations of infidelity that leave the stalking victim and her new husband angry and confused.

The third aspect of borderline personality organisation that facilitates affective violence is developmentally immature defences (Vaillant, 1993). Psychological defences are like the immune system of the soma. They protect us from the attack of internal or external toxins. In stalking cases a wide range of defences may appear, from the most primitive, such as denial and projection, to higher level defences, such as minimisation and rationalisation. What is most germane to affective violence among stalkers is the manner in which defences predispose to violence, or instead, provide plausible explanations for it afterwards. For instance, one stalker, a 38-year-old female divorcee, described her palpable fear as she entered her ex-husband's home and shot him and his new wife to death while they slept in their beds. She was convinced that he controlled the local court system—he was a successful civil lawyer—and was constantly plotting against her, a likely product of her own projective identification.[4]

---

[4] Projective identification is an incomplete projection. An aspect of the self is attributed to and perceived in another, but it is then felt as a threat. In the Broderick case, she attributed her fury to her husband, and then through her magnification of his power, perceived him as a malevolent, omnipotent force in her life. Projective identifications in stalkers contribute to their increased aggressive controlling of the object of the pursuit, as if the latter is the

Subsequent evidence at her trial, despite her histrionics on the witness stand, did not support her perceptions (*People v. Elizabeth Broderick*, San Diego County Superior Court; Stumbo, 1993).

Higher level defences, such as rationalisation and minimisation, will be utilised to explain the violent behaviour in its aftermath. One domestically violent stalker, when confronted with photos of his battered and estranged wife, said that she must have had a "bad makeup" day. O. J. Simpson commented to a reporter four years after he was tried for the murder of his ex-wife: "Let's say I committed this crime...Even if I did do this, it would have to have been because I loved her very much, right?" (*Esquire*, February, 1998, p. 58). In many cases, the excuses prompted by these higher level defences appear plausible, but are ultimately false when considered and weighed with other evidence.

Predatory violence also occurs among stalkers, and typically the motivations are more varied. Fein & Vossekuil (1998) identified a number of motivations in their sample of attackers and assassins of public figures: to achieve notoriety and fame; to bring attention to a personal or public problem; to avenge a perceived wrong; to end personal pain; to save the country or the world; to develop a special relationship with the target; to make money; and to bring about political change. Dietz et al. (1991a, b) reported in two large studies of threatening and otherwise inappropriate letters that subjects who approached Hollywood celebrities were primarily motivated by romantic or sexual fantasies, while those who approached US Congressmen were motivated by a desire for beneficence. Calhoun (1998) studied threats toward federal judicial officials in the US between 1789 and 1993 and found that attacks were invariably motivated by personal anger or a desire for revenge against a specific judge. John Hinckley, Jr., shot President Ronald Reagan in 1981 to win the love of actress Jodie Foster and to be linked with her forever in history (Meloy, 1989; Caplan, 1987). Mark David Chapman assassinated John Lennon in 1980 to become the Holden Caulfield of his generation: "I've always known I'd be different and I've always known I was destined for greatness...I always knew the whole world would know who I was. I always felt different and felt special and felt odd and peculiar" (Jones, 1992, p. 247).

What appears to be shared by stalkers who are predatorily violent is a pathological narcissism that is distinguished from the affectively violent stalker's narcissism in two ways: a grandiose fantasy of shared notoriety is pursued through the attack on the public figure, and a sense of entitlement, often accompanied by a callousness and indifference to the suffering of the targeted person, translates into a belief that he has a right to attack and kill. Because stalkers of public figures are typically not severely

---

principal threat. In some cases this defence has resulted in the stalker seeking a protection order against the victim (Grotstein, 1981; Meloy, 1992a)!

psychopathic (Hare, 1991), these narcissistic traits are often surrounded by emotional turmoil and conflict, such as anxiety and depression, yet may also be burnished by envy: the wish to destroy the goodness of the object of pursuit. Fein & Vossekuil (1999) noted that these subjects are not the high velocity, smoothly functioning, conflict-free assassins of film and cinema, but instead have beleaguered histories of psychiatric impairments and social failures.

Although pathological narcissism appears to play a central role in the psychodynamics of stalkers of both public and private targets, the inflated sense of self in the affectively violent, private stalker is more emotional and *free-floating*: he is vulnerable to painfully felt humiliation in a variety of circumstances because his grandiosity attaches to whatever he says or does. A young woman, for example, characterised her stalker in this manner: "He gets real smart with you about it, like why not me, am I not good enough for you, what's the problem? And when he talks to you he always gets up right in your face and nothing gets on my nerves any more than somebody gets up in my face". Her pursuer, a 32-year-old male, subsequently made obscene calls to her home for a period of several months (author's files).

The predatorily violent, public stalker, on the other hand, has a pathological narcissism that evidences a fantasy-based and *structured* grandiosity: he has given thought to his attack, imagined it in his mind, perhaps delusionally magnified the reasons for its justification, and has attached a specific, grandiose meaning to its outcome. Sirhan Sirhan made the conscious decision to kill Robert Kennedy five months before the assassination when he wrote in his diary, "RFK must die" (Kaiser, 1970, p. 549). He later testified, "how you can install a thought in your mind and how you can have it work and become a reality if you want it to" (*People v. Sirhan Sirhan*, 1969, trial transcript, p. 4905). Svrakic (1989) has elaborated upon this difference between free-floating and structured grandiosity in his excellent theoretical work on pathological narcissism.

COMMUNICATED THREATS

A directly communicated threat is a written or oral communication that implicitly or explicitly states a wish or intent to damage, injure or kill the target (Meloy, 1999a). Communicated threats are expressive or instrumental. Expressive threats are used to regulate affect in the threatener. For example, a spouse ventilates her anger toward her husband by telling him that she'd like to kill him, and then feels both relieved and guilty for expressing herself. Instrumental threats are intended to control or influence the behaviour of the target through an aversive consequence. For example, a physically and sexually abusive husband threatens to murder his wife if she attempts to leave him (Meloy, 1997a).

Mental health and criminal justice professionals believe as a matter of convention that all threats increase the risk of subsequent violence by the threatener. This assumption, however, appears more relative and ambiguous than expected. Macdonald (1968), for instance, found in a study of homicidal threats that 3% of his psychiatrically hospitalised subjects killed someone following return to the community, but in all cases it was not the person threatened. Dietz et al. (1991a, b) found no relationship between threats in letters and approach behaviour among those who inappropriately wrote to Hollywood celebrities, and a negative relationship between threats in letters and approach behaviour among those who inappropriately wrote to members of the US Congress. Recent studies of individuals who stalk, however, have found a positive and significant relationship between communicated threats and violence risk (Harmon et al., 1995, 1998; Meloy et al., 2000, 2001; McNiel & Binder, 1989; Mullen et al., 1999; Palarea et al., 1999). The strength of this relationship, however, appears to be weak, with reported beta weights of 0.15 and 0.26 in two studies (Palarea et al., 1999; Meloy et al., 2001).

One way to empirically approach these data that sheds light on the usefulness of threats in risk managing stalking cases is to study false positive and false negative rates. In this context, a false positive rate represents the proportion of subjects in a sample of stalkers who directly threatened but were not subsequently violent toward the target. A false negative rate represents the proportion of subjects who were violent toward the target but did not directly threaten beforehand. These rates, displayed as percentages, represent predictive failures, and appear in Table 7.3.

Table 7.3. False positive and false negative rates of communicated threats and subsequent violence among various samples of persons who stalk and attack public and private targets

Study	Sample	False positive rate (%)	False negative rate %
Meloy & Gothard (1995)	20	73	22
Harmon et al. (1995)	48	68	13
Kienlen et al. (1997)	25	68	–
Harmon et al. (1998)	175	41	19
Fein & Vossekuil (1999)*	83	–	90
Mullen et al. (1999)	145	52	23
Palarea et al. (1999)	223	75	14
Meloy et al. (2000)	65	72	15

* In this study, the violence was an independent variable, rather than a dependent variable, therefore, false positive rates are unknown (the proportion of subjects who directly threatened and who were not subsequently violent).

I have listed eight studies, which include seven independent samples of stalkers gathered from different research groups in San Diego, New York, Los Angeles, Missouri, Washington and Australia.

As expected, virtually all the studies indicate false positive rates >50% and false negative rates <23% for directly communicated threats and subsequent violence: most individuals who directly threaten are not subsequently violent, and most individuals who do not directly threaten are not subsequently violent.

The one exception to these findings is the study by Fein & Vossekuil (1999) of subjects who near-lethally approached, attacked or assassinated a public figure, wherein the false negative rate was 90%—only one out of ten of their subjects communicated a direct threat to the target or to law enforcement before they were violent. The sensitivity rate—the proportion of violent subjects in their study who directly threatened—was only 10%. The sensitivity rate for the other studies in Table 7.3, excluding Keinlen et al. (1997), averaged 82.3%.

This striking difference between public and private stalkers in their patterns of threatening communications toward the target is more empirical evidence that the mode of violence among public and private stalkers is different. Stalkers of public figures, if they are violent, will engage in a *predatory* mode of attack, as I have theorised above, and will not communicate a threat beforehand to heighten their probability of success. As Fein & Vossekuil (1999) wrote,

> Mounting an attack on a person of public status requires preparation and planning . . . Persons intending to mount attacks follow paths to their attacks. They often engage in "attack related" behaviours, that is, discernible activities that precede an attack. They may demonstrate interest in previous assassins and assassination attempts . . . Similar thinking and analysis may hold true for persons who engage in "stalking" behaviours and for those who commit certain kinds of workplace violence (p. 332).

On the other hand, stalkers of private targets, usually an acquaintance or prior sexual intimate, will engage in an *affective* mode of violence, which is usually unplanned, highly emotional and impulsive. They do not prepare for a violent attack, it is usually a reaction to perceived rejection, and they often have articulated an expressive threat to their object of pursuit before the violence. The private stalker threatens attack, but may not consciously intend to do so. The public stalker does not threaten attack because he intends to successfully carry it out.

PREDICTION OF STALKING VIOLENCE

There have been two studies which have used statistical models to attempt to predict stalking violence. Mullen et al. (1999) used log-linear modelling, a form of regression analysis, to predict the relationship between violence and the independent measures of typology, diagnosis, history of substance abuse, and previous criminal convictions (28% were convictions for interpersonal violence) in a sample of 145 stalkers. Property damage was independently predicted by both substance abuse and previous convictions, although only substance abuse remained significant when all four variables were considered. Assault was predicted by prior criminal convictions and substance abuse, and there was a non-significant trend for typology. Only previous convictions remained significant when all four variables were considered. Although ex-partners were significantly more likely to assault the stalking victim when compared to other relationships, and non-psychotic stalkers were more likely to assault than psychotic stalkers, neither of these dichotomous variables was entered into their regression analysis.

Meloy et al. (2001) studied 59 "obsessional followers" charged with the crime of stalking and related offences to determine risk factors for violence. Six dichotomous variables—prior sexual intimacy with the victim, major mental disorder (e.g. schizophrenia, mood disorder or delusional disorder), explicit threat toward the victim, personality disorder, chemical abuse/dependency, and prior criminal history—were used in a forward stepwise logistic regression to attempt to predict personal and property violence.

Prior sexual intimacy *alone* was the most statistically significant predictor of violence. No other variables were entered into the model. This resulted in a correct classification of 90.20% of the total cases, with a sensitivity of 96.97%, a specificity of 77.78%, a positive predictive power of 88.89%, and a negative predictive power of 93.33%. Even with the most pessimistic estimation, prior sexual intimacy with the victim resulted in an 11-fold increase in the potential for personal and/or property violence.[5] There were no age or gender differences between the violent and the non-violent stalkers. In a separate analysis, the phi coefficient between relationship type and violence was 0.81, indicating a substantial and strong association. The *absence* of a major mental disorder (-0.31, $p < 0.05$), the presence of a personality disorder (0.14), an explicit threat (0.26, $p < .05$), prior criminal history (0.01) and chemical abuse/dependency (0.18) showed much weaker correlations with violence risk.

It appears that the very limited predictive research to date has ferreted out three variables which significantly and strongly predict personal and/or property violence among stalkers: prior criminal convictions, substance abuse and prior sexual intimacy with the victim. Two other variables are significantly, although less strongly, related to violence risk

---

[5] Because the sampling distribution of the odds ratio tends to be skewed when sample sizes are small, the 95% confidence interval for this parameter estimate was calculated. The lower limit was 11.46 and the upper limit was 1093.95.

among stalkers: the absence of a major mental disorder and the articulation of an explicit threat. Both the Mullen et al. (1999) and the Meloy et al. (2001) studies focused upon stalkers who pursued private targets. There is no research to date on predictive factors for violence among stalkers of public targets.

A third study by Menzies et al. (1995), despite its attempt to predict "dangerous behaviour" among erotomanic males, should not be used as a source of knowledge in this area for a number of reasons: it combined two disparate groups of subjects, it included subjects who had only threatened in the "dangerous" group, and it tested an excessive number of predictor variables given its small sample size (n = 29).

RISK ASSESSMENT OF VIOLENCE AMONG STALKERS

The current state of the science in risk of violence among stalkers, and its application to risk assessment, can be summarised through a number of findings and opinions. It is my hope that these points of reference will serve as clinical and forensic guidelines, whether they are formally expressed to a trier of fact, or prove useful in the criminal justice risk management of specific stalking cases.

First, stalkers evidence high frequencies of violence, averaging 25–40%, which is usually directed at the object of pursuit. When samples of stalkers of prior sexual intimates are partialed out from the known universe of stalkers, violence frequencies substantially exceed 50%. Risk management of prior sexually intimate stalking cases should assume that an act of interpersonal violence toward the object of pursuit will occur at some point in the stalking crime.

Second, interpersonal violence in most stalking cases where a private figure is targeted will be done without a weapon, and a minor injury not requiring medical care will result. Homicide rates among stalkers are less than 0.25%, meaning that less than one in four hundred stalking cases will result in the intentional killing of the victim by the stalker.

Third, there is evidence that stalkers of public figures will engage in a mode of violence which is predatory; there is also evidence that stalkers of private figures will engage in a mode of violence which is affective. The latter mode of violence is much more easily managed through criminal justice and mental health intervention, and accounts for most of the stalking violence.

Fourth, most stalkers who are affectively violent toward a private target will have directly communicated a threat to the target beforehand. Most stalkers who are predatorily violent toward a public target will not directly communicate a threat to the target or law enforcement beforehand. In private cases, stalkers who *pose* a threat will often make a threat. In public cases, stalkers who *pose* a threat will usually not make a threat.

Fifth, there are three predictive factors for stalking violence which have been identified: prior criminal history (often interpersonal violence), drug abuse/dependence, and prior sexual intimacy with the victim. There are two other related factors—no mental disorder and threats—which have been associated with an increased risk of violence among stalkers of private targets. Articulated threats should always be taken seriously in risk management of a stalking case, but are typically not acted upon unless the stalker is a prior sexual intimate of the victim.

Sixth, given the limited nature of predictive research on stalking violence, and the likely presence of both psychiatric and criminal histories among stalkers, clinically and actuarially based risk assessment instruments should be utilised, such as the HCR-20 Version 2 (Webster et al., 1997) and the VRAG (Quinsey et al., 1998) in all risk assessments (Meloy, 2000).

Finally, the assessment of violence risk, a continuous process in most cases, should focus on both static (unchangeable) and dynamic (changeable) factors. Two of the three predictive factors currently identified are static (prior criminal history and prior sexual intimacy with the victim). The presence of dynamic factors in a particular stalking case (such as delusions in a schizophrenic stalker of a public figure) bodes well for treatment intervention. As I have noted elsewhere, however, mental health treatment and criminal justice intervention are both necessary, but each alone insufficient, for the effective risk management of most stalking cases (Meloy, 1997b).

Our desire to understand the relationship between the stalker and his violence—and the careful work that will answer our future questions concerning this perplexing and obsessive behaviour—can derive wisdom from the words of William Shakespeare: "Mad in pursuit, and in possession so; Had, having, and in quest to have, extreme" (Sonnet 129).

REFERENCES

American Psychiatric Association (1994). *Diagnostic and Statistical Manual of Mental Disorders*, 4th edn. Washington, DC: APA.

Barratt E, Stanford M, Feltous A & Kent T. (1997). The effects of phenytoin on impulsive and premeditated aggression: a controlled study. *Journal of Clinical Pharmacology*, **17**, 341–9.

Bowlby J (1969). *Attachment and Loss*, Vol. 1: *Attachment*. New York: Basic Books.

Bureau of Justice Statistics (May 2000). *Intimate Partner Violence*. Bureau of Justice Statistics Special Report, NCJ 178247. Washington, DC: US Department of Justice.

Calhoun F (1998). *Hunters and Howlers: Threats and Violence Against Federal Judicial Officials in the United States, 1789–1993*. Arlington, VA: US Marshals Service.

Caplan L (1987). *The Insanity Defense and the Trial of John W. Hinckley, Jr*. New York: Dell.

Cornell D, Warren J, Hawk G, Stafford E, Oram G & Pine D (1996). Psychopathy in instrumental and reactive violent offenders. *Journal of Consulting and Clinical Psychology*, **64**, 783–90.

Dietz PE, Matthews D, Van Duyne C, Martell DA, Parry CDH, Stewart T, Warren J & Crowder JD (1991a). Threatening and otherwise inappropriate letters to Hollywood celebrities. *Journal of Forensic Sciences*, **36**, 185–209.

Dietz PE, Matthews D, Martell D, Stewart T, Hrouda DR & Warren J (1991b). Threatening and otherwise inappropriate letters to members of the United States Congress. *Journal of Forensic Sciences*, **36**, 1445–68.

Eichelman B (1992). Aggressive behavior: from laboratory to clinic. *Archives of General Psychiatry*, **49**, 488–92.

Fein R & Vossekuil B (1998). Preventing attacks on public officials and public figures: a Secret Service perspective. In: J Reid Meloy (ed.) *The Psychology of Stalking: Clinical and Forensic Perspectives* (pp. 176–94). San Diego, CA: Academic Press.

Fein R & Vossekuil B (1999). Assassination in the United States: an operational study of recent assassins, attackers, and near-lethal approachers. *Journal of Forensic Sciences*, **44**, 321–33.

Garrod A, Ewert P, Field G et al. (1995). *The Report of the Criminal Harassment Unit: The Nature and Extent of Criminal Harassment in British Columbia*. Vancouver: Ministry of Attorney General.

Grossman D (1995). *On Killing*. Boston, MA: Little, Brown & Co.

Grotstein J (1981). *Splitting and Projective Identification*. New York: Aronson.

Hare RD (1991). *Manual for the Psychopathy Checklist—Revised*. Toronto: Multihealth Systems.

Harmon R, Rosner R & Owens H (1995). Obsessional harassment and erotomania in a criminal court population. *Journal of Forensic Sciences*, **40**, 188–96.

Harmon R, Rosner R & Owens H (1998). Sex and violence in a forensic population of obsessional harassers. *Psychology, Public Policy, and Law*, **4**, 236–49.

Hempel A, Meloy JR & Richards T (1999). Offender and offense characteristics of a nonrandom sample of mass murderers. *Journal of the American Academy of Psychiatry and the Law*, **27**, 23–32.

Jones J (1992). *Let Me Take You Down*. New York: Random House.

Kaiser R (1970). *"R.F.K. Must Die!"*. New York: Dutton.

Kernberg OF (1984). *Severe Personality Disorders*. New Haven, CT: Yale University Press.

Kienlen K, Birmingham D, Solberg K, O'Regan J & Meloy JR (1997). A comparative study of psychotic and non-psychotic stalking. *Journal of the American Academy of Psychiatry and the Law*, **25**, 317–34.

Macdonald J (1968). *Homicidal Threats*. Springfield, IL: Charles C. Thomas.

McNiel D & Binder R. (1989). Relationship between preadmission threats and later violent behavior by acute psychiatric inpatients. *Hospital Community Psychiatry*, **40**, 605–8.

Meloy JR (1988). *The Psychopathic Mind: Origins, Dynamics, and Treatment*. Northvale, NJ: Aronson.

Meloy JR (1989). Unrequited love and the wish to kill: diagnosis and treatment of borderline erotomania. *Bulletin of the Menninger Clinic*, **53**, 477–92.

Meloy JR (1992a). *Violent Attachments*. Northvale, NJ: Aronson.

Meloy JR (1992b). Revisiting the Rorschach of Sirhan Sirhan. *Journal of Personality Assessment*, **58**, 548–70.

Meloy JR (1996). Stalking (obsessional following): a review of some preliminary studies. *Aggression and Violent Behavior*, **1**, 147–62.

Meloy JR (1997a). Predatory violence during mass murder. *Journal of Forensic Sciences*, **42**, 326–9.

Meloy JR (1997b). The clinical risk management of stalking: "Someone is watching over me . . .". *American Journal of Psychotherapy*, **51**, 174–84.

Meloy JR (ed.) (1998). *The Psychology of Stalking: Clinical and Forensic Perspectives*. San Diego, CA: Academic Press.

Meloy JR (1999a). Stalking: an old behavior, a new crime. *Psychiatric Clinics of North America*, **22**, 85–99.

Meloy JR (1999b). Erotomania, triangulation, and homicide. *Journal of Forensic Sciences*, **44**, 421–4.

Meloy JR (2000). *Violence Risk and Threat Assessment*. San Diego, CA: Specialized Training Services.

Meloy JR & Gothard S (1995). Demographic and clinical comparison of obsessional followers and offenders with mental disorders. *American Journal of Psychiatry*, **152**, 258–63.

Meloy JR & McEllistrem J. (1998): Bombing and psychopathy: an integrative review. *Journal of Forensic Sciences*, **43**, 556–62.

Meloy JR, Davis B & Lovette J (2001). Violence risk factors among stalkers. *Journal of Threat Assessment*, **1**.

Meloy JR, Rivers L, Siegel L, Gothard S, Naimark D & Nicolini JR. (2000). A replication study of obsessional followers and offenders with mental disorders. *Journal of Forensic Sciences*, **45**, 189–94.

Menzies R, Fedoroff JP, Green C et al. (1995). Prediction of dangerous behavior in male erotomania. *British Journal of Psychiatry*, **166**, 529–36.

Mirsky A & Siegel A. (1994). The neurobiology of violence and aggression. In A Reiss, K Miczek & J Roth (eds.) *Understanding and Preventing Violence*, Vol. 2: *Biobehavioral Influences* (pp. 59–111). Washington, DC: National Academy Press.

Mullen P & Pathé M. (1994a). Stalking and the pathologies of love. *Australian and New Zealand Journal of Psychiatry*, **28**, 469–77.

Mullen P & Pathé M. (1994b). The pathological extensions of love. *British Journal of Psychiatry*, **165**, 614–23.

Mullen P, Pathé M, Purcell R & Stuart G (1999). Study of stalkers. *American Journal of Psychiatry*, **156**, 244–49.

Mullen P, Pathé M & Purcell R (2000). *Stalkers and their Victims*. London: Cambridge University Press.

Palarea RE, Zona MA, Lane JC & Langhinrichen-Rohling J (1999). The dangerous nature of intimate relationship stalking: threats, violence and associated risk factors. *Behavioral Sciences and the Law*, **17**, 269–83.

Pathé M & Mullen P (1997). The impact of stalkers on their victims. *British Journal of Psychiatry*, **170**, 12–17.

Quinsey V, Harris G, Rice M & Courmier C (1998). *Violent Offenders: Appraising and Managing Risk*. Washington, DC: American Psychological Association.

Raine A, Meloy JR, Bihrie S, Stoddard J, LaCasse L & Buchsbaum M (1998). Reduced prefrontal and increased subcortical brain functioning assessed using positron emission tomography in affective and predatory murderers. *Behavioral Sciences and the Law*, **16**, 319–32.

Saunders, R (1998). The legal perspective on stalking. In J Reid Meloy (ed.) *The Psychology of Stalking: Clinical and Forensic Perspectives* (pp. 28–51). San Diego, CA: Academic Press.

Schwartz-Watts D & Morgan D (1998). Violent versus nonviolent stalkers. *Journal of the American Academy of Psychiatry and the Law*, **26**, 241–5.

Schwartz-Watts D, Morgan D & Barnes C (1997). Stalkers: the South Carolina experience. *Journal of the American Academy of Psychiatry and the Law*, **25**, 541–5.

Stumbo, B (1993). *Until the Twelfth of Never*. New York: Simon & Schuster.

Svrakic D (1989). Narcissistic personality disorder: a new clinical systematics. *European Journal of Psychiatry*, **3**, 199–213.

Tjaden P & Thoennes N (1997). *Stalking in America: Findings from the National Violence Against Women Survey*. Denver, CO: Center for Policy Research.

Vaillant G (1993). *The Wisdom of the Ego*. Cambridge, MA: Harvard University Press.

Webster C, Douglas K, Eaves D & Hart S (1997). *The HCR-20 Assessing Risk for Violence, Version 2*. Burnaby, BC: Mental Health, Law, and Policy Institute, Simon Fraser University.

CHAPTER 8

Psychopathology and Treatment of Stalking

RICHARD BADCOCK

Rampton Hospital, Retford

INTRODUCTION

"Stalking" has become the accepted English word to describe a style of co-erced and destructive relationship which has exploded into public aware-ness in the western world over the past two decades. It is frightening in its detrimental impact—not only, and obviously, on the lives of victims but also on the lives of stalkers, even though recognition of this impact may be slower. It is threatening because of the degree of overt and covert intrusion into the personal life of the victim, and their experience of fear and dread is heightened by the apparently irrational and implacable way in which the activity is pursued. It is threatening also to a wider sense of social order, because the nature of the activity itself automatically gener-ates offences against the person and because the law can be apparently helpless to consistently prevent it.

"Stalking" is easier to recognise than it is to define in this context. How-ever, the *Oxford English Dictionary* general definition, "to pursue (gain) by stealthy approach for the purpose of (killing or) capture" continues to be apt in its image of a hunter pursuing prey in a sustained but unequal relationship, and it is unlikely that the word will be easily supplanted as a descriptor of this type of offending behaviour.

The majority of reported scenarios involve the stalking of women by men, and this will be taken to be the conventional situation throughout this chapter unless otherwise stated. It is important to recognise at the outset, however, that up to 10% of victims are themselves male, and scenarios of women stalking men, women stalking women, and men stalking men have all been regularly reported.

The purpose of this chapter is to provide an overview of current understanding of the psychopathology of stalking at the level of the individual stalker, together with a review of current approaches to treatment.

NOSOLOGICAL ISSUES

Classification systems and discussion of the types of behaviour exhibited in stalking are not discussed in this chapter because they are covered in detail in other parts of the book, which should be read in conjunction with this chapter. However, a number of additional points also need considering at this stage.

1. It is clinically helpful to distinguish between "stalking" and "prowling" scenarios. Stalking is fixated on the sustained pursuit of a particular relationship with a specific individual. "Prowling" is defined in the *Oxford English Dictionary* as "wandering about in search of plunder or prey or with predatory intent". Prowlers carry out some actions which are similar to stalkers, particularly in terms of covert observation, and taking a specific interest in intruding into the private world of their targeted victim. However, their subjects are selected on a more opportunistic basis and change with greater frequency, as the prowler's main identity is often with the geographical area that he prowls or the action of prowling itself rather than single-minded pursuit over an extended period of a controlling relationship with a particular individual. The relationship with the victim, therefore, differs in quality between the prowler and the stalker. Although the relationship between prowling and stalking is not always clear, they are generally considered to represent differing psychopathologies, and offenders may have preference for one or the other activity but do not generally carry out both simultaneously. Current clinical experience suggests that prowlers are also more likely than stalkers to be involved in other types of offending behaviour which are unrelated to the prowling or stalking, such as burglary or sexual offences.

2. Although stalking is recognised through the presence of certain repeated behaviours which are often shared by other stalkers, it is important to remember that the behaviours themselves are not the psychological "essence" of the disorder. The behaviours commonly observed include telephone calls, unsolicited letters and other personal communications, compiling dossiers of their victim's movements and personal details through

covert observation and sometimes using ingenious information gathering techniques, intrusive following or approaches, either socially or at work, sending unsolicited gifts and reminders of the stalker's presence, and verbally or physically threatening behaviour. Although some of these behaviours are more characteristic of the less threatening phases of stalking and some of more threatening phases, they can change substantially in form if some more convenient way of pursuing the stalker's objective presents itself. Stalking, like pornography, has been quick to avail itself of the opportunities provided by advances in information technology and the use of electronic systems of communication such as email. The essential nature of stalking, therefore, resides not in the behaviours used to pursue it but in the psychological forces that drive it in the mind of the stalker. Stalkers do not always know themselves why they are pursuing their actions in the way that they do, and many give a rationalised and at best partial account of their motivation. The most reliable guide to the motivational structure for individual stalking cases is, therefore, sober inference from reflection about the intrinsic focus of the behaviours exhibited and of the circumstance in which they occur. At a conceptual level, the things that make stalking what it is include:

a. the pursuit of a particular individual by another individual over an extended period of time;
b. the pursuit being focused on gaining the attention and reaction of the individual being pursued;
c. a tendency in the natural history of the condition for the pursuit to become more directly threatening to the integrity and the person of the individual being pursued;
d. significant preoccupation with the pursued by the pursuer (this preoccupation is focused on the relationship between the pursuer and pursued and on maintaining this in the form which is most comfortable to the pursuer);
e. the pursuer's concept of the relationship between himself and the pursued also bearing a significant relationship to his concepts of the relationship that he has with himself.

3. Although stalking is clearly recognisable in its own right, its relationship to other disorders or other offences is not so clear. Medical diagnoses of erotomania or morbid jealousy, for example, can be made in a minority of cases, but the majority of stalkers do not have an identifiable medical condition. Similarly, although stalking has an interesting conceptual relationship with some paraphilic disorders (sexual perversions) in that it has features in common with voyeurism and exhibitionism and some stalking scenarios are intrinsically sadistic in nature, this degree of overlap is no more complete than the overlap with identifiable medical disorders. Since

the essence of stalking is the disturbed relationship it establishes between offender and victim, it is best to conceptualise it in these terms—that is, as a specific form of relationship disturbance which may have associations with other recognisable disorders but stands in its own right as a form of disturbed relationship.

4. The way in which stalking has been classified and subdivided has changed over its lifetime. On the whole, the recognition in early classification systems that obsession was an important feature of cases has remained valid, but attempts have been made to find a more naturalistic system of classification which is easier to work operationally. The "ideal" form of classification, at least in medical terms, would be that which recognised distinct entities or categories based on differences on aetiology, natural history and response to specific rational lines of treatment.

PSYCHOPATHOLOGY OF STALKING

The best starting point for understanding the psychopathology of stalking is to view the behaviours as acts of personal necessity for the individual involved. Other factors may supervene, such as satisfaction in carrying out the process of being controlling and intrusive towards the victim. It is also true that a sense of carrying out the actions in order to fulfil personal needs may be entirely missing from the conscious thinking of the stalker, but stalking usually stems from a state of personal necessity. Understanding the ways in which such necessity arises then becomes the basis for understanding the background to the development of stalking.

The necessity arises from our basic human need to develop and maintain interpersonal relationships. There is a sense of "incompleteness" about each of us as individuals that we look to our relationships with others to remedy and also to help support the relationship we have with ourselves. The need for relationships is deeply embedded in human nature. We might wish to be alone, but the human condition is more accurately described in John Donne's poetic line, "No man is an island". We have a need to love someone, to be loved by someone and to feel that our lives have meaning and purpose. We need to feel that we can influence our environment and those around us and that we can both participate in activities that are greater than we are and avoid the stultifying corrosiveness of monotony and boredom. The most basic issue in all relationships is that of trust, and the struggle between trust and basic mistrust is highlighted by Erikson (1963) as being the first developmental stage in the eight stages of man that he identifies as being required to bring about ego (self) development.

In the development of normal relationships a basic sense of trust allows the relationship to develop on a mutual basis. Built into this mutuality, however, is an implication of potential vulnerability since the more we disclose of ourselves in relationships the more exposed we are to potential harm by the other through criticism, misunderstanding or rejection. This acceptance of vulnerability under the mitigating influence of trust lies at the heart of all genuine human relationships and is one of the important facilitators of personal growth, individuation and development of a stable sense of self-identity.

If, however, there is no basic sense of trust about relationships, this does not mean that relationships can be dispensed with, since the ordinary human need for them is still present, and they still form an important part of the process of self development. What changes instead is the tolerance and acceptance of a necessary sense of vulnerability in relationships. Instead, means are sought whereby a relationship can be attained but the feeling of vulnerability removed or minimised. This in turn requires that the other person not be treated as an equal partner in the relationship but become someone either to be flattered and placated or someone to be controlled. In terms of self development, the only end which can be reached through this process is that of self gratification rather than self individuation. However, the one can become confused with the other, and, in a lifestyle which anticipates rejection and frustration, self gratification can appear the more desired end in any case. Relationships based on controllingness are, therefore, developed in preference to those based on mutual interactivity if the latter appear to fail for any reason. This controllingness can take both active and passive forms.

On the whole, the main behaviours shown in stalking point towards continuing obsession and preoccupation with a particular individual over extended periods of time and to a sustained and often increasing interest in the control of that relationship in an intrusive way, with a tendency also towards increased destructive behaviour over time.

Obsession and preoccupation in human relationships usually indicate the presence of avoided personal anxiety. Dominating thoughts and feelings about another expand the individual's sense of his own world by attempted identification with the other, and he becomes temporarily released from awareness of his own state of personal distress and difficulty. The obsession gives him a mental focus and a sense of direction and purpose. It also provides a stimulus towards action to help overcome a sense of inner emptiness and inertia or disquiet. The activity so generated helps him to feel more effective and less anxious. This process becomes attached to his sense of his own identity and develops a narcissistic quality. In the same way that Narcissus became obsessed with his reflection on the water, so the stalker focuses on the life of his victim in a state of aroused interest and preoccupation. He looks for a reflection of himself in the image which he maintains of his relationship with his victim, and acts out through this relationship something of his inner dilemmas.

Case study

A young, adult, single man developed the habit of stalking teenaged boys, often when they were in groups with their peers. He was intelligent but felt he had poor social skills. As part of his behaviour he would sometimes deliberately place himself at risk of humiliation. For example, he would remain outside the boys' schools, waiting for them to come out, even though he knew from experience he would be jeered at by other children.

He felt that in risking humiliation in this way he was "daring" himself. This raised his levels of anxiety but also made him feel more alive and energetic. Once he could feel "alive" in this way, he could enhance this experience further by telling himself that he no longer cared about the consequences of what he was doing. This state created a sense of omnipotence which, in its turn, was accompanied by a huge sense of relief from personal anxiety.

This experience of relief from anxiety was very similar to the benefits that he had previously hoped for when he had tried to establish more normal social relationships. However, his experience of attempting real relationships had always ended in failure. From his point of view the advantage of his stalking relationships was that, once the process started, he felt that he did not risk any real rebuff or deprivation, since no one could take his feelings away from him. He did find, however, that in order to restore or maintain the state of satisfaction, he had to do more than simply follow the boys. He never tried to assault the boys he was stalking, but would, for example, throw stones at their houses or at public transport which they were using.

* * *

Controllingness and both a desire to control the relationship and satisfaction from the experience of having control of a relationship can arise naturally from obsessing thoughts, since a desire to possess is part of the obsession and control is a form of possession. However, the need for control of the relationship sometimes becomes a necessary precursor to feelings of personal empowerment and can also become either a necessary condition for sexual gratification or an alternative to sexual gratification in generating a sense of personal fulfilment. Power-based behaviours, resulting in controlling actions towards victims, offer a feeling of excitation (through the experience of being in control of another) and a sense of mastery (through the exercise of power). This sense of mastery results in the purging of feelings of personal tension and, although different from the sense of physical and mental relaxation produced by sexual climax, can lead to similar feelings of relaxation and satisfaction. Where a personal or sexual relationship with the victim is denied to an individual, power-based behaviours can offer an alternative route to personal fulfilment.

Relationships in which control becomes a substitute for intimacy also create a need for proof that the person has control over the relationship, because only this gives the reassurance that power over the relationship is maintained. Without such reassurance there is a risk of feeling impotent, unalive and powerless. The proof of control often has to be tangible or visible in order to be satisfying, and this encourages the development of behaviours that impose cruelty, humiliation or degradation on the victim, since these are naturally unwanted experiences and seeing another forced to undergo them assures the individual that he has mastery. The use of such behaviours by the individual is often justified in his own eyes by the victim "deserving" what they get.

Case study

A single woman in her mid-thirties began a relationship with a man 10 years her senior. She was attracted by his attentive, affectionate attitude towards her and because he made her feel that he needed her. Within a short time, however, she noticed that he was becoming increasingly controlling and demanding towards her. He required constant proof of her loyalty and devotion to him. She was required to demonstrate this by making a series of increasing personal sacrifices and disruptions to her normal routines. At the same time, he started to denigrate her personal skills and abilities, and at times seemed to go out of his way in order to humiliate or upset her. It became evident that, even though he claimed he was popular, he had no other close relationships. Moreover, he was unable to sustain normal relationships with members of his own family without the support or intervention of third parties. The pattern also developed of her being expected to accept the full consequences, particularly adverse ones, of any decisions that he himself had made. She found that she was not allowed to discuss issues in her own right. Conversations became largely a matter of him shouting at her. When she tried to discuss their problems, his response was to say that it was her fault that he was constantly under pressure. Further, he accused her of constantly trying to manufacture things in order to make him feel guilty.

She terminated the relationship but shortly afterwards began receiving silent telephone calls. Oil was sprayed on her driveway and her car vandalised. Insulting graffiti were prominently displayed in areas which she frequently, and she received a number of anonymous postings which included chocolates, a bunch of flowers and shotgun cartridges. Various sources of information made it clear that her ex-partner was responsible for these activities. From time to time he would express the wish to restart the relationship and, if they met, he would act as if nothing untoward had troubled their relationship.

APPROACHES TO TREATMENT

Police Intervention

Although this is not a treatment in the conventional sense, police intervention has proved to be an effective measure in reducing the incidence of stalking-related offences. Much of this assessment comes from the work of the Threat Management Unit in Los Angeles. This was set up by the Police Department in 1989 to cope with the rise in high-profile celebrity stalking. The work of the unit broadened to include non-celebrity related cases and other forms of threatening behaviour. Referred cases have the evidence of stalking behaviour collected over-time, and individual cases are monitored both manually and by computer. The main purpose of the unit is to prevent stalking-related crimes from happening in the first place rather than to bring prosecutions once dangerous behaviour has occurred. This is done through planned "interventions" when the unit believes that the stalker is exhibiting potentially dangerous behaviour (Perez, 1993).

Interventions involve confrontation of the stalker by the police. The elements in confrontation that appear to be important are both the police having the power of arrest and the production of tangible evidence of the stalking behaviour. Even though many stalkers will deny that they are involved in such behaviour, the intervention often leads to a change in behaviour patterns, and up to half of those challenged in this way will at least desist from pursuing their current victim as a result. This is a very different result from, for example, victims confronting their stalkers: stalkers then rarely change their behaviour, or, if they do, it is usually to increase the stalking. For this approach to work, therefore, it is important not only that the police be involved as early as possible and evidence of the stalking be collected but that strategies for planned interventions be officially adopted. Such work is, therefore, additional to that of the domestic violence units attached to police forces in the UK, and which cope with many of the similar referrals here.

Psychological Approaches

The application of appropriate psychological treatments offers the best overall approach to stalking both because the majority of stalkers do not have a formal mental illness and because the internal motivational forces underlying the stalking apply to all cases whether other mental disorder is present or not. The only difference is that, if an identifiable mental disorder is present, this may need treatment in its own right before psychological treatment focused on the stalking can begin. Although there is no body of literature on the treatment of stalking, there is relevant literature on the treatment of the sometimes related conditions of morbid jealousy and erotomania (Tarrier, et al., 1990; Taylor et al., 1983).

Although psychological therapies vary in the emphasis they place on the acquisition of insight (a capacity for objective self-reflection), effective personal change in stalkers depends on their developing different ways of thinking about themselves and the ways in which they handle their relationships with others. This, in turn, presupposes that there is acceptance that there is a problem to be tackled and that personal change is necessary. For many stalkers, however, this is simply not the case and the stalking may represent some acted out and maladaptive, but preferred, means of stabilising other personal issues for the stalker which, in turn, present him with a more powerful experience of threat or anxiety. A stubborn denial that stalking is occurring is not uncommon clinically and may be reinforced by the belief that the stalker is himself a victim of the situation.

This problem can be added to by difficulties in conceptualisation in relation to stalking. Individual actions in stalking can often be relatively minor in themselves, and the deep impact on victims comes from their being repeated over time and from the victim's sense of being increasingly and inescapably controlled through the impact of the stalker's actions on their life. Stalking may, therefore, be much easier to recognise than it is to define (and is another reason why it is so important for victims to help the police in collecting evidence in relation to their stalking, even if this runs counter to an intuitive desire to rid themselves of such evidence).

The challenge, therefore, is to find psychological treatments that are robust enough to accommodate a degree of denial that will enable stalkers to reorientate themselves without inducing a massive sense of personal threat and that cannot be simply subverted by stalkers and used to reinforce preferred but maladaptive beliefs. The main treatments in current use are cognitive behavioural therapy and variants of traditional psychotherapy.

Cognitive Behavioural Therapy

Cognitive behavioural therapy is developed from the perception that abnormal behaviours associated with abnormal emotional states are often in turn related to specific distortions in thinking and reasoning. The thought patterns in cognitive processes are capable of being identified, and the subject can then use this information to learn to change. People can be destructive in their behaviour because of negative convictions about themselves, their world and their future. These negative cognitions develop through learning (upbringing, life experience and self-directing) and are maintained by reinforcing behaviour such as ruminations, selectively seeking confirmatory behaviour for beliefs and (ironically in the present context) avoidance of provoking situations. Cognitive therapy aims to identify and then challenge negative assumptions that the individual has and encourages them to develop new cognitions and ways of thinking about problems and to reinforce these new cognitions and monitor their responses using techniques such as record-keeping, modelling, directed imagination and real-world practice.

The most influential model has been that of Beck (Beck, 1967), which was developed from his work on the treatment of depression. He drew attention to the importance of the development of idiosyncratic cognitive structures (described as "schemas"), which consisted of pervasive negative ideas of the individual's worth and expectations and yet became the determining value system in the way he recognised, thought about and identified his experiences. As a result of such attitudes, a depressed person becomes sensitive to specific stresses of being deprived or rejected and responds with disproportionate ideas about personal deficiency, self-blame and pessimism. Although such schemas may be inactive for periods of time, a recurrence of specific stress or circumstances can trigger automatic negative thoughts, which then in turn reactivate the schemas. If the process goes unchecked, it has a tendency to perpetuate itself and thus intensify the experience of depression and lead to its continuance.

The schema in stalking (for example, in ex-partner harassment) might include a belief that a stalker's ex-partner has betrayed the trust he placed in her with the automatic negative thought that the loss to him was deliberately contrived to weaken his own position. The model has to be modified slightly for stalking to take account of situations in which the stalker avoids awareness of his own self-weakness or sensitivity to ridicule by adopting a defiant attitude towards the victim or a conscious preference for a controlling stalking relationship with the victim over any other. Nevertheless, the model retains its overall coherence and applicability.

A study of the effectiveness of cognitive therapy in the treatment of nonpsychotic morbid jealousy (Dolan & Bishay, 1996) suggested that identifying schemata related to feelings of inferiority or unattractiveness, and that identifying the environmental precipitating factors associated with the schemata being activated, with subsequent work on these along behaviour lines, led to a substantial reduction of jealousy-associated behaviours in those who completed their treatments. This improvement was sustained over an average follow-up period of five months. The group of subjects was, however, not typical in that the majority were female and already in long-term relationships. Their jealous behaviour was creating difficulties which they were trying to change. The selection procedure meant that they were already motivated to change, and it is probably significant that even in these circumstances almost a quarter of the study group dropped out before the end of treatment.

Although cognitive behavioural therapies require skill and training to successfully carry out, they are nevertheless widely available and can be undertaken in a variety of situations including, if necessary, penal establishments. Other potential advantages that they have in relation to stalking include a concentration and focus on "here and now" interactions, an emphasis on setting practicable tasks during the course of the treatment and the active involvement in the treatment in a way which nevertheless leaves the individual in substantial charge of the rate at which work proceeds.

Conventional Psychotherapies

Conventional psychotherapies mainly comprise psychoanalytic or psychodynamic therapies based on models of psychopathology and treatment derived from Freudian, neo-Freudian, Kleinian or Jungian sources (Stevens, 1998). The aim of therapy is to gain insight into conscious and unconscious motivation of problematic thoughts, emotions or behaviour with the aim of resolving the conflicts considered responsible for these. Although the therapy has an important "here and now" element to it, there is a substantial focus on tracing back and re-experiencing the origins of difficulties with the aim of cathartic release of repressed material in order to allow more adaptive and naturalistic personal development.

Although forms of relatively brief psychodynamic therapy are available (Malan, 1979) and attempts have been made in the UK to make these as widely available as possible under the National Health Service, the time required and cost of conventional psychotherapeutic treatment as well as the high levels of training involved for its practitioners severely limit its availability. However, the theories on which these treatments are based are widely influential in their own right and arise in acknowledged or unacknowledged form in a wide variety of therapies.

There is no written-up analysis of a case of stalking in the psychoanalytic literature. There are in Freud's writings descriptions of developmental psychopathology which perhaps give an indication of the concepts he would have brought to bear. Writing in his introductory lectures on psychoanalysis (see Nagera, 1969) about early ("pregenital") sexual and personal development, when sadistic and anal instincts are believed to be prominent, he wrote:

> The contrast between masculine and feminine plays no part here as yet. Its place is taken by the contrast between "active" and "passive"... What appears to us as masculine in the activities of this phase... turns out to be the expression of an instinct for mastery which easily passes over into cruelty. Trends with a passive aim are attached to the erotogenic zone of the anal orifice... The instincts for looking (scopophilia) and for gaining knowledge (epistomophilia) are powerfully at work... The component instincts of this phase are not without objects but those objects do not necessarily converge into a single object.

Although it is not a part of psychotherapy as such, it is worth noting at this stage that the taking of a detailed history, a process common to psychotherapy and conventional medical practice, is itself often a valuable aid to building up a degree of therapeutic rapport. It allows patients to see how their problems have been taken seriously and treated dispassionately whatever their particular circumstances. Many stalkers appreciate this, as their actions can be as much a puzzle to themselves as to others.

Drug Treatments

Drug treatments, unlike psychological treatments, can only be applied to selected cases of stalking where a diagnosis of a specific and recognised medical condition can be made. The exact types of drugs that can be used are specific to the diagnosis made and therefore vary with it. When a medical diagnosis has been made, there has usually been a historical presumption that this diagnosis is supraordinate to the stalking behaviour and that the stalking is a function of the underlying diagnosed condition. Experience suggests, however, that this is an unsafe assumption and that it is much better to think of the stalking and the diagnosed condition as being comorbid states, each of which requires separate treatment. It is true to say, however, that where such comorbidity exists it is usually preferable to treat the medical condition as fully as possible before fully instituting appropriate psychological work.

Although some studies, particularly American ones, show a high apparent level of identified mental illness or disorder in stalkers (e.g. Zona et al., 1993), general experience suggests that the majority of stalkers do not have such a condition. In Sheridan & Boon's study of 124 stalking cases (this volume, Chapter 5), the category of "delusional fixation stalking" accounted for only 15% of the sample yet included all the cases of identified mental disorder, in addition to cases where no diagnosis had been made. This is likely to be a more accurate reflection of the proportion of stalkers with mental illness or disorder in the UK.

The medical condition perhaps most consistently recognised as being associated with stalking is that of erotomania, previously known as de Clerambault's syndrome. The condition has been recognised for at least 80 years, and the central symptom is the delusional belief that one is passionately loved by another. The main criteria of the condition have been consistently recognised as:

1. A delusion that the subject is loved by an "other".
2. The subject has had little previous contact with the other.
3. The other is unattainable—usually because of their elevated social position but sometimes because of marriage.

4. The other is nevertheless regarded as watching over and protecting the subject.
5. The subject remains chaste.

Historically the condition was seen as primarily affecting women with the unattainable object of desire being male. More recently, however, it has been recognised that men are also subject to the condition and that, although clinical studies identify female sufferers in the majority, forensic samples suggest that most subjects with this condition are male and that they are much more likely to come into conflict with the law, either through trying to pursue the object of their desire, or through misguided interventions to rescue the object of their desire from perceived danger. The bond between subject and object is often perceived in terms of spiritual union or an idealised form of love rather than sexual attraction.

Despite the historical recognition of the condition, it has proved difficult to consistently locate it in diagnostic systems. At various times it has been seen as being linked to both schizophrenic and affective psychoses, and its current ranking in DSM-IV is as a subtype of delusional disorder, which is distinguished as separate from both schizophrenic and affective psychosis (American Psychiatric Association, 1994).

In a study of men with psychotic illnesses who were charged with violent offences, Taylor et al. (1983) found four cases of male erotomania. All had been previously diagnosed as suffering from paranoid schizophrenia but none showed evidence of schizophrenic features outside the symptoms of erotomania. They also all had marked disturbance of affect. They had all been treated with phenothiazines for their presumed schizophrenia and the authors commented:

> Phenothiazines or related medication was helpful in all cases in controlling tension and mood disturbance. The men seemed to become more relaxed and communicative and more willing to consider their situations as problematical when on these drugs. In no case, however, was there an early resolution (of their erotomanic symptoms). These diminished only after lengthy separation, usually of more than one kind, such as job loss combined with imprisonment or hospitalisation. They returned with any renewed proximity of the women (who were the objects of their erotomanic attachment). Symptom relief does seem possible in the long term and safety can probably be ensured by encouraging the natural tendency to separate rather than by attempting direct confrontation... Cure or the attainment of a full and happy life without further episodes has not been achieved with any of them. Long-term psychotherapy may offer some hope but their defences of silence and evasion are hard to penetrate. Their response to therapeutic approaches is passively cooperative rather than one of active involvement.

Although this was a small study, the findings are consistent with general clinical experience.

At least one study (Rudden et al., 1990) emphasises that, although many patients with erotomania have features reminiscent of schizophrenia, a substantial number (a quarter of the 28 patients in their study) have marked affective features, including both manic and depressive symptoms. While the patients with schizophreniform illnesses tended to have chronic refractory conditions, those with more marked components appeared to do better in treatment generally and responded to conventional treatments for affective disorders including antidepressants and lithium. The overall course of their condition was less predictable and there was better preservation of higher levels of social functioning, even though symptoms could recur.

Several papers refer to the desirability of combining drug treatment with forms of psychotherapy. For example, Mullen & Pathé (1994) feel that low-dose antipsychotics, combined with supportive psychotherapy, are helpful in ameliorating problems related to erotomania, while Dolan & Bishay (1996) feel that a combination of antidepressants and cognitive therapy would be a sensible combined treatment approach in the management of non-psychotic morbid jealousy. While these findings may not be applicable to stalkers as a whole, they do point out the clinical wisdom of thinking about combined approaches to treatment in such cases. Although this ideal may be unattainable in the present context, the classification introduced by Sheridan & Boon in this volume represents a helpful step forward, since it produces categories which have differing recognisable aetiologies, pursue difference courses over time and offer the prospect not only of targeted investigative interventions but also of differing rational approaches to wider management and treatment. However, it should be recognised that cases will not necessarily easily slot into just one of the four categories as the second case study described in this chapter demonstrates.

This case has features which would qualify it for inclusion under either ex-partner harassment or sadistic stalking. From the point of view of using the typology clinically (not, admittedly, its primary purpose) it would be unsafe to exclude either classification. It would be necessary, therefore, to regard this case as being appropriate to both categories. However, both investigatively and clinically, priority would be given to the sadistic elements of the stalking because of its significance in prognostication and management.

REFERENCES

American Psychiatric Association (1994). *Diagnostic and Statistical Manual of Mental Disorders*, 4th eds. Washington, DC: APA.

Beck, A. T. (1967). *Depression—Clinical, Experimental and Theoretical Aspects*. New York: Harper & Row.

Dolan, M. & Bishay, N. (1996). The effectiveness of cognitive therapy in the treatment of non-psychotic morbid jealousy. *British Journal of Psychiatry*, **168**, 588–93.

Erikson, E. (1963). *Childhood and Society*. New York: Norton.

Malan, D. H. (1979). *Individual Psychotherapy and the Sciences of Psychodynamics*. London: Butterworth.

Mullen, P. & Pathé, M. (1994). The pathological extensions of love. *British Journal of Psychiatry*, **165**, 614–23.

Nagera, H. (ed.) (1969). *Basic Psychoanalytic Concepts on the Libido Theory/ Theory of Instincts vols I and III*. London: Hampstead Clinic Psychoanalytic Library, George Allen & Unwin.

Perez, C. (1993). Stalking: when does obsession become a crime? *American Journal of Criminal Law*, **20**, 263–80.

Rudden, M., Sweeney, J. & Allen, F. (1990). Diagnosis and clinical course of erotomanic and other delusional patients. *American Journal of Psychiatry*, **147**, 625–8.

Stevens, A. (1998). *An Intelligent Person's Guide to Psychotherapy*. London: Duckworth.

Tarrier, N., Beckett, R., Harwood, S. & Bishay, N. (1990). Morbid jealousy: a review and cognitive behavioural formulation. *British Journal of Psychiatry*, **157**, 319–26.

Taylor, P., Mahendra, B. & Gunn, J. (1983). Erotomania in males. *Psychological Medicine*, **13**, 645–50.

Zona, M. A., Sharma, K. K. & Lane, J. C. (1993). A comparative study of erotomanic and obsessional subjects in a forensic sample. *Journal of Forensic Sciences*, **38**, 894–903.

CHAPTER 9

Managing Stalkers: Coordinating Treatment and Supervision

P. Randall Kropp

Forensic Psychiatric Services, Vancouver

Stephen D. Hart, David R. Lyon

Simon Fraser University, Burnaby

and

Douglas A. LePard

Vancouver Police Department

INTRODUCTION

As is made abundantly clear in other chapters in this book, stalking is a complex phenomenon and stalkers are heterogeneous with respect to motive, victimology and psychosocial adjustment. In this chapter, we focus on the management of stalkers. We start with a review of the relevant literature. Next, we outline key principles for effective case management of stalkers. Finally, we present a case study that illustrates these principles in action.

Before we begin, we should advise readers of two factors that influence our thinking about stalkers. First, because we all live and work in Canada, our review focuses on Canadian law and empirical research. As Canadian criminal law with respect to stalking is very similar to that in other anglo-American jurisdictions, as well as that of western European nations, we do not think the focus on Canadian experiences will limit the usefulness of

Stalking and Psychosexual Obsession: Psychological Perspectives for Prevention, Policing and Treatment.
Edited by J. Boon and L. Sheridan. © 2002 John Wiley & Sons, Ltd.

our comments. Second, each of us approaches this problem from a different perspective: Randall Kropp works as a clinical-forensic psychologist, working primarily with mentally disordered offenders in an outpatient setting; Stephen Hart is a university professor whose teaching and research focuses on clinical-forensic psychology; David Lyon is trained as an experimental psychologist and a lawyer, and has a strong interest in public policy; and Doug LePard is a police officer with a background in criminology who for several years directed a specialized anti-stalking unit. Despite our diverse backgrounds, we collaborate on evaluative research and professional training activities, and we share a belief that such interdisciplinary liaison is essential for the effective management of stalkers.

REVIEW OF LEGAL AND SCIENTIFIC ISSUES

Canadian Law

Section 264 of the *Criminal Code of Canada* (CCC) defines criminal harassment, or stalking, as follows:

> 264. (1) No person shall, without lawful authority and knowing that another person is harassed or recklessly as to whether the other person is harassed, engage in conduct referred to in subsection (2) that causes that other person reasonably, in all the circumstances, to fear for their safety or the safety of anyone known to them. (2) The conduct mentioned in subsection (1) consists of (a) repeatedly following from place to place the other person or anyone known to them; (b) repeatedly communicating with, either directly or indirectly, the other person or anyone known to them; (c) besetting or watching the dwelling-house, or place where the other person or anyone know to them, resides, works, carries on business or happens to be; or (d) engaging in threatening conduct directed at the other person or any member of their family.

This law has been in place since 1993, was modelled after previously existing laws in the United States, and, like those statutes, the Canadian law broadly defines stalking behaviours and requires a test of "reasonable fear" for the victim's physical and psychological safety. Importantly, the CCC provides other criminal remedies for stalking behaviour, including harassing phone calls (s. 372), threatening (s. 264.1), intimidation (s. 423), assault (s. 265), and any attempt to commit these offences (s. 24). Many other stalking cases are not reported, not prosecuted, or are dealt with in the civil courts (Cornish et al., 1999). While lifetime prevalence rate statistics are not available in Canada, other North American estimates suggest that this form of criminal behaviour is very common. For example, Tjaden & Thoennes (1998) estimate that 8–12% of women and 4% of men will be stalked during their lifetime. Moreover, stalking behaviour has been linked in Canada to spousal violence in general (Canadian Centre for Justice Statistics, 2000) and spousal homicide specifically (Cooper, 1994a,b;

Wilson & Daly, 1994). All considered, stalking represents an important legal, health and social problem for Canadian society, and the criminal justice response to manage victim safety has been significant.

Research on Stalking in Canada

Research in Canada suggests that stalkers are a very heterogeneous group with respect to motivations, nature/severity of violence, risk factors, and so forth. According to one criminal statistics report (Kong, 1996), most victims of criminal harassment in Canada are female (80%) and most perpetrators are male (90%). In approximately 90% of the cases the perpetrator is known to the victim and in 58% of the cases the perpetrator and victim are former or current intimate partners. The remainder of cases involve either some type of casual social acquaintanceship between the perpetrator and victim, work-related conflict, or stranger stalking often secondary to a major mental illness (Kong, 1996; Lyon, 1997). Stranger perpetrated stalking appears to be relatively rare in Canada, and celebrity and political figure obsessional pursuit behaviours are seldom publicized.

There have been few Canadian studies on risk factors associated with persistent harassing behaviours and/or violence. We have conducted some preliminary research on a sample of those arrested for criminal harassment or another harassment-related charges such as harassing phone calls (Lyon et al., 1999). We identified all police investigational files (n = 230) for the year 1997 in a large urban centre. Analyses of perpetrator demographics, and behavioural, criminological and psychological characteristics sketch a number of possible risk factors for stalking behaviour. For example, many in this sample were unemployed (40%), living alone (63%), single (64%) and male (91%). The victim knew the stalker in 86% of cases, and the two were current or former intimate partners in 58% of cases. Some type of angry or persecutory attachment was present in 68% of cases, and this type of attachment was common in both non-romantic and romantic relationships. Past or recent violence appeared to be most prevalent in a group of stalkers who had had a prior romantic relationship with the victim. These findings are consistent with international studies documenting characteristics and risk factors associated with stalking behaviour (Harmon et al., 1998; Mullen et al., 1999; Palarea et al., 1999; Westrup & Fremouw, 1998), readers are referred elsewhere in this volume for more detailed discussions of stalker characteristics.

We have also examined risk factors in a sample of stalkers referred for psychiatric/psychological evaluations (Kropp, 1999; Kropp et al., 1999a). In this study, 106 forensic psychiatric patients who were charged with criminal harassment were evaluated according to existing risk-related assessment tools including the Psychopathy Checklist—Screening Version (PCL-SV; Hart et al., 1995), the Spousal Assault Risk Assessment

Guide (SARA; Kropp et al., 1995, 1999b; Kropp & Hart, 2000), and the HCR-20 (Webster et al., 1997). Like our larger police sample, many in this group were male (88%), single (66%), living alone (49%) unemployed (60%) and, somewhat to our surprise, well educated, with 45% of the sample possessing some post-secondary education. Again, the most common form of victim–perpetrator relationship was ex-intimate. These data point to certain implications for risk management. First, it suggests that social isolation and poor social skills might be related to excessive ruminating and an absence of challenges from others to the offender's distorted thinking. Moreover, these factors, combined with high education and relatively strong verbal skills, suggest that many of these offenders are difficult to treat due to their strong psychological defenses and ability to rationalize their behaviour. Based on this research, management options worth considering are social skills training, vocational counselling, and specialized treatment programmes for relationship pathology.

Our data allowed us to consider whether or not psychopathic personality is a prevalent risk factor in stalkers. Psychopathy, as defined by Hare (1991) and others, is a constellation of interpersonal (e.g. superficiality, grandiosity, deceitfulness, lack of empathy, lack of remorse) and behavioural (e.g. impulsivity, poor behavioural controls, irresponsibility, antisocial behaviour) features that, taken together, have been strongly associated with violent behaviour (Hemphill et al., 1997; Salekin et al., 1996). We found that the mean PCL-SV total score of 10.8 (s.d. $= 5.2$) was far below reported norms for forensic psychiatric inpatients (M $= 16.6$) and outpatients (M $= 13.7$). Thus, the average stalker in this sample was not particularly psychopathic, suggesting that psychopathy might not play as significant a role in stalking-related violence as it does with other forms of violence (Hart, 1998). On the HCR-20 and SARA measures, ex-intimate and "grudge"-related (i.e. angry, persecutory) stalkers were more likely than stranger and casual acquaintance stalkers to have a history of criminal behaviour, including violence, suggesting that the type of victim–perpetrator relationship might be related to risk.

Finally, a subsample of ex-intimate stalkers (n $= 42$) was compared on the SARA to a sample of spousal assaulters with no documented history of stalking (n $= 102$). Analyses indicated that ex-intimate stalkers were on average to be considered the same level of risk for spousal assault as the spousal assault group. Of note was that approximately half of the offenders in each group (50% of ex-intimate stalkers; 46% of spousal assaulters) were judged to be of high risk for future domestic violence based on a consideration of the SARA risk factors. Ex-intimate stalkers had, on average, fewer risk factors than the spousal assaulters, and showed non-significant statistical trends to be (a) less likely to be violent outside relationships, (b) less likely to have substance abuse, (c) more likely to have recent relationship problems, (d) more likely to have employment problems and (e) more likely to be suicidal and/or homicidal.

Based on a coding of certain DSM-IV personality disorder symptoms, there was evidence that the ex-intimate stalkers often possessed borderline and narcissistic personality traits, although we did not have this type of information for the spousal assault comparison group. In general, the results again point to some considerations for managing ex-intimate stalkers. First, these offenders are probably more difficult to treat than most spousal assaulters due to a greater degree of psychopathology and, possibly, personality disorder traits. Ex-intimate stalkers might not neatly fit into traditional batterer treatment programmes due to their relationship pathology. Crisis intervention for suicidal and homicidal ideation or intent might also be more commonly implicated. These conclusions and observations are largely preliminary, but they have guided our thinking with respect to managing these individuals.

Influential International Research

Our work is also influenced by a number of international efforts to treat and manage stalkers. There are three small bodies of literature that are relevant. The first group of studies focuses on the psychological and, more commonly, psychiatric treatment of stalkers. Much of this literature is anecdotal in nature, focusing on the clinical management of specific cases, and much of this area was summarized usefully by Cooper (1994). She noted that although there are no well-documented treatment techniques for stalking per se, many of the psychiatric and medical conditions associated with stalking—i.e. erotomanic or jealous delusions, affective disorders, obsessive compulsive disorders, intellectual disabilities—might be treatable with appropriate medications or specific therapeutic techniques. Her conclusions are echoed elsewhere, with most authors noting the necessary diversity and complexity of treatment approaches (Lindsay et al., 1998; Meloy, 1997; Meyers, 1998; Mullen & Pathé, 1994; Noone & Cockhill, 1987; Zona et al., 1998). Specific treatment strategies will generally be determined by the nature and severity of mental illness (Meloy, 1997). Examples of specific treatments are psychopharmocological interventions for obsessional thinking and delusions (Gross, 1991; Mullen & Pathé, 1994), supportive counselling for acculturation stressors (Meyers, 1998) and cognitive approaches for intellectual disabilities (Lindsay et al., 1998).

The second body of knowledge comes from the extensive literature on the assessment and treatment of domestic violence. Given the high prevalence of intimate or ex-intimate stalking in virtually every jurisdiction, there is much to borrow from this field. Many have argued that intimate partner stalkers and spousal assaulters have much in common with respect to their motivations, their personality characteristics, their abuse of power and control, and their attitudes about women and relationships. Burgess et al. (1997) found that 30% of a sample of spousal batterers in treatment self-reported stalking behaviours. They described three stages of post-separation stalking, which involve (a) repeated attempts to contact an ex-partner, (b) conversion of positive emotion of love to the negative of hate, and (c) a move from clandestine to public stalking and violence. Similarly, Kurt (1995) has discussed "stalking as a variant of domestic violence" and Walker & Meloy (1998) have reviewed the relevant issues in some detail. We have also discussed the similarities—and differences—between stalkers and spousal batterers (Kropp, 1999; Kropp et al., 1999b). Thus, in many cases existing assessment (Dutton & Kropp, 2000) and treatment (Healy et al., 1998) techniques used with batterers are applicable to stalkers. Attention must be paid to proper assessment and screening of factors that may preclude such treatment, such as personality, psychotic and cognitive disorders.

The third area we reviewed relates to police intervention strategies and targeted threat management techniques. With certain exceptions (Borum et al., 1999), much of the knowledge in this area remains unpublished in the professional literature, but it has been discussed and widely disseminated at professional conferences (De Becker, 1994; Hart et al., 1998), published as government reports (e.g. Fein et al., 1995) and distributed on the Internet. These approaches typically focus on targeted threat assessment, identification of risk factors and approach behaviours, and the development of a management plan that directly addresses relevant risk factors (Fein et al., 1995; White & Cawood, 1998). Most emphasize the importance of assessing and managing approach behaviour in the offender, and working with the victim to ensure that appropriate security measures are in place. This thorough, idiographic and context-specific approach has greatly influenced our own thinking regarding risk management of offenders.

Recently, some efforts have called for integrated approaches to the management of offenders that incorporate various levels of the criminal justice and health sectors (Cornish et al., 1999; Meloy, 1997, 1998; Westrup & Fremouw, 1998). Meloy, for example, notes that: "In most cases, mental health and criminal justice responses are both necessary, but each insufficient" (p. 181). White and Cawood (1998) emphasize that case management must often involve agencies with "different perspectives, goals, and tools regarding violence prevention" (p. 312). These integrated approaches are consistent with our own approach to managing stalking and other forms of violence (Boer et al., 1997; Hart, 1997; Hart et al., 1998; Kropp et al., 1999b).

EFFECTIVE MANAGEMENT OF STALKERS

To mental health professionals, "treatment" is (re-)habilitative and involves delivering services to people who are suffering from symptoms of mental disorder, usually with their consent or cooperation, to relieve distress, dysfunction or disability. In the case of stalking, however, the primary goal of treatment is to stop people from committing violence rather than to alleviate their symptoms; thus, the treatment is preventive rather than rehabilitative. Furthermore, the actions taken to prevent violence often include interventions that are not solely or even primarily within the domain of the mental health professions and that may be delivered by people who are agents of the criminal justice system. Finally, the people being "treated" may be nonconsenting and uncooperative. For this reason, we prefer the term "case management" to "treatment". In the remainder of this section, we will identify some key principles of and strategies for effective case management, drawing upon the empirical and professional literature wherever possible. Anyone familiar with recent discussions of "threat assessment" by Robert Fein, Bryan Vossekuil and others associated with the United States Secret Service (e.g. Fein & Vossekuil, 1998; Fein et al., 1995; Borum et al., 1999; Pynchon & Borum, 1999) will recognize their influence on our thinking.

Principle 1: Case Management Should Focus on Risk

The first principle is that case management should focus on identifying, assessing and containing risk. A risk is a hazard that can be forecast only with uncertainty. Violence risk management is the process of speculating in an informed way about the aggressive acts a person might commit and to determine the steps that should be taken to prevent those acts and minimize their negative consequences (Hart, 1998).

Risk identification involves making an inventory of the feared outcomes—that is, determining what we are trying to prevent. As risk is a complex and multi-dimensional construct, evaluators should consider the following facets of risk:

- *Nature*. What might motivate the stalking—past or present conflict, desire to establish or re-establish a romantic relationship, desire for fame or infamy, or something else? Who are the likely targets of the stalking? Will the stalking include indirect communications, following, direct confrontation, threats of harm or actual harm? Are there several distinct scenarios of potential stalking behaviour?
- *Severity*. What level of fear or other psychological harm is the stalking likely to cause to victims? Will the stalking cause physical harm and, if so, might it include life-threatening physical harm (either intended or unintended)?
- *Imminence*. How soon might the person engage in stalking? Is there any reason to believe that the stalking might occur sooner rather than later—that is, next week or next month rather than, say, next year or sometime in the next ten years? Are there any "red flags"—factors that might

indicate that the person's risk for stalking is escalating or becoming imminent?

- *Frequency/duration.* How frequently might the person engage in stalking behaviours, and how long might the stalking behaviour persist? Is there any reason to believe that the person may commit acts on a frequent (e.g. daily or weekly) basis, as opposed to an occasional (e.g. monthly or yearly) basis? Is there any reason to believe that the person's obsession with the target is lessening over time, or instead that the obsession is likely to persist well into the future (e.g. for years to come)?
- *Likelihood.* What is the likelihood that the person will engage in stalking behaviours of various sorts? On the basis of this person's past behaviour, and in light of any relevant scientific data, can the evaluator estimate the probability that the various scenarios of violence will occur over various periods of time?

Risk assessment involves evaluating an individual to determine which factors are present in that case that might increase or enhance risk, typically referred to simply as *risk factors*, as well as factors that might decrease or diminish risk, often called *protective factors*. The presence of risk and protective factors should be determined from a review of case history information concerning the individual (e.g. law enforcement, corrections and mental health records), interviews with or statements by collateral informants (e.g. victims, as well as the individual's family, friends or co-workers), and interviews with or statements by the individual. Assuming the individual is cooperative, direct psychological or psychiatric assessment of the individual is always desirable.

Risk management involves developing a set of intervention strategies targeted at specific risk factors and designed to prevent the feared outcomes. Evaluators should specify whether the individual requires monitoring and if so, the kind and frequency required (e.g. weekly face-to-face visits, daily phone contacts, monthly assessments). Whenever possible, they should specify any "triggers" or "red flags" that might indicate that the individual's risk of violence is imminent or escalating. The intervention strategies recommended should take into account the individual's plans or goals, the availability of professional resources, and the likelihood that the individual will cooperate with and respond to case management efforts.

Note that risk identification, assessment and management are inherently subjective and speculative processes. They require considerable judgement and discretion. At present, there are no useful procedures to assist evaluators in this work. Existing actuarial tests of violence risk focus on general violence or sexual violence rather than stalking. They may be inappropriate in cases where the perpetrator knows the likely victim and may even have had a pre-existing relationship with the victim. Evaluators may find more helpful structured professional guidelines for assessing risk of spousal violence (in the case of ex-intimate stalkers; see Kropp et al., 1995, 1999b) or violence by people suffering from mental illness or personality disorder (in the case of erotomanic, "love obsessional" or grudge stalkers; see Webster et al., 1997). For the purposes of this chapter, we have used risk factor terminology that is consistent with our previous work (e.g. Kropp et al., 1995).

There are a number of risk factors that relate to risk in all forms of stalking due to their relationship to violent behaviour in general. These include *criminal history* variables such as past violence against strangers or acquaintances, past violence against family members, and past violation of conditional release. These factors reflect the axiom that past behaviour predicts future behaviour. Another category of risk factors relates to *psychosocial adjustment*. These factors include recent relationship and employment instability, being the victim or witness to family violence as a child or adolescent, substance abuse, suicidal/homicidal ideation or intent, major mental illness (with paranoid or manic symptoms) and personality disorder such as psychopathy or borderline personality disorder. All of these risk factors have been reviewed with respect to their relevance to general violence, sexual violence and domestic violence elsewhere (Boer et al., 1997; Kropp et al, 1999a; Webster et al., 1997). There are other risk factors commonly related to most forms of stalking, which include obsessional thinking (Cooper, 1993; Meloy, 1999), anger or persecutory thinking (White & Cawood, 1998), attachment pathology (Meloy, 1992; Skoler, 1998), and access to weapons (Fein et al., 1995).

As noted earlier, because of the high prevalence of (ex-) intimate partner stalking, another significant group of risk factors is that believed to be related to *spousal assault* specifically. These include past evidence of physical or sexual violence in relationships, past violence in the context of sexual jealously, past use of weapons or credible threats of death, past violations of no-contact orders, recent escalation in the severity or frequency of violence, extreme minimization or denial of violence history, and attitudes that support or condone the use of violence in relationships (Campbell, 1995; Dutton & Kropp, 2000; Kropp et al., 1999b).

After considering the presence/absence of individual risk factors, and each factor's relevance to the case at hand, it is recommended that risk management strategies be devised. Risk management strategies should be explicitly tied to risk factors, ensuring that each risk and need factor of the individual is addressed in some constructive manner. If the important risk factors are static or historical in nature, such as past criminal behaviour or conditional release violations, management strategies will likely be police- or corrections-based, involving, for example, strict release or custodial conditions. More dynamic, psychosocial variables will typically be addressed by health professionals and will include medical, psychological, occupational and social work interventions. Examples of some of these linkages are included in Table 9.1.

Table 9.1.   Risk factors and related management strategies

Risk factor	Strategies
1. Past assault of family members	• Incarceration • Intensive supervision • Family treatment • Parenting skills training
2. Past assault of strangers or acquaintances	• Incarceration • Intensive supervision • Correctional treatment for violence
3. Past violations of conditional release or community supervision	• Incarceration • Intensive supervision • Correctional recidivism programme
4. Recent relationship problems	• Dispute resolution • Spousal assault group programme • Couples counselling • Financial counselling • Legal advice/Family court • Restraining orders
5. Recent employment problems	• Vocational counselling • Financial counselling • Drug/alcohol treatment • Social work intervention
6. Victim of and/or witness to family violence as a child or adolescent	• Individual therapy • Posttraumatic stress treatment • Spousal assault group programme • Family treatment • Parenting skills
7. Recent substance abuse/dependence	• Drug/alcohol treatment • Court-ordered abstinence • Urine screening
8. Recent suicidal or homicidal ideation/intent	• Crisis counselling • Hospitalization • Psychotropic medication • Cognitive-behavioural therapy • Weapons restrictions • Individual treatment • Drug/alcohol restrictions
9. Recent psychotic and/or manic symptoms	• Hospitalization • Psychotropic medication • Individual treatment • Drug/alcohol restrictions
10. Personality disorder with anger, impulsivity, or behavioural instability	• Long-term individual therapy • Intensive supervision • Specialized therapy for personality disorders (e.g. dialectical behaviour therapy, therapeutic communities) *continues overleaf*

Table 9.1. *(continued)*

Risk Factor	Strategies
11. Past physical assault	• Incarceration • Intensive supervision • Psycho-educational programme • Anger management treatment
12. Past sexual assault/sexual jealousy	• Incarceration/supervision • Sexual deviance assessment • Sex offender treatment • Spousal assault group treatment with emphasis on power and control • Anger management treatment
13. Past use of weapons and/or credible threats of death	• Incarceration • Intensive supervision • Weapons restrictions
14. Recent escalation in frequency or severity of assault	• Crisis intervention • Increased supervision
15. Past violations of no-contact orders	• Incarceration • Intensive supervision • Discourage reliance on future no-contact orders
16. Extreme minimization or denial of spousal assault history	• Spousal assault group treatment to break down defensiveness • Psycho-educational group
17. Attitudes that support or condone spousal assault	• Spousal assault group treatment with emphasis on power and control • Psycho-educational group
18. Obsessional thinking	• Medication • Cognitive-behavioural treatment
19. Anger/persecution	• Medication • Anger management programming
20. Attachment pathology	• Specialized treatment • See factor 10
21. Access to weapons	• Incarceration • Weapons restrictions

Principle 2: Form a Multidisciplinary Case Management Team

The second principle is that case management should begin with the formation of a multidisciplinary case management team. The team should comprise, where appropriate and possible, people with diverse training or expertise, including mental health, law enforcement, security, legal, and management or human resources professionals. Of course, the composition of the team will depend on the nature and context of the allegation or suspicion.

One of the primary duties of the case management team is the initial investigation of alleged or suspected stalking (e.g. Fein et al., 1995). The team should be responsible for reviewing all available evidence (including, as noted previously, records, statements and interviews) to reach an opinion regarding whether there are reasonable grounds to believe that stalking has occurred. (The investigation should never rely solely on interviews with the individual, as stalkers typically engage in severe minimization or denial of harassing behavior; Rosenfeld, 2000). If the answer is affirmative, the team then should make recommendations concerning further investigation (the conduct of which will be determined by relevant law or policy) and any steps that should be taken to ensure the immediate safety of the complainants pending the outcome of the investigation. Once the final investigation is complete, the team should be responsible for developing and implementing a case management plan and for reviewing the adequacy of the management plan on a regular basis.

It is important to emphasize here that the effectiveness of all subsequent case management depends on the adequacy of the team's investigations. Good investigation not only protects the safety of the complainants; it also protects the liability of the people and agencies involved in case management should the alleged stalker initiate legal proceedings against them. The use of a multidisciplinary team demonstrates a good faith attempt on the part of the agencies involved to consider all relevant information; it also helps to foster an integrated and systematic approach to case management (discussed in the next section) that hopefully will persist beyond the preliminary investigation.

Principle 3: Case Management Should Deliver Comprehensive and Integrated Services

The third principle is that case management should involve the delivery of a wide range of services in a coordinated manner. Because the phenomenon of stalking is so complex and heterogeneous, no single system, agency or profession can claim to have the knowledge or ability necessary to manage stalkers on its own. Accordingly, case management services should include, where appropriate and possible, treatment, supervision and victim safety planning. These services are discussed in greater detail below.

Integrating the delivery of diverse services is a challenge. At a minimum, integration requires that every agency involved in case management has clearly defined roles and responsibilities, including guidelines for proper documentation, communication and coordination. Integration of services is best accomplished through the development of policy and procedure manuals. Various agencies should either be familiar with each other's policies and procedures, or be governed by the same inter-agency policy. The nature of the policy and procedure manuals depends, of course, on the nature and context in which the stalking occurs; a stalking complaint made to a local police force may be handled very differently from one made in the workplace or at school. Even in the workplace, stalking by an employee at a high-tech firm likely will be handled differently from stalking by a patient at a maximum security forensic psychiatric hospital. Good examples of policy and procedure manuals that focus, inter alia, on stalking and threat assessment are available for those working in the criminal justice system (British Columbia Ministry of Attorney General, 1997), in the workplace (US Office of Personnel Management, 1998), and in schools (Olweus, 1993). An excellent policy for coordinated case management of violent offenders—in this case, sexual offenders—in the criminal justice system is the "containment model" developed in the State of Colorado (English et al., 1996).

Principle 4: Treatment Services Should Focus on Improving Psychosocial Adjustment

The fourth principle is that treatment of stalkers should focus on attempting to ameliorate dynamic risk factors related to psychosocial adjustment. Treatment services typically are delivered by health care professionals working at inpatient or outpatient clinics. Experience suggests that in most cases the treatment is involuntary; that is, the stalker is civilly committed to inpatient or outpatient care under a mental health act, is being treated in a forensic psychiatric facility following a finding of incompetence (unfitness) to stand trial or legal insanity, is required to attend assessment or treatment as part of an employee assistance programme, or is ordered to attend treatment as a condition of bail, probation or parole (e.g. Rosenfeld, 2000).

One of the most important goals in the management of stalkers is the treatment of mental disorder related to the stalking behaviour. As Ronsenfeld (2000) notes, mental disorder often plays an important causal role in stalking. Major mental illnesses, such as psychotic or mood disorders, may be associated with erotomanic or persecutory delusions. Similarly, chronic mental disorders, such as personality disorders or mental retardation, may be associated with problematic personality traits such as impulsivity, hostility or dependency. Other mental disorders, such as substance use and psychosexual disorders, may lead to further instability or impulsivity. Although there is no direct evidence suggesting that various treatments for mental disorder decrease stalking behaviour, it is possible—and even likely—that they will have a beneficial impact. Treatment may include individual or group psychotherapy, psychoeducational programmes designed to change attitudes towards violence, training programmes designed to improve interpersonal, anger management and vocational skills, psychoactive medications, such as antipsychotics or mood stabilizers, and chemical dependency programmes.

Another important goal of management is the reduction of acute life stresses. Life stress can trigger or exacerbate mental disorder. But it can also lead to transient symptoms of psychopathology even in people who are otherwise mentally healthy. Stress plays an especially important role in grudge stalking, where it may be associated with an ongoing conflict between the stalker and victim. The most effective way to reduce psychological stress is to eliminate the stressor (i.e. stressful event); to this end, dispute resolution mechanisms may be helpful. These might include referral of the stalker to crisis management services or legal counselling and even, when comprehensive assessment indicates it is likely to be helpful for both parties, a recommendation for stalker and victim to participate in arbitration, mediation or conferencing.

Principle 5: Supervision Services Should Focus on Containing Risk Through Monitoring and Restriction of Activity

The fifth principle is that supervision of stalkers should focus on monitoring and restriction of activity at an intensity commensurate with the level of risk they pose. Supervision is essential because treatment is relevant only for certain dynamic risk factors and its effectiveness at reducing or preventing stalking is unknown. The goals of supervision are to make it difficult for a perpetrator to engage in further stalking behaviour and to make it easier to detect any further stalking behaviour that does occur. Supervision services typically are delivered by law enforcement, corrections, and legal and security professionals working in institutions or in the community. (Keep in mind that individuals can engage in stalking behaviour even when imprisoned or hospitalized.)

Monitoring—repeated evaluation of the stalker—is always a part of good supervision. Monitoring should include contact with the stalker as well as with the victims and other relevant people (e.g. therapists, correctional officers, family members, co-workers) in the form of face-to-face or telephonic meetings. Where appropriate, it should also include surveillance in the form of field visits (i.e. at home or work), electronic monitoring, polygraphic interviews, drug testing (urine, blood or hair analysis), and inspection of mail or telecommunications (telephone records, fax logs, email, etc.). Frequent contacts with health care and social service professionals are an excellent form of monitoring; missed appointments with treatment providers are a warning sign that the stalker's compliance with supervision may be deteriorating.

The most common restriction of activity is no contact with victims. These restrictions should be broad, including prohibition of all direct or indirect communications and prohibition of travel or movement within a fixed distance of the victims and their places of work and residence. Stalkers should be informed that any communications with or about the victims required as part of legal proceedings should be directed to the police, private security or the victims' lawyers. More general restrictions on travel and speech (e.g. house arrest, no travel to a particular city, county or state, deportation, gag orders) should be considered, but, to prevent infringement of the stalker's civil rights and to reduce risk of liability for people involved in supervision, implemented only when it is reasonable to conclude that they are necessary to protect victims from serious harm.

Principle 6: Victim Safety Planning Should Focus on "Target Hardening"

The sixth principle is that safety planning should focus on improving the victim's dynamic and static security resources, a process sometimes referred to as "target hardening". The goal is to ensure that if stalking behaviour resumes despite treatment and supervision, any negative impact on the victim's psychological and physical well-being is minimized. Victim safety planning services may be delivered by a wide range of social service, human resource, law enforcement and private security professionals. These services can be delivered regardless of whether the stalker is in an institution or the community.

Dynamic security is a function of the social environment. It is provided by people—the victim and others—who can respond rapidly to changing conditions. The ability of these people to respond effectively depends, critically, on the extent to which they have accurate and complete information concerning the risks posed to victims. This means that good victim liaison is the cornerstone of victim safety planning. Counselling with victims to increase their awareness and vigilance may be helpful, particularly in the case of former intimate stalkers who, in our experience, often greatly minimize the seriousness of the stalker's behaviour. Treatment designed to address deficits in adjustment or coping skills that impair the ability of victims to protect themselves (e.g. psychotherapy to relieve anxiety or depression) may be indicated. Training in self-protection should be considered, such as protocols for handling telephone calls and mail or classes in physical self-defence. Finally, information concerning the stalker (including a recent photograph), the risks posed to victims, and the steps to be taken if the stalker attempts to approach the victims should be provided to people close to the victims and those responsible for their safety. This information will allow law enforcement and private security professionals to develop proper security plans.

Static security is a function of the physical environment. It is effective when it improves the ability of victims to monitor their environment and impedes stalkers from engaging in stalking behaviour. The case management team should consider whether it is possible to improve the static security where victims live, work and travel. Visibility can be improved by adding lights, altering gardens or landscapes, and installing video cameras. Access can be restricted by adding or improving door locks and security checkpoints. Alarms can be installed, or victims can be provided with personal alarms. In some cases, it is impossible to ensure the safety of victims in a particular site and the case management team may recommend extreme measures such as relocation of the victims' residences or workplaces.

CASE STUDY: GRUDGE STALKING

The following case study illustrates the application of the principles discussed above. The details are factual, with the exception that names and certain identifying details have been disguised.

Background: Initial Complaint

Ms Ryan, the owner of an exclusive physical fitness studio in a large Canadian city, approached a consulting firm that specializes in the management of workplace conflict, including workplace violence. Ms Ryan described a pattern of unusual and concerning behavior by one of her firm's clients, Mr Maraun. Mr Maraun was a 40-year-old single male, self-employed as a public relations consultant. He joined the fitness studio in January 2000 and expressed interest in attending an early evening aerobics group. Shortly afterwards, a long-time client approached Ms Ryan in a state of distress. The client, a 38-year-old female physician, claimed that Mr Maraun had harassed her a little more than a year earlier. The harassment stemmed from a work-related conflict and culminated in accusations of sexual impropriety with patients made in a letter of complaint to the medical licensing board (although these accusations had nothing to do with the original conflict). The licensing board dismissed the complaints, but Mr Maraun continued to harass the physician by phone and mail. Eventually, the physician laid a complaint of stalking with the local police. The police investigated and determined that there were insufficient grounds to lay criminal charges at the time. The matter was resolved after Mr Maraun entered into an undertaking in which he agreed not to have further contact with the physician for a period of one year. The physician was very disturbed that Mr Maraun had joined the studio and now was a fellow student in the aerobics classes she had been attending for more than a decade. Ms Ryan was sympathetic to her client's concerns and agreed to talk to Mr Maraun. She met with him, politely explained the physician's concerns, and asked him to attend a different aerobics class, either one hour earlier or one hour later. Mr Maraun agreed, but was very angry that the physician had "publicly slandered" him and demanded an opportunity to explain the background of the incident to the staff of the studio. Ms Ryan explained that she had not discussed the incident with anyone else, so addressing the staff was unnecessary.

Within a week, several staff members approached Ms Ryan—independently and unknown to each other—to express their concerns that Mr Maraun's behaviour was "odd" and inappropriate. One female aerobics instructor complained that Mr Maraun was somewhat uncoordinated and impulsive in his movements, frequently moving close to other students in the class or touching them; several students had commented to the instructor that they found Mr Maraun to be "creepy" or "scary". Another instructor complained that Mr Maraun gave her a "pat on the bum" after one class. She immediately gave Mr Maraun a polite but firm direction that such physical contact was inappropriate, but he expressed surprise at her "over-reaction". Finally, the receptionist at the studio complained that Mr Maraun had been asking questions of a personal nature about Ms Ryan, including whether she was currently involved in a romantic relationship and where she lived.

Ms Ryan once again asked to meet with Mr Maraun. When she explained about the new complaints, he was immediately enraged and accused her of "spreading lies" about him to the staff and clients at the studio. He began to shout, paced in the office, and waved his arms wildly. Ms Ryan told him his behaviour was inappropriate and asked him to leave immediately. Mr Maraun phoned her later that day, apologized profusely, and asked that he be allowed to attend the studio again. He insisted that Ms Ryan contact the police officer who had investigated him following the physician's complaint of harassment, saying the officer would provide her with information that would "vindicate" him. Ms Ryan and Mr Maraun agreed to speak about the matter further after a "cooling-off period" of two weeks, which would give her an opportunity to determine what she should do. Despite Mr Maraun's promise not to visit or contact the studio during the cooling-off period, he sent lengthy faxes, dropped off letters, and made telephone calls on an almost daily basis. Ms Ryan called the police, who advised her that there were insufficient grounds to lay criminal charges. She then contacted the workplace conflict consultants for advice.

Preliminary Investigation and Development of Case Management Plan

Ms Ryan met with two members of the workplace conflict consulting firm, a lawyer and a psychologist. She explained the situation, answered questions posed by the consultants, and provided them with records (including the faxes and letters from Mr Maraun). The consultants then contacted the police officer involved in the physician's complain of harassment, as well as the officer with whom Ms Ryan had spoken. The consultants decided not to speak with Mr Ryan at that time. On the basis of their investigation, they advised Ms Ryan that there was no reason to believe that Mr Maraun was an imminent risk of physical violence to staff or clients at the studio, although they believed that he was at high risk to continue his pattern of disturbing behaviour. Available evidence, including the review of documents and the descriptions of staff and police who had dealt with him, suggested that Mr Maraun was an intelligent and mostly pro-social man with no acute mental illness but with pronounced obsessive-compulsive personality traits. The consultants developed a case management plan that included four steps:

1. *An official letter from the lawyer.* Ms Ryan retained the lawyer to write a letter on her behalf stating that his behaviour had caused clients at the studio to fear for their safety and that his relationship with staff members had deteriorated to the point where they felt unable to work with him. Regrettably, the letter continued, he was no longer welcome at the studio. Mr Maraun was also instructed to have no direct contact with the studio or with members of its staff; he was told that correspondence should be through the lawyer. The letter was polite and respectful, contained no threats of legal action or police involvement, made no mention of the physician's allegations, and included a full refund of his membership fees.
2. *An official memo from Ms Ryan to staff members regarding Mr Maraun.* The memo informed staff that he was no longer welcome at the studio because of his behaviour, but reassured them that there was no reason to believe that he posed a risk for physical violence. The memo also informed staff to call the police emergency line if Mr Maraun entered the studio and to inform Ms Ryan if they received any other communication from him.
3. *Development of a workplace violence prevention programme.* The programme included a review of static and dynamic security procedures, development of new procedures for documenting security-related concerns, holding a two-hour education and training session for staff members, and developing a brief workplace violence policy to include in the studio's staff training and orientation manual.
4. *Liaison with police.* The consultants spoke with police by telephone to inform them of the steps they were taking and provided them with a copy of the letter from Ms Ryan's legal counsel. The police offered to send an officer from the community policing division to perform a free inspection of physical security.

Response to Case Management

Mr Maraun responded to the lawyer's letter by "testing the limits": he sent a fax to the fitness studio in clear violation of the lawyer's request and walked past the studio's front window several times. The lawyer responded immediately by stating that further violations of his request would result in civil action or referral of the matter to police, as appropriate. Mr Maraun apologized in a phone call to the lawyer, and over the next few weeks sent several polite letters and faxes to the lawyer in which he discussed the possibility of launching legal action against Ms Ryan or the fitness studio. The lawyer did nothing to discourage such communications, as they provided an excellent means of monitoring any changes in Mr Maraun's mental state.

After about three months, the fitness studio received a courier package from Mr Maraun containing three open tins of cat food. The staff were distressed by this contact, which they perceived to be "crazy". The lawyer contacted Mr Maraun and asked him to explain his actions, which he refused to do. The consultants immediately contacted the police, who agreed that the situation now required more formal action. A police officer interviewed Mr Maraun, explained the criminal law pertaining to stalking, notified him that a file had been opened concerning the case, and warned him that any further contact would result in criminal charges in addition to any civil remedies sought by the victims. Mr Maraun apologized for his actions and has not contacted Ms Ryan, her studio or the lawyer since.

Commentary

As this case makes clear, even a relatively minor case of stalking or harassment can cause significant disruption of victims' lives. Although Ms Ryan was a skilled and experienced businesswoman, she was unable to successfully resolve the conflict with Mr Maraun on her own. Working with the consultants, she undertook a course of action that was fair and reasonable in its treatment of Mr Maraun, protected the safety and well-being of her staff and clientele, and protected her in terms of legal liability. The case management plan addressed monitoring, supervision and victim safety planning, reflected the advice of experienced legal and mental health professionals, and included close cooperation with law enforcement. The plan allowed prompt and effective response to continued harassment and ultimately was effective in stopping the harassment altogether without the need for arrest or civil action—both of which can be necessary in certain circumstances but require considerable time and effort to pursue and may even escalate the level of conflict.

CONCLUSION

Although there is no good research on the "treatment" of stalkers at the present time, research on stalking behaviour, combined with knowledge of risk management of other violent offenders, provides a basis for delineation of several general principles for effective case management. We hope that our views, based on our experiences working as a multidisciplinary team in Canada, stimulate others to share their experiences on case management.

NOTE

Preparation of this chapter was supported in part by a grant from the British Columbia Institute Against Family Violence to P. R. Kropp and a Simon Fraser University President's Research Grant to S. D. Hart. The opinions expressed herein are those of the authors and do not reflect official policy of the British Columbia Forensic Psychiatric Services Commission, Simon Fraser University or the Vancouver Police Department. Address correspondence to Dr P. R. Kropp, Adult Forensic Outpatient Services, Suite 300, 307 West Broadway, Vancouver, British Columbia, Canada V5Y 1P8. Email should be addressed to rkropp@sfu.ca.

REFERENCES

Boer, D. P., Hart, S. D., Kropp, P. R. & Webster, C. W (1997). *Manual for the Sexual Violence Risk—20: Professional Guidelines for Assessing Risk of Sexual Violence*. Burnaby, British Columbia: The Mental Health, Law, & Policy Institute, Simon Fraser University, and the BC Institute Against Family Violence.

Borum, R., Fein, R., Vossekuil, B. & Berglund, J. (1999). Threat assessment: defining an approach for evaluating risk of targeted violence. *Behavioral Sciences and the Law*, **17**, 323–37.

British Columbia Ministry of Attorney General (1997). *Violence Against Women in Relationships Policy*. Victoria, BC: Queen's Printer.

Burgess, A. W., Baker, T., Greening, D., Hartman, C. R., Burgess, A. G., Douglas, J. E. & Halloran, R. (1997). Stalking behaviors within domestic violence. *Journal of Family Violence*, **12**(4), 389–403.

Campbell, J. C. (1995). Prediction of homicide of and by battered women. In J. C. Campbell (ed.), *Assessing Dangerousness: Violence by Sexual Offenders, Batterers, and Child Abusers* (pp. 96–113). Thousand Oaks, CA: Sage.

Canadian Centre for Justice Statistics (2000). *Family Violence in Canada: A Statistical Profile*. Ottawa: Minister of Industry.

Cooper, M. (1993). *Assessing the Risk of Repeated Violence Among Men Arrested for Wife Assault: A Review of the Literature*. Vancouver, BC: British Columbia Institute Against Family Violence.

Cooper, M. (1994a). *Wasted Lives: The Tragedy of Homicide in the Family*. Vancouver, BC: BC Institute Against Family Violence.

Cooper, M. (1994b). *Criminal Harassment and Potential for Treatment: Literature Review and Annotated Bibliography*. Vancouver, BC: BC Institute Against Family Violence.

Cornish, J. L., Murray, K. A. & Collins, P. I. (1999). *The Criminal Lawyers' Guide to the Law of Criminal Harassment and Stalking*. Aurora, Ontario: Canada Law Book Inc.

De Becker, G. (1994). *A White Paper Report—Intervention Decisions—The Value of Flexibility*. Draft prepared for the attendees of the Threat Management Conference, Anaheim, CA.

Dutton, D. & Kropp, P. R. (2000). A review of domestic violence risk instruments. *Trauma, Violence, & Abuse*, **1**(2), 171–81.

English, K., Pullen, S. & Jones, L. (1996). *Managing Adult Sex Offenders: A Containment Approach*. Lexington, KY: American Probation and Parole Association.

Fein, R. & Vossekuil, B. (1998). *Protective Intelligence and Threat Assessment Investigations: A Guide for State and Local Law Enforcement Officials*. NIJ/OJP/DOJ publication no. NCJ 170612. Washington, DC: US Department of Justice.

Fein, R., Vossekuil, B. & Holden, G. (1995). *Threat Assessment: An Approach to Prevent Targeted Violence*. Washington, DC: US Department of Justice.

Gross, M. D. (1991). Treatment of pathological jealousy by fluoxetine. *American Journal of Psychiatry*, **148**(5), 683–4.

Hare, R. D. (1991). *Manual for the Hare Psychopathy Checklist—Revised*. Toronto: Multi-Health Systems, Inc.

Harmon, R. B., Rosner, R. & Owens, H. (1998). Sex and violence in a forensic population of obsessional harassers. *Psychology, Public Policy, and Law*, **4**(1/2), 236–49.

Hart, S. D. (1998). The role of psychopathy in assessing risk for violence. *Legal and Criminological Psychology*, **3**, 121–37.

Hart, S. D., Cox, D. N. & Hart, R. D. (1995). *The Hare Psychopathy Checklist: Screening Version*. Toronto: Multi-Health Systems, Inc.

Hart, S. D., Kropp, P. R. & LePard, D. (1998). *Stalking in Canada: Characteristics of Offenders and Offences*. Paper presented at the Eighth Annual Threat Management Conference, Anaheim, California.

Healey, K., Smith, C. & O'Sullivan, C. (1998). *Batterer Intervention: Program Approaches and Criminal Justice Strategies*. NCJ publication no. 168638. Washington, DC: National Institute of Justice.

Hemphill, J. F., Hare, R. D. & Wong, S. (1997). Psychopathy and recidivism: a review. *Legal and Criminological Psychology*, **3**, 141–72.

Kong, R. (1996). Criminal harassment. *Juristat*, **16**(12).

Kropp, P. R. (1999). *Risk in a Forensic Psychiatric Sample of Stalkers*. Paper presented at the Conference on Risk Assessment and Risk Management: Implications for the Prevention of Violence. Vancouver, British Columbia.

Kropp, P. R. & Hart, S. D. (2000). The Spousal Assault Risk Assessment (SARA) guide: reliability and validity in adult male offenders. *Law and Human Behavior*, **24**, 101–18.

Kropp, P. R., Hart, S. D., Webster, C. W. & Eaves, D. (1995). *Manual for the Spousal Assault Risk Assessment Guide* (2nd edn). Vancouver, British Columbia: British Columbia Institute on Family Violence.

Kropp, P. R., Lyon, D., Hart, S. D., & LePard, D. (1999a). *Assessing Risk in Stalkers*. Paper presented at the Psychology and Law International Conference, Dublin, Ireland.

Kropp, P. R., Hart, S. D., Webster, C. W. & Eaves, D. (1999b). *Spousal Assault Risk Assessment: User's Guide*. Toronto: Multi-Health Systems, Inc.

Kurt, J. L. (1995). Stalking as a variant of domestic violence. *Bulletin of the American Academy of Psychiatry and Law*, **23**(2), 219–30.

Lindsay, W. R., Olley, S., Jack, C., Morrison, F. & Smith, A. H. (1998). The treatment of two stalkers with intellectual disabilities using a cognitive approach. *Journal of Applied Research in Intellectual Disabilities*, **11**(4), 333–44.

Lyon, D. (1997). *The Characteristics of Stalkers in British Columbia*. Unpublished master's thesis. Simon Fraser University, Burnaby, British Columbia.

Lyon, D., Kropp, P. R., Hart, S. D. & LePard, D. (1999). *Assessing Risk in Cases of Stalking: Preliminary Data*. Paper presented at the Conference on Risk Assessment and Risk Management: Implications for the Prevention of Violence. Vancouver, British Columbia.

Meloy, J. R. (1992). *Violent Attachments*. North Vale, NJ: Aronson.

Meloy, J. R. (1997). The clinical risk management of stalking: "Someone is watching over me . . . ". *American Journal of Psychotherapy*, **51**(2), 174–84.

Meloy, J. R. (1998). *The Psychology of Stalking: Clinical and Forensic Perspectives*. New York: Academic Press.

Meloy, J. R. (1999). Stalking: an old behavior, a new crime. *Psychiatric Clinics of North America*, **22**(1), 85–99.

Meyers, J. (1998). Cultural factors in erotomania and obsessional following. In J. Reid Meloy (ed.), *The Psychology of Stalking: Clinical and Forensic Perspectives* (pp. 214–24). San Diego, CA: Academic Press.

Mullen, P. E. & Pathé, M. (1994). Stalking and the pathologies of love. *Australian and New Zealand Journal of Psychiatry*, **28**, 469–77.

Mullen, P. E., Pathé, M., Purcell, R. & Stuart, W. (1999). Study of stalkers. *American Journal of Psychiatry*, **156**, 1244–9.

Noone, J. A. & Cockhill, L. (1987). Erotomania: the delusion of being loved. *American Journal of Forensic Psychiatry*, **8**, 23–31.

Olweus, D. (1993). *Bullying at School: What We Know and What We Can Do*. Oxford: Blackwell.

Palarea, R. E., Zona, M. A., Lane, J. C. & Langhinrichsen-Rohling, J. (1999). The dangerous nature of intimate relationship stalking: threats, violence, and associated risk factors. *Behavioral Sciences and the Law*, **17**, 269–83.

Pynchon, M. & Borum, R. (1999). Assessing threats of targeted group violence: contributions from social psychology. *Behavioral Sciences & the Law*, **17**, 339–55.

Rosenfeld, B. (2000). Assessment and treatment of obsessional harassment. *Aggression and Violent Behavior*, **5**, 529–49.

Salekin, R., Rogers, R. & Sewell, K. (1996). A review and meta-analysis of the Psychopathy Checklist and Psychopathy Checklist—Revised: predictive validity of dangerousness. *Clinical Psychology: Science and Practice*, **3**, 203–15.

Skoler (1998). The archetypes and the psychodynamics of stalking. In J. Reid Meloy (ed.), *The Psychology of Stalking: Clinical and Forensic Perspectives* (pp. 295–315). San Diego, CA: Academic Press.

Tjaden, P. & Thoennes, N. (1998). *Stalking in America: Findings from the National Violence Against Women Survey*. Washington, DC: US Department of Justice.

US Office of Personnel Management (1998). *Dealing with Workplace Violence: A Guide for Agency Planners*. Washington, DC: Office of Workforce Relations.

VandenBos, G. R. & Bulatao, E. Q. (eds). *Violence on the Job: Identifying Risk and Developing Solutions*. Washington, DC: American Psychological Association.

Walker, L. E. & Meloy, J. R. (1998). Stalking and domestic violence. In J. Reid Meloy (ed.), *The Psychology of Stalking: Clinical and Forensic Perspectives* (pp. 140–60). San Diego, CA: Academic Press.

Webster, C. D., Douglas, K. S., Eaves, D. & Hart, S. D. (1997). *HCR-20: Assessing Risk for Violence*. Burnaby, BC: Mental Health, Law, & Policy Institute, Simon Fraser University.

Westrup, D. & Fremouw, W. J. (1998). Stalking behavior: a literature review and suggested functional analytic assessment technology. *Aggression and Violent Behavior*, **3**(3), 255–74.

White, S. G. & Cawood, J. S. (1998). Threat management of stalking cases. In J. Reid Meloy (ed.), *The Psychology of Stalking: Clinical and Forensic Perspectives* (pp. 295–315). San Diego, CA: Academic Press.

Wilson, M. & Daly, M. (1994). Spousal homicide. *Juristat*, **14**(8).

Zona, M. A., Palarea, R. E. & Lane, J. (1998). Psychiatric diagnosis and the offender–victim typology of stalking. In J. Reid Meloy (ed.), *The Psychology of Stalking: Clinical and Forensic Perspectives* (pp. 69–84). San Diego, CA: Academic Press.

Zona, M. A., Sharma, K. K. & Lane, J. (1993). A comparative study of erotomanic and obsessional subjects in a forensic sample. *Journal of Forensic Sciences*, **38**, 894–903.

CHAPTER 10

Erotomania in Women

PAUL FITZGERALD

Dandenong Psychiatric Research Centre

and

MARY V. SEEMAN

Centre for Addiction and Mental Health, Ontario

LOVE AND THE PATHOLOGIES OF LOVE

The emotion of love is a crucial one for human evolution. It is the emotion that brings and bonds two human beings together, that ensures sufficient proximity for procreation to take place, that endures through time so that children of the union can be cared for until the age of maturity, that retains its exclusivity so that disputes over paternity do not disrupt it. On average, in order for the human race to survive, feelings of love need to be powerful enough to result in sexual union, enduring enough to weather the disharmonies of child rearing and exclusive enough to shelter the family unit from the dangers of envy, jealousy and hostility. The saliency of love over other emotions must be securely coded into our genetic material. We would not have survived had the genes that constitute the motivation to fall in love not been widely distributed throughout the DNA. Consequently, in any given population, the push to love is probably stronger than the social opportunities for individuals within the population to develop reciprocal, socially acceptable, love relationships. Hence the pathologies of love.

The emotion that we call love has been studied intensively and is the main theme of history, myth, literature and art. It encompasses sexual

Stalking and Psychosexual Obsession: Psychological Perspectives for Prevention, Policing and Treatment.
Edited by J. Boon and L. Sheridan. © 2002 John Wiley & Sons, Ltd.

passion (eros), romance (ludus), caring (caritas) possessiveness (mania) and self-sacrifice (agape). It has various dimensions of intensity, involvement, exclusivity, adulation, ambivalence. It exists in the context of pleasure and pain, security and anxiety. The subject, the person who loves, can be clear-headed or blinded by love. The object, the person who is loved, can be deserving or unworthy. Love may be mutual or one-sided, declared or undeclared, consummated or not, short-lived or constantly evolving. There are cognitive, affective and behavioural components to love, and each of these components undergoes its own pathology, although it is the behavioural component that leads to trouble with the law. Cognitive and affective aspects are the ones that bring individuals to seek help from mental health professionals (Critelli et al., 1986; Hendrick & Hendrick, 1991).

The pathologies of love are extensions of common, everyday experience, most evident in adolescence when it is acceptable and probably necessary to experiment with a variety of "pretend" relationships, crushes, infatuations, idealizations of public figures, pop singers and movie idols. These precursors to adult love are safe and, in some ways, prepare adolescents for the real world of adult relationships. They are replete with beliefs in telepathy, magic communication and irrational daydreams. They are self-centred in the sense that they fulfil the need to be in love rather than function in response to any real characteristic of the love object. The Greek myth of Psyche and Eros encompasses much of what adolescent love is about, the invisible object whose reality vanishes when light is cast upon its face (Seeman, 1971). The pathologies of love are elaborations, longer lasting and more intractable, of adolescent infatuations. In adulthood, they often emerge in the context of love loss, the sequelae of rejection and humiliation (Seeman, 1975).

Erotomania, defined as obsessive, excessive, unwanted or delusional love, when ascertained by the courts as a result of its behavioural manifestations, is primarily a syndrome of men. When seen in psychiatric offices, for its subjectively worrisome cognitive and affective dimensions, it is primarily a syndrome of women. As a gross generalization, women obsess about love; love permeates their thinking, motivates them, worries them, distracts them, devastates them. Men act on love, often impulsively and boldly, sometimes disastrously. Men do not think about love as much as women; they do not speak about love as often as women do, but obsessive stalking, for instance, is relatively more common among men. The link between women and love can be seen in the names parents give to children (Lawson, 1974; Seeman, 1972, 1976, 1980, 1983). Names linked to love, in all languages, are the almost exclusive domain of women, for example Aimee, Amy, Desiree, Luba, Cara and Cherie.

By its very nature, love is not always reciprocated. Physical attraction, sympathy for another person, interest in the other person, sexual desire and identification with another person can and do flourish without necessitating a response or return of affection from the object of interest. Because feelings of love seem naturally to lead to a wish for proximity, pursuing the person you fancy, putting yourself in the presence of the person in the hope of kindling an interest, finding out all you can about the person, asking friends about the person, telephoning, sending flowers, sending notes, asking others for introductions— all of these activities fall within the realm of the everyday. Unrequited love can and frequently does continue for long periods of time. Even in the face of a rebuff, hope may linger. There are many, many examples in literature of the patient lover who suffers rejection silently for years but ultimately wins the attention of the beloved (Fisher, 1990). This may also sometimes happen in examples from real life and, thus, convey hope and encourage perseverance on the part of the unrequited lover.

Such feelings, however, begin to edge toward the pathological when they persist in the face of long-term lack of interest, especially when there is a direct plea from the love object to cease and desist. Constant rumination and obsession with unrequited love can be seen as a form of masochism. It is not uncommon, particularly among women, to habitually select unavailable and unsuitable love objects in a repeated pattern of painful heartbreak (Mintz, 1980).

The next grade of pathology expresses itself in behaviour. It encompasses an insistence on the part of the subject on being seen repeatedly and repeatedly heard out. Demands for closeness become more assertive, even aggressive, despite repeated rejection. This has been called "borderline erotomania" (Meloy, 1989)—the subject knowing that his (or her) interest is not returned but determined that it will be, that the chosen person will eventually be made to love. There is not yet a loss of reality testing but the behaviour has strayed beyond the acceptable and can escalate to violence. Usually, there has been some form of real attachment between subject and object in the past, although it may not have amounted to more than a friendly smile. Nevertheless, there has been enough for the subject to feel the rejection keenly, to experience abandonment and, depending on many internal and external variables, to potentially become violent. The violence, more often than not, is turned on the person "in the way", not the beloved, but a third party seen to be the obstacle preventing the relationship from developing.

A more severe distortion of reality is the delusion that love is, indeed, requited but that the beloved cannot acknowledge and is not free to act on his (or her) desires, that someone or something constantly interferes. Frequently, there has been no prior real attachment between subject and object, although they may be known to one another.

HISTORICAL DESCRIPTION

The clinical condition that is now commonly known as erotomania was referred to in early literature by Hippocrates, Erisistratus, Plutarch and Galen. It was first described in the psychiatric literature in 1623 in a treatise by Jacques Ferrand on Maladie d'Amour ou Melancolie Erotique (Hunter & MacAlpine, 1963). This clinical presentation gained considerable attention in the German psychiatric literature in the early 20th century with descriptions by Kretschmer, Keher and Kraepelin (Keher, 1922; Kraepelin, 1909–1915; Kretschmer, 1918). A number of terms were coined in this period including erotic self-reference delusions (Kretschmer, 1918), old maid's psychosis (Hart, 1921), erotic paranoia (Krafft-Ebing, 1879) and erotomania (meaning to be loved in secret) (Kraepelin, 1909–1915). The syndrome gained its eponymous name following a review by de Clerambault, *Les Psychoses Passionelles* (de Clerambault, 1942) which brought together all the then published clinical material.

In the syndrome as described by de Clerambault, almost all the patients were women. Typically, the subject reports that the object, usually a person of high social standing, has made it known that he (or she) loves and desires the affection of the subject. This is made clear to the subject by a variety of means. The subject is, initially, surprised, even shocked. At first very uncomfortable, the subject grows to appreciate the attention and to feel sorry for the object's evidently unsuccessful attempts to fight off an uncontrollable passion. Gradually, the subject begins to return the affection and to try to communicate to the object that he (or she) need not be so circumspect, so indirect, that the suit will be welcome. The subject interprets innocuous remarks, gestures, facial expressions, happenstance, to signify that the object is in love. The subject then begins to say things back, write notes, telephone, take out advertisements, clamour for the object to declare himself publicly, and openly. Any denial is taken as evidence that the truth is too explosive to be told. Any negative statement is rationalized. De Clerambault speaks of three stages. The first is the stage of hope. The second stage is despair. Intermediaries are blamed. The person's standing in the community is held responsible for his inability to be forthright. The need to force the person to tell the "truth" becomes an obsession. The third stage is one of revenge sometimes leading to physical confrontation, accusation and violence (de Clerambault, 1942; Hollender & Callahan, 1975; Lovett-Doust & Christie, 1978).

De Clerambault described two varieties of the syndrome. The first springs up de novo in an otherwise well person. The second variety is superimposed on a pre-existing paranoid disorder. In de Clerambault's syndrome, there is usually no real prior attachment between subject and object but there may be a longstanding attachment to a representation of a public figure, embellished by reference to photographs in the press, replies to fan letters, the fantasy made real by arranged encounters, imagined exchanges, improvised dialogues narrated to others.

A number of attempts have been made to refine and/or confirm the description of de Clerambault. A number of studies have confirmed that there appear to be two varieties of the syndrome but there has been dispute over the nature of the distinction between the two clinical types. For example, Seeman (1978) described a group of women, predominately with schizophrenia and who were poorly integrated, with fixed delusions about a phantom individual (phantom lover syndrome). A second group consisted of more integrated women (considered as "erotomania proper") who had recurrent delusions focused on prominent powerful individuals. Clinically, these women had a mixture of mood, psychotic and personality disorders.

Recent literature has attempted to delineate more clearly the boundaries of erotomania and other pathologies of love. There is no universally accepted classification or conceptualization of these syndromes although, in general, patients with psychotic love syndromes tend to be considered as suffering from erotomania. A considerable body of this research has occurred in forensic settings where female patients are underrepresented. For example, Zona et al. (1993) have described two groups, the "love obsessional" and "simple obsessional", and compared these with an erotomanic group from the files of a "threat management" police unit. The love obsessional group consisted of patients with an erotomanic delusion as only a single feature of a multifaceted psychotic disorder as well as patients considered non-delusional but in love with an individual and fanatical in their pursuit of the object of their desire. The simple obsessional group consisted of individuals who stalk to gain retribution for perceived maltreatment or to rectify a schism in a prior real relationship. Erotomania was considered the diagnosis if the individual had the classical delusion of being the object of another (usually prominent) individual's love. Females comprised 88% of patients in the erotomanic group but only 12% of the "love obsessional" and 40% of the "simple obsessional" groups.

The delusional patients in the love obsessional group described by Zona et al. (1993) and the erotomanic patients appear to make up what is being increasingly considered the primary and secondary subtypes of erotomania. This distinction is drawn between a pure or primary form of the disorder, which is limited to erotomania and has a sudden onset, and the secondary form, which is of gradual onset and the erotomania is superimposed upon a pre-existing psychotic illness (Hollender & Callahan, 1975). Although most of the studies published in the literature are limited by sample size and methodology, this distinction appears to hold. In particular, a number of studies have confirmed that there is a distinction between the majority of patients with erotomanic delusions, who have these in the context of a pre-existing psychotic illness, often schizophrenia, and a small number of patients with "pure" erotomanic delusional disorder (Gillett et al., 1990; Mullen & Pathé, 1994; Rudden et al., 1990). The existence of the pure form of the disorder has been questioned by several authors (Ellis & Mellsop, 1985; Lehman, 1980) although its consistent appearance in a small percentage of patients in more recent studies appears to have confirmed its "true" existence and led to its recognition as a subtype of delusional disorder in DSM-III-R and DSM-IV.

PRIMARY EROTOMANIA

The current conceptualization of the pure or primary form of erotomania is relatively consistent with the classical description of erotomania arising de novo made by de Clerambault. This syndrome is best seen as a subtype of delusional disorder and is uncommon (Gillett et al., 1990; Mullen & Pathé, 1994; Rettersol & Opjordsmoen, 1991; Rudden et al., 1990). These patients, who are predominately women, typically develop the delusional belief that an older and prominent male is in love with them. The onset of the belief is rapid and they believe that the object of their affection has initiated advances towards them. The object of the delusion stays constant and the patient does not experience other psychotic symptoms such as hallucinations. Even within patients who experience a pure erotomania in the absence of other psychotic symptoms, it is unusual for all of these features to be found and several, such as the rapid onset, have been disputed.

The onset of erotomania appears to be at times precipitated by a loss or narcissistic wound (Evans et al., 1982; Mullen & Pathé, 1994), and both primary and secondary erotomania have been reported after a variety of triggering incidents, including substance use, the development of brain disease and childbirth (Lovett-Doust & Christie, 1978; Murray et al., 1990). It has repeatedly been reported to occur more frequently in women who lack a satisfying intimate relationship. These women often have pre-existing personality difficulties that result in interpersonal isolation. These characteristics may include suspiciousness, narcissism, avoidance, schizoid withdrawal, shyness and timidity (Enoch & Trethowan, 1979; Krafft-Ebing, 1879; Rettersol & Opjordsmoen, 1991; Seeman, 1978). These women are often described as having a lonely, isolated existence with the desire for a relationship balanced by the fear of emotional intimacy (Mullen & Pathé, 1994). They are also consistently noted to show interpersonal hypersensitivity and a tendency to misinterpret the actions, comments and intentions of others.

The working of a number of psychological mechanisms has been proposed in erotomania. These include deviant responses to mourning, separation and loss (Evans et al., 1982). Another interpretation is that the psychological fixation on another person reflects a form of "twinship alliance", meaning that the object appears to mirror qualities in the subject, either real qualities or wished for qualities. This encourages illusions of merging and fusion in personalities which are immature, illusions which are experienced as love. Envy of the person whose social standing is superior has also been identified as a trigger, with love serving as an acceptable denial of an otherwise unacceptable emotion such as envy. There may be a narcissistic feeling of being "as good as" or superior to the love object. Alternatively, the driving force may be a masochistic subjugation to an unattainable object, accompanied by a sense of pride at being able to endure unbearable suffering at the hands of an unrequited lover (Meloy, 1989). It has been proposed that these mechanisms may exist in both psychotic forms of erotomania and a variety of "borderline" states which are characterized by a severe but non-psychotic disorder of attachment.

Some biological mechanisms have been suggested to account for the female preponderance of erotomania. Recent work on brain laterality suggests that syndromes of misidentification (Capgras syndrome) and hypersexuality (into which erotomania loosely fits) are disorders of the right cerebral hemisphere responsible for spatial organization, a function in which men are reported to excel. In the absence of frank psychosis, reported experiences of both strangeness and odd familiarity when in the presence of the love object, hallucinations of smell, episodic outbursts of anger, otherwise well-preserved emotional tone and coherent spoken and written language point to the possibility of psychomotor epileptic phenomena deriving from the right temporal lobe (Barton, 1978).

SECONDARY EROTOMANIA

The secondary forms of erotomania are considerably more common and delusions of these type have been found in a considerable proportion of women with psychotic disorders. For example, one study has found delusions of erotomania in 14% of psychotic women studied (Rudden et al., 1983). Whereas primary erotomania appears predominately in women, this is less the case in secondary erotomania. Although there have been no systematic epidemiological studies, there appears to be an increasing proportion of male patients in the secondary group and a substantial increase in the proportion of males when non-psychotic disorders of attachment are considered (Zona et al., 1993). The results of the limited studies available, however, appear to be substantially influenced by ascertainment, there being a female over-representation in clinical populations and a substantial over-representation of males in forensic settings.

Erotomanic delusions have been reported in a wide variety of disorders. These include schizophrenia, schizoaffective disorder, major depressive disorder, bipolar disorder, intellectual disability and dementia (Drevets & Rubin, 1987; Evans et al., 1982; Greyson & Akhtar, 1977; Raskin & Sullivan, 1974; Remington & Book, 1984). They have been reported in both homosexual and heterosexual individuals and in a variety of cultures (Dunlop, 1988; El-Assra, 1989). There has been increasing recognition that erotomanic delusions are not uncommon in mood disorders, and one study indicates that the diagnoses of schizoaffective disorder and bipolar disorder are relatively frequent in women with erotomania (Rudden et al., 1990).

The variety in clinical presentations of women with secondary erotomania may be illustrated with the following case studies.

Case 1

A well-functioning woman in her mid-thirties, a single mother with a prior history of depression, is finally able to attain her goal of returning to school for a postgraduate degree. In class, she meets and has a few brief exchanges with a fellow student who subsequently leaves the class and emigrates to another country. Not immediately, but soon after he leaves, she imagines that he is spying on her, hovering around her, encouraging her, inordinately interested in her. She begins to feel his physical presence, to experience somatic hallucinations of his presence in her bed at night, engaging her in sexual intercourse producing multiple unwanted orgasms. She begins to hear his voice in her head. This woman sought treatment for what were experienced as unpleasant sexual feelings and frightening thoughts. She was diagnosed as having a schizoaffective disorder and was treated with antipsychotic medication and mood stabilizers. She was able to complete her doctoral degree but has been unable to obtain employment in her field. The feelings in her body and the voices in her head continue to bother her and she is puzzled by the events. She realizes they are illogical but cannot explain why they are happening.

Case 2

A single school teacher in her forties with no prior psychiatric history but with a history of multiple impulsive moves and changes of employment settles down to a relatively permanent position as an adult educator. She meets and befriends a woman student roughly her own age who is married to a prominent person in the community. They spend much time together and the patient helps her friend through pregnancy, childbirth and the early years of looking after her child. There is upheaval and threat of termination on the job; at the same time, the patient becomes involved in astrology, numerology and other forms of New Age spirituality. From the insights she gains in practising these magic arts, she becomes convinced that her friend is dying of an incurable illness and that she needs to be there, close to her, protecting her, nurturing her, sheltering her. She begins to call frequently, to write letters, to visit her friend at all hours, to continue doing so after being asked to stop. She begins to feel there is an erotic bond between the two of them; her letters to her friend become filled with sexual connotations. Her friend issues a restraining order which she ignores. She is finally arrested, charged and convicted of harassment. She is seen by a psychiatrist who diagnoses a psychotic illness, probably in the context of mania. After starting antipsychotic medication, the patient realizes the impropriety and illogicality of her beliefs and perceptions. Her voices stop and she becomes seriously depressed. A year later, she is just now beginning to recover from depression.

Case 3

A 45-year-old woman with a delusional disorder of many years has spent the last 15 years of her life fighting to regain custody of her children whose care had been awarded to her sister. The children are now at the age of majority and, although they still live with her sister, she is able to see them. In general, they avoid her as much as possible because she tends to pester them with advice and reprimands. Because she now spends less time writing legal briefs with respect to custody, she has been able to return to postgraduate school, where she is doing extremely well academically. After several months in school, she became convinced that she was the special pet of one of the teachers. She knew he was married but, nevertheless, was convinced that he took a special interest in her. She became so excited by the prospect of a romance between them that she was unable to sleep and, for the first time, asked for medication (she had adamantly refused any form of medication prior to this). After a short period of antipsychotic treatment, she realized that the teacher's interest in her was based solely on the fact that she was a rather good student. Interestingly, her rigid stand vis-à-vis her children and sister also softened and she appeared to blossom at school and in her family life. Unfortunately, she stopped her medication because it was making her put on weight.

* * *

These cases illustrate a number of the features of secondary erotomania. Firstly, they indicate the range of diagnoses that may be apparent in these patients. The three patients appear to have diagnoses of schizoaffective disorder, bipolar disorder and delusional disorder, respectively. Clearly the patients here all had a psychotic illness and the nature of any underlying character difficulties is less apparent. Secondly, we can see that the diagnosis is predominately determined on the presence of other mood or psychotic symptoms, such as the experience of hallucinations in the first patient and mood disturbance in patient 2. Additionally, the character of the erotomanic delusions differs from the classical description, with variable onset, often unremarkable individuals as the object of the fixation and the possibility of the recurrence of the delusion involving another individual when a fresh episode of the underlying illness recurs.

In regards to the object of the delusion, the range may be from a nonexistent imaginary figure whose characteristics change over time, to a real but unattainable celebrity whose only contact with the subject is through the media. Frequently, the object may have had some brief relationship with the patient that is distorted and altered by the patient's psychotic thought process. It is not uncommon for erotomanic delusions to arise during the course of treatment for an ongoing disorder, with the therapist becoming the object for the delusional ideation. In this context the borderline between erotomania and erotic transference may become blurred. This is illustrated by two further cases.

Case 4

An elderly married woman came for treatment for depression and alcohol abuse. Because she had had problems for many years, a very long psychotherapy ensued with a strongly positive transference rapidly evolving into an erotic one. The patient was convinced that the (female) therapist loved her but that professional barriers prevented her from saying so. The therapy continued, for the most part successfully, but whenever there were health crises—which occurred with increasing frequency as the patient grew older—there was a resurgence of insistence that the therapist disclose her love, a demand for more time, more physical closeness. Kindness was read as encouragement; demurral precipitated depression.

Case 5

A 50-year-old married woman was in long-term psychotherapy for subclinical mood swings and mixed phobias. Attachment to the therapist fluctuated but often had a pronounced erotic tinge, with reports of many sexually explicit dreams, frequent love letters, requests for extra time and prolonged dips of mood when appointments were spaced further apart. The eroticized transference grew stronger whenever the patient confronted previously avoided phobic activities.

* * *

In both patients, the erotic transference was accompanied by embarrassment and discomfort. Actual fulfillment of erotic wishes was never sought, only a persistent demand for a verbal statement of reciprocation. When this was not stated by the therapist, it was taken as true. Enquiries about health were taken as tokens of affectionate interest, telephone calls to change appointment times were interpreted as signs of specialness.

Erotic transference may, in many instances, be a defence against other feelings, such as competition and envy. This is true for relatively well-functioning patients in response to the intimacy of a therapeutic relationship. It is probably also true for delusional patients with erotomania. In the patients described above, eroticism increased with a threat to body integrity in the first case and a confrontation with a fearful object or activity in the second. Others have noted that eroticized transference can mask hostility or grief (Gabbard, 1994). For many, it is more comfortable to express sexual wishes than to admit the childlike wish of wanting to be looked after or held. As with delusional erotomania, eroticized transference is more common in women than in men (Lester, 1985; Person, 1985).

EROTOMANIA, WOMEN AND VIOLENCE

Various attempts have been made to ascertain the risk of violence associated with erotomanic delusions. The studies published are difficult to compare due to divergent methodologies. One study has indicated that the rate of violence may be as low as 5% of patients (Dietz, quoted in Meloy, 1989) with data gathered from the studies of letters sent to celebrities and politicians. A number of case series and reports from the forensic psychiatric literature document cases of significant violence associated with erotomania and perpetrated by both male and female patients (for example, see Mullen & Pathé, 1994). Both the object of the delusional love and those who are perceived to stand in the way of the relationship are at risk (Goldstein, 1978; Meloy, 1989; Taylor et al., 1983). Interestingly, the rate of violence in patients with erotomanic delusions may actually be less than the rate of those with non-delusional attachment disorders (Kienlen et al., 1997). Most studies have described both male and female patients who have responded violently to erotomanic delusions, although the numbers of patients in these studies make it difficult to compare the sexes accurately. Certainly the over-representation of male patients in forensic samples indicates that the rate of violence for female patients is substantially lower.

The mechanism through which erotomanic love transforms to violence varies with the pathology of the individual and the disorder. One conceptualization considers a process by which the love object is first idealized, then in an abrupt turnaround, is ragefully devalued. One of the motives for inflicting pain is to convey to the object an inkling of the suffering he (or she) has caused the subject. Violent crime has been attributed to a wish to be co-identified with the object forevermore in history, an attempt to enhance the grandiosity of the subject. Alternatively, the aggression may be toward an individual, such as the spouse of the object, who is perceived as preventing fulfillment of the desired relationship.

TREATMENT, COURSE AND OUTCOME

There is a considerable lack of systematically gathered information about the course and treatment of erotomania. What is known is predominately based upon case series and retrospective reports. Fortunately, studies published since the advent of modern psychopharmacology have tended to be consistent in their observations and recommendations.

In general, the course and outcome for erotomania is mixed and dependent on the underlying diagnosis. The best prognosis appears to be for patients with bipolar disorder, in whom the delusion usually, but not always, responds as the mood normalizes with treatment (Gillett et al., 1990; Mullen & Pathé, 1994; Rettersol & Opjordsmoen, 1991; Rudden et al., 1990). Patients with schizoaffective disorder appear to have an intermediate prognosis and the worst prognosis is seen in patients with treatment-resistant schizophrenia.

The prognosis for patients with primary erotomania appears to be similar to that of other patients with delusional disorders. These patients often continue to experience delusional ideation for a considerable period of time but may retain a higher functioning level than those patients with secondary forms of the disorder. In at least one study (Rudden et al., 1990), these patients had the overall highest level of functioning, although in another the outcome was mixed, with a range of responses over time (Gillett et al., 1990).

The treatment of erotomania is based upon the appropriate management of the underlying condition with consideration of some of the unique issues that arise with this particular form of psychopathology. Appropriate pharmacotherapy will usually involve low-dose antipsychotic medication (e.g. 2–4 mg of pimozide or haloperidol) with a mood stabilizer or antidepressant for patients with mood disorder (Gillett et al., 1990; Mullen & Pathé, 1994; Rettersol & Opjordsmoen, 1991). Response to antipsychotic medication may be slow but improvement may continue over several months. There are no data on the use of the newer atypical antipsychotics in these patients but these should be considered if patients do not respond to initial treatment. Several of the atypical antipsychotics are particularly useful in women since they do not elevate prolactin levels and thus do not disrupt menstruation.

Pharmacotherapy should be combined with an appropriate consideration of the psychological issues facing the individual. It has been suggested that supportive and gentle challenging of the delusional ideation will aid recovery once the patient has begun to respond favourably to medication (Mullen & Pathé, 1994). Additionally, it may be useful to involve a spouse or family member in this process (Mullen & Pathé, 1994) although these individuals may be more appropriately targeted for supportive therapy to help them cope with the difficulties of their experience. It is important to be mindful of the nature of the patient's defences and personality structure. Often these patients will have difficulties with interpersonal relationships and they will benefit from a supportive and consistent individual relationship. More in-depth analysis of defences and personality structure is usually inappropriate.

Finally, it is important to remember that erotomania can be associated with violence, and the management of an individual patient may require a period of containment. There may be a need for a warning to be issued to those at risk from potentially harassing or violent behaviour.

CONCLUSION

Erotomania is a relatively common syndrome in women with psychotic disorders. It may appear de novo, as the primary presenting symptom of a delusional disorder, or as one feature of a major psychiatric disorder such as schizophrenia or mania. There is a significant association between the development of erotomanic delusions and violent behaviour, although the risk of violent acts appears to be less a problem of women than of men. Erotomania can be distinguished from a variety of other pathologies of love, all of which may also contribute to stalking behaviour. Erotomania, whether it is primary or secondary, requires treatment with antipsychotic medication in combination with adequate attempts to deal with psychological, social and environmental issues.

REFERENCES

Barton, J. L. (1978). Neurological basis for syndromes and symptoms of disordered recognition? *American Journal of Psychiatry*, **135**, 11.

Critelli, J. W., Myers, E. J. & Loos, V. E. (1986). The components of love: romantic attraction and sex role orientation. *Journal of Personality*, **54**, 354–70.

de Clerambault, G. (1942.). Les Psychoses Passionelles, *Oeuvre* (pp. 311–455). Paris: Presses Universitaires de France.

Drevets, W. C. & Rubin, E. H. (1987). Erotomania and senile dementia of Alzheimer type. *British Journal of Psychiatry*, **151**, 400–2.

Dunlop, J. L. (1988). Does erotomania exist between women? *British Journal of Psychiatry*, **153**, 830–3.

El-Assra, A. (1989). Erotomania in a Saudi woman. *British Journal of Psychiatry*, **155**, 553–5.

Ellis, P. & Mellsop, G. (1985). De Clerambault's syndrome—a nosological entity? *British Journal of Psychiatry*, **146**, 90–5.

Enoch, M. D. & Trethowan, W. H. (1979). *Uncommon Psychiatric Syndromes*. Bristol: John Wright.

Evans, D. L., Jechel, L. L. & Slott, N. E. (1982). Erotomania: a variant of pathological mourning. *Bulletin of the Menninger Clinic*, **46**, 507–20.

Fisher, M. (1990). *Personal Love*. London: Duckworth.

Gabbard, G. (1994). *Psychodynamic Psychiatry in Clinical Practice. The DSM-IV Edition*. Washington, DC: American Psychiatric Press,.

Gillett, T., Eminson, S. R. & Hassanyeh, F. (1990). Primary and secondary erotomania: clinical characteristics and follow-up. *Acta Psychiatrica Scandinavica*, **82**, 65–9.

Goldstein, R. L. (1978). De Clerambault in court: a forensic romance. *Bulletin of the American Academy of Psychiatry and the Law*, **6**, 36–40.

Greyson, B. & Akhtar, S. (1977). Erotomanic delusions in a mentally retarded patient. *American Journal of Psychiatry*, **134**, 325–6.

Hart, B. (1921). *The Psychology of Insanity*. Cambridge: Cambridge University Press.

Hendrick, C. & Hendrick, S. S. (1991). Dimensions of love: a sociobiological interpretation. *Journal of Social & Clinical Psychology*, **10**, 206–30.

Hollender, M. H. & Callahan, A. S. I. (1975.). Erotomania or de Clerambault syndrome. *Archives of General Psychiatry*, **32**, 1574–6.

Hunter, R. & MacAlpine, I. (1963). *Three Hundred Years of Psychiatry: 1535–1860*. London: Oxford University Press.

Keher, F. (1922). Erotische Wahnbildungen sexuell unbefriedigter weiblicher Wesen. *Archiv für Psychiatrie und Nerven Krankh Eiten*, **65**, 315–85.

Kienlen, K. K., Birmingham, D. L., Solberg, K. B., O'Regan, J. T. & Meloy, J. R. (1997). A comparative study of psychotic and non-psychotic stalking. *Journal of the American Academy of Psychiatry and the Law*, **25**, 317–34.

Kraepelin, E. (1909–1915). *Psychiatrie. Ein Lehrbuch fur Studierene und Arzte*. (8th edn). Leipzig: Barth.

Krafft-Ebing. (1879). *Text Book of Insanity* (C. G. Chaddock, 1904, Trans.). Philadelphia, PA: F.A. Davies.

Kretschmer, E. (1918). *Der sensitive Beziehungswahn*. Berlin: Springer.

Lawson, E. (1974). Women's first names: a semantic differential analysis. *Names*, **22**, 52–8.

Lehman, H. E. (1980). Unusual psychiatric disorders, atypical psychoses and brief reactive psychoses. In H. I. Kaplan, A. M. Freedman & B. J. Saddock (eds), *Comprehensive Textbook of Psychiatry* (3rd edn). Baltimore, MD: Williams & Wilkins.

Lester, E. P. (1985). The female analyst and the eroticized transference. *International Journal of Psycho-Analysis*, **66**, 283–93.

Lovett-Doust, J. W. & Christie, H. (1978). The pathology of love: some clinical variants of de Clerambault's syndrome. *Society Science & Medicine*, **12**, 99–106.

Meloy, J. R. (1989). Unrequited love and the wish to kill. *Bulletin of the Menninger Foundation*, **53**, 477–92.

Mintz, E. E. (1980). Obsession with the rejecting beloved. *Psychoanalytic Review*, **67**, 480–92.

Mullen, P. E. & Pathé, M. (1994). The pathological expressions of love. *British Journal of Psychiatry*, **165**, 614–23.

Murray, D., Harwood, P. & Eapen, E. (1990). Erotomania in relation to childbirth. *British Journal of Psychiatry*, **156**, 896–8.

Person, E. S. (1985). The erotic transference in women and men: differences and consequences. *American Academy of Psychoanalysis*, **13**, 159–80.

Raskin, D. E. & Sullivan, K. E. (1974). Erotomania. *American Journal of Psychiatry*, **131**, 1033–5.

Remington, G. & Book, H. (1984). Case report of de Clerambault's syndrome, bipolar affective disorder and response to lithium. *American Journal of Psychiatry*, **141**, 1285–7.

Rettersol, N. & Opjordsmoen, S. (1991). Erotomania erotic self-reference psychosis in old maids: a long term follow-up. *Psychopathology*, **24**, 388–97.

Rudden, M., Sweeney, J., Frances, A. et al., (1983). A comparison of delusional disorders in women and men. *American Journal of Psychiatry*, **140**, 1575–8.

Rudden, M., Sweeney, J. & Frances, A. (1990). Diagnosis and clinical course of erotomanic and other delusional patients. *Americal Journal of Psychiatry*, **147**, 625–8.

Seeman, M. V. (1971). The search for cupid or the phantom lover syndrome. *Canadian Psychiatic Association Journal*, **16**, 183–4.

Seeman, M. V. (1972). Psycho-cultural aspects of naming children. *Canadian Psychiatic Association Journal*, **17**, 149–51.

Seeman, M. V. (1975). Psychotherapy of love loss. *American Journal of Psychotherapy*, **29**, 558–66.

Seeman, M. V. (1976). The psychopathology of everyday names. *British Journal of Medical Psychology*, **49**, 89–95.

Seeman, M. V. (1978). Delusional loving. *Archives of Psychiatry*, **35**, 1265–7.

Seeman, M. V. (1980). Name and identity. *Canadian Journal of Psychiatry*, **25**, 129–37.

Seeman, M. V. (1983). The unconscious meanings of personal names. *Names*, **31**, 237–44.

Taylor, P., Mahendra, B. & Gunn, J. (1983). Erotomania in males. *Psychological Medicine*, **13**, 645–50.

Zona, M. A., Sharma, K. K. & Lane, J. (1993). A comparative study of erotomanic and obsessional subjects in a forensic sample. *Journal of Forensic Sciences*, **38**, 894–903.

CHAPTER 11

The Phenomenon of Stalking in Children and Adolescents

Joseph T. McCann

United Health Services Hospitals, Binghampton

Many pathological behaviours that have often been viewed as typically occurring only in adults have been studied in children and adolescents with greater frequency in recent years. For example, juvenile sex offending (Barbaree et al., 1993), sexual aggression in children (Araji, 1997), juvenile homicide (Ewing, 1990; Heide, 1999), and sexual homicide in adolescents (Myers, 1994; Myers et al., 1998) have been systematically studied over the last decade. Stalking is similar to these other social problems in that evidence exists that children and adolescents engage in this repetitive and threatening form of harassment (McCann, 1998, 2000, 2001).

Although the notion that stalking can be perpetrated by juveniles may seem unusual to some individuals, stalking is similar to other forms of obsessive harassment that have long been recognised as problematic behaviours among children and adolescents. For instance, legal definitions of stalking include repetitive following or harassment of another person in which there is a credible threat of bodily injury (Saunders, 1998). Likewise, Meloy (1996, 1998) has used the term "obsessional following" to describe the behaviour used by stalkers to harass their victims, defined as "an abnormal or long-term pattern of threat or harassment directed toward a specific individual" (Meloy, 1996, p. 148). These definitions are similar to other forms of repetitive harassment that have been observed among young people, such as bullying (Olweus, 1993), sexual harassment (Roscoe et al., 1994), and certain forms of dating violence and sexual aggression in

Stalking and Psychosexual Obsession: Psychological Perspectives for Prevention, Policing and Treatment.
Edited by J. Boon and L. Sheridan. © 2002 John Wiley & Sons, Ltd.

children. Among college students, Cupach & Spitzberg (1998) have studied the phenomenon of *obsessive relational intrusions*, which are defined as "repeated and unwanted pursuit and invasion of one's sense of physical or symbolic privacy by another person, either stranger or acquaintance, who desires and/or presumes an intimate relationship" (pp. 234–5).

One of the risks inherent when discussing the problem of stalking among children and adolescents is that relatively innocuous forms of infatuation and benign relationship intrusions that are common among young people, such as sending "love notes", "crushes" and song dedications, may be mistakenly characterised as stalking or menacing. However, concepts such as Cupach & Spitzberg's (1998) "obsessive relational intrusion" are useful for conceptualising obsessive forms of harassment because they view intrusive behaviours along a continuum, from those that are relatively benign to those that are more threatening and harassing.

The preliminary evidence that stalking occurs in children and adolescents has come primarily from scattered case reports in the media and professional literature. Urbach et al. (1992) reported a case of pure erotomania, defined as the delusional belief that one is loved by another person (American Psychiatric Association, 1994), in a 13-year-old female who maintained a romantic fixation on her teacher and later transferred it to a physician. Over time, the girl's fixation evolved into an extensive delusional system in which she believed that her teacher was in love with her and began writing love letters to the teacher. A perceived rejection that involved reporting the letter writing to school officials precipitated suicidal behaviour and depression, which resulted in a psychiatric hospitalisation.

This case of erotomania in adolescence represents one of three types of stalking that were identified by Zona et al. (1993). Based on a study of the first 74 cases investigated by the Threat Management Unit of the Los Angeles Police Department, Zona and colleagues outlined three major subtypes of stalking in adults: erotomania, love obsessional and simple obsessional. Love obsessional stalking is characterised by a fanatical love for another person and differs from erotomania because the delusional beliefs in love obsessional stalking are one symptom of a severe mental illness. Simple obsessional stalking is characterised by a prior relationship that existed between the victim and perpetrator, usually a sexually intimate relationship, and often involves feelings of having been wronged or rejected by the victim that motivate revenge or retribution. Aside from the case of erotomania in adolescence discussed by Urbach and colleagues (1992), McCann (1998) discussed two additional cases of stalking in adolescents that represented love obsessional and simple obsessional stalking. One case involved a 15-year-old male with a severe mental illness who wrote sexually explicit letters to several girls in his class; these letters became increasingly bizarre and threatening. In a different case, another 15-year-old male repeatedly followed, threatened and harassed his ex-girlfriend after she ended their relationship. This case resulted in the girl taking out an order of protection which the boy violated; he was involuntarily hospitalised after threatening to kill his parents, whom he perceived as preventing him from having contact with the ex-girlfriend.

In one study of 13 documented cases of stalking in children and adolescents, McCann (2000) provided further evidence that stalking occurs in younger populations. Many of the findings from this study were consistent with research on adult stalking offenders (Meloy, 1996, 1998) in that most perpetrators were male, most victims were female, over half of the cases involved an explicit threat toward the victim, and a variety of behaviours were used by young perpetrators to stalk their victims, including telephone calls, repetitive letter writing and physical approach. Interestingly, the victims of young stalking perpetrators were about evenly split between same-age peers and adults, and 31% of the cases involved violence toward the victim, which is also consistent with the prevalence of violence in adult stalking cases (Meloy, 1996).

Although individual case reports and small sample sizes prevent broad generalisations from being made, McCann (2001) has provided an integrated review of the literature on stalking in children and adolescents. Overall, stalking appears to be a behavioural aberration arising in late latency or early adolescence that involves disturbances in both attachment (Kienlen, 1998; Kienlen et al., 1997; Meloy, 1998) and identity. Disruptions in the formation of healthy attachments in early childhood may preclude the development of resiliency in the face of personal rejection or loss and may predispose the individual to maintain fixations on a person as a way of maintaining narcissistic linking fantasies (Meloy, 1996, 1998). In addition, identity disturbances and deficits in the person's capacity to tolerate and resolve feelings of envy and jealousy may predispose the individual to select a particular victim or maintain multiple or fluctuating object fixations (McCann, 2001).

THE EXTENT OF THE PROBLEM

It is difficult to determine the extent of stalking among children and adolescents because no formal research has been conducted on the prevalence of stalking specifically among younger populations. Some research provides indirect support for the notion that stalking is a problem among younger individuals. One study in the United States that examined a broad range of issues pertaining to violence in 8000 women and 8000 men revealed that 8% of women and 2% of men reported having been stalked at some time in their lives (Tjaden, 1997). These figures correspond roughly to about 1.4 million individuals in the United States being stalked each year. In another study reported by the Violence Against Women Grants

Office (1998), data on 797 male and female stalking victims revealed that 12% (or about one in eight) were first stalked before reaching the age of 18. While it is not possible to discern from this study the number of young victims that were stalked by an adult or young perpetrator, these data suggest that stalking is a significant but unrecognised problem among children and adolescents.

There is additional research to support the notion that stalking is a problem among younger individuals. For instance, data on the prevalence of stalking among college students is informative because the college years represent a transitional developmental phase between late adolescence and early adulthood. In addition, this period represents a time of more extensive exploration in intimate relationships, in a setting where there is closer proximity to people other than the student's immediate family. Fremouw et al. (1997) found in a sample of 593 college students that about 24% reported being stalked, with 35% of females and 17% of males reporting being victims of stalking. McCreedy & Dennis (1996) found in a sample of 760 college students that 6% reported having been stalked at some time in their lives. While these two studies examined the number of students who reported being stalked, Gallagher et al. (1994) approached the issue of stalking on college campuses differently in that they sampled 590 student affairs officers from 2- and 4-year colleges in the United States. Their findings revealed that about 35% of the officers reported having to intervene in one or more stalking cases over the previous year. In 15% of these cases a verbal warning was sufficient to stop the harassment while in an additional 21% of the cases both a warning and mandated counselling for the offender were warranted. Of particular note is the fact that in 57 stalking incidents reported by the student affairs officers the victim was injured, and five homicides were reported. Moreover, the number of officers who had to intervene in stalking cases increased as the size of the academic institutions increased.

It is difficult to derive accurate prevalence estimates from these studies given the differences in sampling techniques used and wide range in prevalence estimates obtained across studies. However, these findings lend strong support to the conclusion that stalking is a pervasive problem among college students.

In younger populations, including elementary and high school students, the data on stalking prevalence is much more limited and indirect. One relevant study reported by the National Victim Center (1995) indicated that during a ten-month period in the state of Massachusetts, there were 757 restraining orders issued against adolescents for threatening, stalking and abusive behaviours. It remains unclear how many of these protective orders were issued specifically for stalking; however, these data suggest a significant problem with stalking and threatening behaviour among high school students.

Despite the sparse literature on the prevalence of stalking among children and adolescents, there are related forms of obsessional harassment that have been studied more extensively. Other types of harassment in young people include bullying, sexual harassment, and dating or courtship violence. Research on the nature and extent of these problematic behaviours provides indirect evidence that stalking is a subtype of particularly severe harassment in children and adolescents.

STALKING AND RELATED FORMS OF HARASSMENT IN YOUNG PEOPLE

Bullying

Bullying is a form of harassment that has long been recognised as a problem in social relationships among children. Many interesting parallels exist between bullying and stalking with respect to how each is defined and conceptualised. For instance, bullying is generally defined as "repeatedly (not just once or twice) harassing others" using "physical attack . . . words, actions, or social exclusion" (Hazler, 1996, p. 6). Likewise, Olweus (1993) defines bullying as when a student "is exposed, repeatedly and over time, to negative actions on the part of one or more other students" (p. 9). These definitions of bullying mirror the "course of conduct" requirement in legal definitions of stalking (McCann, 2001). Moreover, many of the behaviours bullies and stalkers use to threaten their victims are similar, including intimidation, verbal threats and physical following in order to evoke fear in the victim. Additionally, bullying and stalking each require that the victim have some awareness of the perpetrator's threatening actions.

The parallels between bullying and stalking have also been recognised legally in cases where anti-stalking laws have been used to address chronic bullying that has occurred among children. In a case from the United States, the North Dakota Supreme Court upheld the legality of a two-year restraining order issued under the state's anti-stalking law which barred one youth from engaging in bullying toward a peer (*Svedberg v. Stamness*, 1994). This case arose when the victim's parents sought court action after the school failed to stop the bully from threatening, harassing, teasing and assaulting their child; the bullying had occurred over a two-year period. In a case from the United Kingdom, three youths (ages 12, 13 and 15) from Leicestershire, England had repeatedly harassed and teased two neighbourhood children for several years (Bowcott, 1998). One of the victims was ultimately treated for depression, yet no significant legal action was taken until the Protection From Harassment Act was passed in 1997. Thereafter, the youths were prosecuted under this law as a test case to determine if chronic bullying could be addressed using anti-stalking legislation.

There are some interesting observations that can be made about these two cases. First, they demonstrate how anti-stalking legislation has been used to address chronic bullying, thus providing legal recognition of the similarities that exist between bullying and stalking. Second, these cases arose in two independent legal jurisdictions in two different countries, providing further support for the fact that the overlap between bullying and stalking does not represent a legal anomaly and appears to generalise to other settings. Finally, both cases reflect how schools and other community agencies may be powerless to deal with severe forms of bullying unless some legal basis, such as anti-stalking laws, can be used to address these problems.

Since bullying and stalking are conceptually similar (McCann, 2001), research on the prevalence of bullying may offer indirect evidence for the notion that stalking and obsessional harassment are significant problems in children and adolescents. The problem of bullying among school age children appears to be pervasive. It has been noted, for instance, that 15% of students in Norway encounter problems with bullying (Olweus, 1993); 23% of students in the United Kingdom have experienced bullying in school (Oliver, et al. 1994), and 75% of students in the United States report having been bullied with 14% reporting severe trauma from their bullying experiences (Oliver et al., 1994). This latter figure may be somewhat inflated, since Duncan (1999) found in a sample of 375 children in the United States that 25% reported being the victim of bullying, a figure that is more consistent with those found in other studies. Nevertheless, it appears that about one-quarter of students report being the victims of bullying, making repetitive harassment a significant problem among school age children.

Sexual Harassment

In recent years, considerable attention has been given to the problem of sexual harassment among school age children, and findings from research on this problem reveals that stalking-related behaviours appear to be a subtype of sexually harassing behaviour. The most comprehensive study of sexual harassment in schools was conducted by the American Association of University Women Educational Foundation (1993). Findings from this study reveal that 81% of school age children in the United States report having experienced some form of sexual harassment during the school years, with the most common form being peer-on-peer harassment and unwanted sexual advances. Some sexually harassing behaviours are less severe (e.g. mooning, name calling, sexual jokes) and would not necessarily amount to stalking. However, some forms of sexual harassment reflect serious obsessional harassment, such as receiving unwanted pictures or notes, being spied upon while dressing or showering at school, and being the target of rumours. Moreover, 6% of those students who admitted engaging in sexually harassing behaviour wanted the victim to think that he or she had control, 23% of victims avoided familiar places, 10% of victims stopped attending specific activities, and 10% of victims altered their route to and from school. These findings suggest that a subset of sexually harassing behaviours in schools overlap with stalking.

Other studies provide support for the seriousness of sexual harassment in school settings. Roscoe et al. (1994) found among 561 students, aged 11 to 16, that 50% of females and 27% of males had experienced some form of sexual harassment. Of the harassing behaviours that students had experienced, two of those studied (telephone calls and letter/note writing) have been observed to be quite common among stalking offenders, including adults (Meloy, 1998) and children and adolescents (McCann, 1998, 2000; Urbach et al., 1992).

Dating Violence

In adult populations, the most common form of stalking is an obsessional male who repeatedly follows and harasses a female with whom he has had a prior intimate sexual relationship (Meloy, 1998). As such, stalking has often been associated with domestic, dating, or courtship violence. In fact, stalking has been construed as one form of courtship disorder (Freund et al., 1983) in which there is a disturbance in the location of potential mating partners and the successful attainment of a romantic attachment (Meloy, 1996, 1998). Therefore, research on the extent of violence in dating relationships of adolescents may provide some insight into the extent of stalking as a problem in younger populations.

Overall, there is strong evidence indicating that dating and sexual violence among adolescents is comparable to the rate of such violence among adults (McCann, in 2001). For instance, Roscoe and Callahan (1985) found in one sample of 204 high school students that 35% knew of another student who had been in a physically violent dating relationship and 9% reported having experienced physical violence by a dating partner. Similarly, O'Keefe et al. (1986) found in another sample of 256 high school students that about 36% experienced some form of dating violence. Bennett & Fineran (1998) found a higher rate of self-reported victimisation of dating violence (43%) among 463 high school students.

Furthermore, some of the violent behaviours reported in adolescent dating relationships reflect stalking-related behaviour. For instance, jealousy and possessiveness are cited by adolescents as the most common causes of violence in dating relationships of teenagers (Laner, 1990; Roscoe & Callahan, 1985; Stets & Pirog-Good, 1987). Moreover, in the study by

O'Keefe et al. (1986), 4.5% of a subsample of dating violence victims reported being threatened with a weapon and 45.5% were threatened with physical assault. Likewise, Bergman (1992) found that victims often failed to disclose dating violence, leading to lower prevalence estimates, and that 11.3% of victims reported being the target of verbal threats.

These data provide indirect, but not confirmatory, support for the notion that since the rate of dating and relationship violence is similar in both adult and adolescent populations that stalking may also occur in younger populations at rates that mirror the rate of stalking in adult populations. However, further survey and epidemiological data are needed.

SEXUAL AGGRESSION IN CHILDREN

Another form of interpersonal violence that is related in some respects to stalking and which has been studied, particularly in children under the age of 12, is sexual aggression (Araji, 1997). According to Araji, sexually aggressive behaviours lie at the extreme end of a continuum of sexual behaviour in children and often involve an organised pattern of coercive and aggressive behaviour. Moreover, the manner in which Araji described sexually aggressive behaviour reveals parallels to stalking in that sexual aggression has "a compulsive, obsessive nature . . . and may be opportunistic . . . planned, calculated, and predatory" (p. 36).

The prevalence of sexually aggressive behaviour among children has been shown to be high. For instance, Pithers & Gray (1998) suggested that about 13–18% of all substantiated reports of child sexual maltreatment are perpetrated by children between the ages of 6 and 12. Araji (1997) also provided comparable data suggesting that sexual aggression among children is quite prevalent in juvenile sexual offenders under the age of 13. Although these data do not provide any direct indication of the prevalence of stalking in younger children, it has been argued by McCann (2001) that stalking appears to be developmentally feasible in the late latency or early adolescent stages of development when the youth begins to explore attachments outside of the immediate family. As such, evidence of sexually aggressive behaviour in children merely provides corroborative support for the notion that obsessive and coercive harassment occurs in younger age groups.

PATTERNS AND DYNAMICS

Although there is limited research on stalking in younger populations, some of what is currently known about the dynamics and patterns of stalking behaviour in adults has also been observed in child and adolescent stalkers. McCann (2000) found in a small sample of stalking cases involving perpetrators ranging in age from 9 to 18 years that most of these young stalking offenders were male, most victims were female, and the behaviours most commonly used to harass victims included physical approach, repetitive telephone calls and letter writing. These findings are consistent with the adult stalking research (Meloy, 1996, 1998). In addition, McCann (2000) found the motivations for stalking to include a desire for sexual contact, anger and revenge, which reflect the two major motivations for stalking behaviour studied in adults by Harmon et al. (1995).

Among adult populations, stalking has also been associated with domestic violence in that the prototypical case of stalking often involves a male who stalks and harasses a female victim with whom he has had a prior intimate sexual relationship (Meloy, 1996). However, in younger populations, the perpetrator–victim dynamics mirror, but are slightly different from, those that have been observed in adult populations. For instance, McCann (2001) has noted that the most common form of stalking in juvenile cases appears to involve a young male making repeated and unwanted sexual advances towards either a female adult or same-age female peer. This trend can be interpreted as reflecting differences in social and psychosexual development between adults and adolescents; inasmuch as adolescents are generally less certain about their identity than are adults and because their sexual exploration and capacity for long-standing intimate relationships is inchoate, there is a greater tendency for adolescents to express sexual feelings toward casual acquaintances rather than intimate partners as do adults.

In addition, McCann (2001) has discussed an unusual pattern of stalking behaviour involving adolescents, *intrafamilial stalking*, that parallels, but is slightly different from, stalking between prior intimate adult partners. The phenomenon of intrafamilial stalking generally involves stalking behaviour that occurs between a parent and child; in some cases the stalking perpetrator may be the child and the victim the parent, whereas in other cases the parent may be the stalker and the child a victim. One highly publicised case of intrafamilial stalking occurred several years ago when a famous gymnast was reportedly stalked by her estranged father and had to file for a court order of protection to keep her father from harassing her and her friends. It is interesting to note that three general classes of stalking victims have been identified—prior intimate partners, prior acquaintances and strangers (Meloy, 1998)—yet intrafamilial patterns of stalking involving a parent and child are perhaps unique in that they do not fit neatly into one of these perpetrator–victim relationships. McCann (2000, 2001) has argued that intrafamilial stalking cases appear to more closely fit the prior intimate partner classification in that there has been a non-sexual, live-in relationship between the stalker and the victim. Moreover, because various behavioural difficulties and family conflicts can involve threatening or harassing behaviour, there is a risk that these cases may be inappropriately classified as stalking. To provide a more accurate definition of intrafamilial stalking cases, McCann (2001) has outlined three criteria for defining stalking cases in which the perpetrator and victim are a child and his or her parent: (1) the pattern of threatening and harassing behaviour in which the child or parent engages should meet the formal legal definition of stalking, (2) some legal action (e.g. court order of protection, police notification) should be taken in response to the stalking behaviour, and (3) the stalking should occur during a period of time when the parent and child are living apart. These criteria may serve to help identify cases of stalking between a parent and child, while recognising conflicted or abusive behaviour in a family as a separate issue.

One form of behaviour that is common in children and adolescents, but which can overlap somewhat with stalking, is an obsessive preoccupation with a public figure. Among young people, it is normal to identify closely with a particular celebrity, musical group or popular media figure. The large teen magazine market, numerous fan clubs, and other forms of idolisation of public figures among young people reveal that such preoccupations are common. However, there is anecdotal case evidence that reveals some notorious adult stalking offenders began exhibiting obsessive fixations on public figures in adolescence, suggesting that quasi-stalking behaviour in adolescence may be an early indicator of stalking behaviour later in life (McCann, 2001). Leets et al. (1995) found that the self-reported reasons among college students for seeking contact with a celebrity were a need for information, expression of praise and admiration, or some specific request such as an autograph, letter or money for a fund-raising drive. Moreover, seeking contact with a celebrity appeared to be a relatively normal behaviour. Nevertheless, certain factors appear to be useful in differentiating between benign fixations and maladaptive preoccupations with public figures among younger people (Leets et al., 1995; McCann, 2001). These factors include: (1) the person's capacity to distinguish between unrealistic (e.g. marriage) and realistic (e.g. autograph) expectations, (2) pathological reactions (e.g. suicide attempts) in response to rejection or some change in the public figure's life, (3) approach behaviours that are poorly organised or have a low likelihood of success (e.g. spurious bus trip to visit a celebrity), (4) impairment in school performance or family relationships as a result of the fixation, and (5) serious psychopathology (e.g. delusions) associated with the preoccupation. Once again, differentiating developmentally normal behaviour from more pathological forms of obsessive preoccupation is important when dealing with stalking behaviours among young people.

THREATS AND VIOLENCE IN JUVENILE STALKING CASES

Because stalking behaviour is threatening in nature, a major concern in these types of cases is whether or not the perpetrator will act violently toward the victim or some third person who is viewed as preventing access to the victim (Meloy, 1999). The relationship between threats and subsequent violence is equivocal, and some research points to either the absence of any association (Dietz et al., 1991b; Fein & Vossekuil, 1999) or a negative association between threats and approach behaviour toward the victim (Dietz et al., 1991a). Contributing to the lack of any clear relationship between threats and violence is the fact that those individuals who are intent on harming their victim are not likely to communicate their intentions directly.

In cases where stalking is perpetrated by a child or adolescent, there is no empirical evidence currently available on the relationship between threats and subsequent violence. However, preliminary evidence suggests that the prevalence of threats and violence in juvenile stalking cases is similar to the prevalence of such behaviours in adult stalking cases. Whereas Meloy (1999) found in a review of adult stalking research that about 50–75% of perpetrators make a threat, McCann (2000) found similarly that just over 50% of young stalking perpetrators made a threat toward the victim. Likewise, McCann found a violence base rate of 31% in his small sample of child and adolescent stalking perpetrators, which is consistent with Meloy's (1996) finding of an average rate of violence in adult stalking cases ranging from 25% to 35%.

More extensive research is needed to examine the relationship, if any, between threats and violence in juvenile stalking cases. Despite the lack of such research, however, individual case reports indicate that there are parallels in the types of threats and violence that may be perpetrated by young stalkers, including attack with a weapon, physical assault, threats against third parties who impede contact with the victim, and property damage (McCann, 1998, 2000, 2001; Urbach et al., 1992).

Until such research is forthcoming, the clinical and forensic assessment of violence potential in young stalking perpetrators should be guided by general principles of risk assessment of juveniles. These guidelines include the fact that: (1) specific risk factors (e.g. substance abuse) should have some clinical or research evidence to support their relationship to violence, (2) the social context and setting in which violence might occur should be appraised, (3) general estimates of risk (e.g. high, moderate, low) should be offered instead of definitive predictions, (4) recognition should be given to the fact that delinquency is heterogeneous and broad predictions of violence across all youths should be avoided, and (5) recognition should be given to the fact that delinquent and violent behaviour often stops after adolescence (Grisso, 1998; Moffitt, 1993). Another important component of violence risk assessment of children and adolescents is the potential impact of mitigating, or risk-reducing factors (e.g. existence of a supportive family environment; strong bonding to school; absence of substance abuse) that may also be relevant when evaluating the risk for violence in young offenders (Witt & Dyer, 1997).

YOUNG STALKING VICTIMS

The impact of stalking on victims is quite significant and many factors determine the severity and intensity of disruption that can occur as a result of being stalked, including the nature of the harassment, the length of time the stalking endures, the responsiveness of police and the legal system, social supports, and the individual resiliency of the victim. When the victim of stalking is a child or adolescent, other considerations must also be taken into account, including the maturity of the victim and availability of environmental supports.

According to a recent study of 797 male and female stalking victims by the Violence Against Women Grants Office (1998), 12% of all victims reported having been first stalked prior to reaching the age of 18. Although these data suggest that about one in eight stalking victims are first stalked in childhood or adolescence, they do not specify how many young victims are targeted by another child or adolescent. Furthermore, much of the empirical literature on the impact of stalking on victims has focused on adult samples, although a few studies include samples of stalking victims where the age range extends into middle or late adolescence.

For instance, Hall (1998) reported results from a study on victims of stalking (n = 145) where 3% of the sample was under the age of 18. Many victims reported feeling less sociable, more cautious, and easily startled as a result of being stalked. There were also higher levels of suspiciousness as a result of being stalked. The victims in Hall's study often reported that the experience of being stalked felt like a form of "psychological terrorism" in which their lives were significantly disrupted such that many had to change or leave their jobs, change residences, or change their names to avoid their stalkers. Among female college undergraduates, Westrup et al. (1999) found that stalking victims experienced a greater number and more severe symptoms of posttraumatic stress disorder than did other students who had been harassed or who were in the control group. Other adverse effects of stalking reported by the subjects in the study by Westrup and her colleagues included greater interpersonal sensitivity, depression and general feelings of distress. About half (46.7%) of stalking victims on college campuses report long-lasting adverse effects (McCreedy & Dennis, 1996).

Although there is no research specifically on younger child and adolescent victims of stalking, findings from the effects of related forms of harassment such as bullying, dating violence and sexual harassment reveal that stalking is likely to have a significant adverse impact on the psychological and social functioning of younger victims as well. For instance, children who are the victims of bullying are much more likely to become clinically depressed and to experience low self-esteem or helplessness (American Psychological Association, 1993; Kolko, 1998), suicidal ideation (Olweus, 1993) and unstable peer relationships (Slaby, 1998).

Despite these empirical findings, research that examines the impact of stalking specifically on children and adolescent victims is needed. Until such research is available, however, clinicians should still be cognisant of the fact that young stalking victims are likely to experience a broad range of adverse psychological symptoms as a result of being stalked. Therefore, clinical and forensic evaluations of child or adolescent stalking victims should include an assessment of symptoms associated with anxiety, depression, posttraumatic stress disorder, relationship problems and behavioural difficulties (McCann, 2001). Many standardised clinical interviews (Rogers, 1995) and psychometric instruments (McCann, 2001) are available for evaluating the psychological difficulties and personality dynamics of young stalking victims. Treatment interventions should include supportive psychotherapy for the victim, reduction of symptom severity and frequency through targeted interventions such as medication or psychotherapy, referral to community supports, and family consultation (McCann, 2001). In addition to traditional forms of psychological assessment and treatment, stalking cases should also include specific case management strategies that educate the victim and his or her family, as well as other individuals who interact with the victim, such as school officials and law enforcement agencies.

INTERVENTIONS AND CASE MANAGEMENT

Stalking cases involving a child or adolescent victim are perhaps unique in that there are several individuals and agencies that are either directly or peripherally involved. In addition to the victim and stalking perpetrator, consideration must also be given to the victim's parents and family, the perpetrator's parents and family, school officials, teachers, peers and law enforcement officials. Different interventions and case management strategies in juvenile stalking cases may be directed at each of these individuals, depending on the particular issues that need to be addressed.

With respect to the young stalking victim and his or her family, it is important that they be provided with useful information on how to deal with persistent harassment and stalking behaviour. Among legal interventions that are possible is the obtaining of a court order of protection, which is a legal step intended to provide legal authority prohibiting the perpetrator from engaging in specific harassing behaviours or coming within a specific distance of the victim. Concerns have been raised over the appropriateness of protective orders in stalking cases because such orders are believed to risk provoking anger and retaliation by the perpetrator or they are seen as being of limited efficacy (Hart, 1996). However, research demonstrates that protective orders are generally effective (Carlson et al., 1999; Meloy et al., 1997), although in some cases they do not dissuade stalking or harassing behaviour. While research on the efficacy of restraining orders has been conducted on adult samples, there is evidence that family courts issue a significant number of such protective orders against adolescents who have harassed, abused or stalked a peer (National Victim Center, 1995). Therefore, while further research is needed on the efficacy of these orders in younger populations, they continue to be viewed as one legal method for protecting young victims from persistent harassment.

Aside from individual and family therapy for stalking victims, there are personal protection measures which have been proffered that may prove useful in cases involving younger victims (McCann, 2001; National Victim Center, 1995). Among the personal protective measures that have been suggested are: (1) adequate lighting around the victim's home, (2) maintaining an unlisted telephone number, (3) having parents screen incoming calls for their child, (4) taking all threats seriously and reporting them to police, school officials or legal authorities, (5) varying travel routes to and from school, (6) having a contingency plan for transportation to and from school when parents are unable to pick up their child, (7) enlisting a small group of trusted peers to accompany the student when walking to and from school or between classes, (8) keeping emergency numbers (e.g. parents' work numbers, police) available, (9) using pagers or cellular phones for emergencies, and (10) maintaining an open and supportive relationship with family, school officials and support agencies. In addition, de Becker (1999) offers some practical suggestions to parents and their children for identifying signs early in dating relationships that may forecast potential difficulties later on. These include being aware of unsolicited promises of help, someone being unable to accept "no" for an answer, offering and soliciting too many details about one's personal life, and intrusive efforts to build trust using excessive charm. Professionals who work with young stalking victims and their families can provide education and advice on measures that can be taken to reduce the threat and potential risk to victims.

It has also been noted by McCann (1998) that school officials are often in a position to first observe stalking behaviour among children and adolescents, since school settings permit students to interact closely with one another over long periods of time. As such, teachers, administrators, and guidance counsellors should be attuned to various forms of harassment that occur in stalking cases and should take appropriate action, including referral of the perpetrator for appropriate treatment and providing victims with necessary support and direction. In recent years, schools in the United States have been legally mandated to respond to claims of teacher-on-student and peer-on-peer sexual harassment (McCann, 2001), and other forms of obsessive harassment, such as stalking, could be readily viewed as also raising a duty to respond. Schools are encouraged to adopt clear policies which reinforce the need for an education environment in which students are free from all forms of harassment. Moreover, appropriate response procedures should be outlined, including how claims of stalking and harassment should be reported, how they will be investigated, and various responses that may result from validated claims. Overall, it is important for school officials not to discount reports of stalking behaviour as "teenage infatuation gone awry" and to investigate all claims thoroughly.

Finally, an equally important component of managing stalking cases involving children and adolescents is providing treatment for the young stalking perpetrator. Although research is scant, there is evidence that some forms of psychopathology found among adult stalking offenders are also found among young offenders, including substance abuse (McCann, 2000) and erotomania (Urbach et al., 1992), as well as mental disorders that are commonly found in children and adolescents in mental health settings such as conduct disorder (McCann, 1998) and attention deficit hyperactivity disorder (Johnson & Becker, 1997; McCann, 2000). Therefore, the treatment of young stalking perpetrators should be guided by the clinical diagnosis and specific symptomatology present in individual cases, as occurs in the treatment of adult stalking perpetrators (Meloy, 1997). Specific treatment interventions may include medication directed at symptoms that are amenable to pharmacological agents, as well as individual psychotherapy that addresses personality disturbances, deficits in the young stalking perpetrator's capacity to tolerate and deal with feelings of envy and jealousy, poor social skills, and other forms of psychological disturbance that may be contributing to the stalking behaviour (McCann, 2001).

CONCLUSION

The phenomenon of stalking has emerged as a significant social problem that is the focus of serious scholarly study. While most research on stalking has been devoted to understanding the characteristics of adult stalking victims and perpetrators, as well as the dynamics and motivations of stalking behaviour, there is convincing evidence that stalking is a behavioural aberration that can emerge in late childhood or adolescence. There are several reasons for expanding the research on stalking to include populations of child and adolescent perpetrators and victims. By studying obsessive forms of harassment in young people, we may better learn how stalking develops, what early warning signs are present that can guide treatment and prevention programmes, and how the stalking behaviours among adults and juveniles are similar to and different from one another. This chapter has provided an overview of what is currently known about stalking in children and adolescents, as well as how stalking overlaps with other forms of repetitive harassment that are more widely acknowledged to be problems in the social relationships of young people, including bullying, dating violence and sexual harassment. Clearly there is a need for more research, yet current cases in which children or adolescents are either engaging in stalking behaviour or being victimised by this troubling form of threatening and harassing behaviour require intervention and management. Hopefully, this chapter will call attention to the need for research on this issue, as well as provide some guidance for treatment and case management.

REFERENCES

American Association of University Women Educational Foundation (1993). *Hostile Hallways: The AAUW Survey on Sexual Harassment in American's Schools*. Washington, DC: AAUW.

American Psychiatric Association (1994). *Diagnostic and Statistical Manual of Mental Disorders*, 4th edn. Washington, DC: APA.

American Psychological Association (1993). *Violence and Youth: Psychology's Response*. Vol. 1: *Summary of the American Psychological Association Commission on Violence and Youth*. Washington, DC: American Psychological Association.

Araji, S. K. (1997). *Sexually Aggressive Children: Coming to Understand Them*. Thousand Oaks, CA: Sage.

Barbaree, H. E., Marshall, W. L. & Hudson, S. M. (eds) (1993). *The Juvenile Sex Offender*. New York: Guilford.

Bennett, L. & Fineran, S. (1998). Sexual and severe physical violence among high school students: power beliefs, gender, and relationship. *American journal of Orthopsychiatry*, **68**, 645–52.

Bergman, L. (1992). Dating violence among high school students. *Social Work*, **37**, 21–7.

Bowcott, O. (1998). Three boys convicted of bullying neighbours. *The Guardian*, 28 April, p. 9.

Carlson, M. J., Harris, S. D. & Holden, G. W. (1999). Protective orders and domestic violence: risk factors for re-abuse. *Journal of Family Violence*, **14**, 205–26.

Cupach, W. R. & Spitzberg, B. H. (1998). Obsessive relational intrusions and stalking. In B. H. Spitzberg & W. R. Cupach (eds), *The Dark Side of Close Relationships* (pp. 233–63). Mahwah, NJ: Lawrence Erlbaum.

de Becker, G. (1999). *Protecting the Gift: Keeping Children and Teenagers Safe (and Parents Sane)*. New York: Dial Press.

Dietz, P., Matthews, D., Martell, D., Stewart, T., Hrouda, D. & Warren, J. (1991a). Threatening and otherwise inappropriate letters to members of the United States Congress. *Journal of Forensic Sciences*, **36**, 1445–68.

Dietz, P., Matthews, D., van Duyne, C., Martell, D., Parry, C., Stewart, T., Warren, J. & Crowder, D. (1991b). Threatening and otherwise inappropriate letters to Hollywood celebrities. *Journal of Forensic Sciences*, **36**, 185–209.

Duncan, R. D. (1999). Peer and sibling aggression: an investigation of intra- and extra-familial bullying. *Journal of Interpersonal Violence*, **14**, 871–86.

Ewing, C. P. (1990). *When Children Kill: The Dynamics of Juvenile Homicide*. Lexington, MA: Lexington.

Fein, R. A. & Vossekuil, B. (1999). Assassination in the United States: an operational study of recent assassins, attackers, and near-lethal approachers. *Journal of Forensic Sciences*, **44**, 321–33.

Fremouw, W. J., Westrup, D. & Pennypacker, J. (1997). Stalking on campus: the prevalence and strategies for coping with stalking. *Journal of Forensic Sciences*, **42**, 666–9.

Freund, K., Sher, H. & Hucker, S. (1983). The courtship disorders. *Archives of Sexual Behavior*, **12**, 369–79.

Gallagher, R. P., Harmon, W. W. & Lingenfelter, C. O. (1994). CSAO's perception of the changing incidence of problematic college student behaviour. *NASPA Journal*, **32**(1), 37–45.

Grisso, T. (1998). *Forensic Evaluation of Juveniles*. Sarasota, FL: Professional Resource Press.

Hall, D. M. (1998). The victims of stalking. In J. Reid Meloy (ed.), *The Psychology of Stalking: Clinical and Forensic Perspectives* (pp. 113–37). San Diego, CA: Academic Press.

Harmon, R., Rosner, R. & Owens, H. (1995). Obsessional harassment and erotomania in a criminal court population. *Journal of Forensic Sciences*, **40**, 188–96.

Hart, B. (1996). Battered women and the criminal justice system. In. E. S. Buzawa & C. G. Buzawa (eds), *Do Arrests and Restraining Orders Work?* (pp. 98–114). Thousand Oaks, CA: Sage.

Hazler, R. J. (1996). *Breaking the Cycle of Violence: Interventions for Bullying and Victimisation*. Washington, DC: Accelerated Development.

Heide, K. M. (1999). *Young Killers: The Challenge of Juvenile Homicide*. Thousand Oaks, CA: Sage.

Johnson, B. R. & Becker, J. V. (1997). Natural born killers? The development of the sexually sadistic killer. *Journal of the American Academy of Psychiatry and the Law*, **25**, 335–48.

Kienlen, K. K. (1998). Developmental and social antecedents of stalking. In J. Reid. Meloy (ed.), *The Psychology of Stalking: Clinical and Forensic Perspectives* (pp. 51–67). San Diego, CA: Academic Press.

Kienlen, K. K., Birmingham, D. L., Solberg, K. B., O'Regan, J. T. & Meloy, J. R. (1997). A comparative study of psychotic and nonpsychotic stalking. *Journal of the American Academy of Psychiatry and the Law*, **25**, 317–34.

Kolko, D. (1998). Treatment and intervention for child victims of violence. In P. K. Trickett & C. J. Schellengach (eds), *Violence against Children in the Family and the Community* (pp. 213–49). Washington, DC: American Psychological Association.

Laner, M. R. (1990). Violence or its precipitation: which is more likely to be identified as a dating problem? *Deviant Behavior*, **11**, 319–29.

Leets, L. de Becker, G. & Giles, H. (1995). Fans: exploring expressed motivations for contacting celebrities. *Journal of Language and Social Psychology*, **14**, 102–23.

McCann, J. T. (1998). Subtypes of stalking/obsessional following in adolescents. *Journal of Adolescence*, **21**, 667–75.

McCann, J. T. (2000). A descriptive study of child and adolescent obsessional followers. *Journal of Forensic Sciences*, **45**, 195–9.

McCann, J. T. (2001). *Stalking in Children and Adolescents: The Primitive Bond*. Washington, DC: American Psychological Association.

McCreedy, K. R. & Dennis, B. G. (1996). Sex-related offenses and fear of crime on campus. *Journal of Contemporary Criminal Justice*, **12**, 69–80.

Meloy, J. T. (1996). Stalking (obsessional following): a review of some preliminary studies. *Aggression and Violent Behaviour*, **1**, 147–62.

Meloy, J. R. (1997). The clinical risk management of stalking: "Someone is watching over me . . ." *American Journal of Psychotherapy*, **51**, 174–84.

Meloy, J. R. (1998). The psychology of stalking. In J. Reid Meloy (ed.), *The Psychology of Stalking: Clinical and Forensic Perspectives* (pp. 1–23). San Diego, CA: Academic Press.

Meloy, J. R. (1999). Stalking: an old behaviour, a new crime. *Psychiatric Clinics of North America*, **22**, 85–99.

Meloy, J. R., Cowett, P. Y., Parker, S. B., Hofland, B. & Friedland, A. (1997). Domestic protection orders and the prediction of subsequent criminality and violence toward protectees. *Psychotherapy*, **34**, 447–58.

Moffitt, T. E. (1993). Adolescence-limited and life-course persistent antisocial behaviour: a developmental taxonomy. *Psychological Review*, **100**, 674–701.

Myers, W. C. (1994). Sexual homicide by adolescents. *Journal of the American Academy of Child and Adolescent Psychiatry*, **33**, 962–9.

Myers, W. C., Burgess, A. W. & Nelson, J. A. (1998). Criminal and behavioural aspects of juvenile sexual homicide. *Journal of Forensic Sciences*, **43**, 340–7.

National Victim Center (1995). *School Crime: K-12*. Arlington, VA: NVC.

O'Keefe, N. K., Brockopp, K. & Chew, E. (1986). Teen dating violence. *Social Work*, **31**, 465–8.

Oliver, R., Hoover, J. H. & Hazler, R. (1994). The perceived roles of bullying in small-town midwestern schools. *Journal of Counselling & Development*, **72**, 416–20.

Olweus, D. (1993). *Bullying at School: What We Know and What We Can Do*. Cambridge, MA: Blackwell.

Pithers, W. D. & Gray, A. (1998). The other half of the story: children with sexual behaviour problems. *Psychology, Public Policy, and Law*, **4**, 200–17.

Rogers, R. (1995). *Diagnostic and Structured Interviewing: A Handbook for Psychologists*. Odessa, FL: Psychological Assessment Resources.

Roscoe, B., Strouse, J. S. & Goodwin, M. P. (1994). Sexual harassment: early adolescents' self-reports of experiences and acceptance. *Adolescence*, **29**, 515–23.

Roscoe, B. & Callahan, J. E. (1985). Adolescents' self-report of violence in families and dating relations. *Adolescence*, **20**, 545–53.

Saunders, R. (1998). The legal perspective on stalking. In J. Reid Meloy (ed.), *The Psychology of Stalking: Clinical and Forensic Perspectives* (pp. 25–49). San Diego, CA: Academic Press.

Slaby, R. G. (1998). Preventing youth violence through research-guided intervention. In P. K. Trickett & C. J. Schellenbach (eds), *Violence against Children in the Family and Community* (pp. 371–99). Washington, DC: American Psychological Association.

Stets, J. E. & Pirog-Good, M. A. (1987). Violence in dating relationships. *Social Psychology Quarterly*, **50**, 237–46.

Svedberg v. Stamness, 525 N.W.2d 678 (N.D. 1994).

Tjaden, P. (1997). *The Crime of Stalking: How Big is the Problem?* Washington, DC: United States Department of Justice.

Urbach, J. T., Khalily, C. & Mitchell, P. P. (1992). Erotomania in an adolescent: clinical and theoretical considerations. *Journal of Adolescence*, **15**, 231–40.

Violence Against Women Grants Office (1998). *Stalking and Domestic Violence: The Third Annual Report to Congress under the Violence Against Women Act.* Washington, DC: United States Department of Justice.

Westrup, D., Fremouw, W. J. & Thompson, N. (1999). The psychological impact of stalking on female undergraduates. *Journal of Forensic Sciences*, **44**, 554–7.

Witt, P. H. & Dyer, F. J. (1997). Juvenile transfer cases: risk assessment and risk management. *Journal of Psychiatry & Law*, **25**, 581–614.

Zona, M. A., Sharma, K. K. & Lane, J. (1993). A comparative study of erotomanic and obsessional subjects in a forensic sample. *Journal of Forensic Sciences*, **38**, 894–903.

CHAPTER 12

Cyberstalking

ANN WOLBERT BURGESS and TIMOTHY BAKER

Boston College School of Nursing, Chestnut Hill, MA

INTRODUCTION

In the last two decades of the 20th century the terms stalking and cyberstalking have become part of the common parlance as well as new classifications of crime. Stalking, in contrast to a direct physical attack, involves pursuit of a victim and is the act of following, viewing, communicating with, or moving threateningly or menacingly toward another person. Stalking behaviour has many dimensions that include written and verbal communications, unsolicited and unrecognised claims of romantic involvement on the part of victims, surveillance, harassment, loitering and following that produce intense fear and psychological distress to the victim. In addition, these behaviours can take the form of telephone calls, vandalisms and unwanted appearances at a person's home or workplace. When it occurs through the Internet, e.g. electronic stalking or cyberstalking, the acts include unsolicited email, negative messages in live chat rooms, hostile Internet postings, spreading of vicious rumours, leaving abusive messages on site guestbooks, impersonating a person online and saying negative things, and electronic sabotage (sending viruses, spamming etc.)

While the Internet is viewed as an information superhighway and an invaluable communication tool, it also provides a new environment for harassers and criminals to target victims. As US Attorney General Janet Reno noted in the report prepared by the Department of Justice (1999), many of the attributes of this technology—low cost, ease of use

Stalking and Psychosexual Obsession: Psychological Perspectives for Prevention, Policing and Treatment.
Edited by J. Boon and L. Sheridan. © 2002 John Wiley & Sons, Ltd.

and anonymous nature—make it an attractive medium for fraudulent scams, child sexual exploitation and cyberstalking. She also noted that while some conduct involving annoying or menacing behaviour might fall short of illegal stalking, such behaviour may be a prelude to stalking and violence and should be treated seriously.

Cyberstalking, also called online stalking or online victimisation, shares important characteristics with offline stalking. The similarities are that, first, the majority of cases involve stalking by former intimates, although stranger stalking certainly occurs in the real world and in cyberspace; second, most victims are women and most stalkers are men (for exceptions, see Novell, cited in Hall & Karl, 1999; Romans et al., 1996); and third, stalkers are believed to be motivated by the desire to control the victim. Major differences include, first, offline stalking requires the stalker and victim to be located in the same geographic area whereas cyberstalkers may be located in the same city or across the country; second, technologies make it easier for a cyberstalker to encourage third parties to harass and/or threaten a victim; and third, technologies lower the barriers to harassment and threats, and a cyberstalker does not need to physically confront the victim (Reno, 1999).

Understanding cyberstalking is to understand stalking in general. Cyberstalking may be viewed as simply another phase in an overall stalking pattern or it may be viewed as a regular stalking behaviour using new, high-technology tools. In some reported studies, both offline and online behaviours are surveyed, making it difficult to separate the behaviours. Thus, this chapter reviews the literature and cases on cyberstalking in the following sections: youth online victimisation, collegiate stalking and cyberstalking, adult cyberstalking, child pornography and paedophiles on the Internet, law enforcement response to illegal sex on the Internet, and victim services.

YOUTH ONLINE VICTIMISATION

The United States Congress became aware of the misuses of the Internet to prey upon children and quickly took action through implementation of the Child On-line Privacy Protection Act to help safeguard children from unsavoury advertising practices and the registration of personal information without parental consent. Congress also enhanced Federal law-enforcement resources such as the Federal Bureau of Investigation's (FBI) Innocent Images Task Force and the US Customs Service's Cybersmuggling Unit, both of which have successful records of investigating and arresting online predators. One of the most important tools for law enforcement staff and families has been the development of the National Center for Missing and Exploited Children's (NCMEC) CyberTipline, a resource that has initiated numerous investigations and arrests of child predators. However, the Congress's strong message of intolerance for online predators was not enough without information regarding the number of children victimised on the Internet and the various ways in which they are approached. Thus, Congress commissioned a study to identify the threats, incidence rates, and victim responses to online predators and illegal content . This initial report (Gregg, 2000) provides a starting point in better understanding what children face online. As noted in the introduction to the report, nearly 24 million young people aged between 10 and 17 were online regularly in 1999, and millions more are expected to join them shortly. But not every online adventure is stress free. The Internet has a seamier side that young people can encounter. A telephone survey (the Youth Internet Safety Survey) yielded a representative national sample of 1501 young people in the 10 to 17 age bracket, who reported using the Internet at least once a month for a six-month period on a computer at home, at school, someone else's home, or some other place. This definition was chosen to exclude occasional users, while including both "heavy" and "light" users. The survey asked about three different types of online victimisation: sexual solicitations and approaches, unwanted exposure to sexual materials, and harassment.

The Report provides a foundation for understanding youth experiences on the Internet. Approximately 19% or one in five youths reported receiving an unwanted sexual solicitation or approach in the last year. Girls were targeted at almost twice the rate as boys. Almost half (48%) of the perpetrators were under the age of 18, with 24% aged between 18 and 25, and 27% were age unknown. One-quarter of the aggressive episodes were from females. Thus, not all of the sexual solicitors on the Internet fit the media stereotype of an older, adult male.

The descriptions given appeared to be propositions for cybersex, a form of fantasy sex, which involves interactive chat-room sessions where the participants describe sexual acts and sometimes disrobe and masturbate. In almost half of the incidents (49%) the youth did not tell anyone of the incident and even when the incident was aggressive, the young person did not tell in 36% of the situations. In 24% of the incidents, a youth told a parent and in 29% of the cases, the young person told a friend or sibling. Only 10% were reported to an authority such as a teacher, Internet service provider or law enforcement. Some of this non-reporting resulted from most of the young people brushing off the encounter and treating it as a minor annoyance. Only 20% of the sample said they were very or extremely upset.

Many parents are concerned about their child's exposure to unwanted sexual material. Almost a quarter of all youths in the survey were exposed to such material, usually by conducting Internet searches, misspelling addresses or clicking on links. Such exposure occurred primarily in the

15 years and older group but some children as young as 11 had experiences to report. The concern of this issue is two-fold: first, what is the influence, traumatic or otherwise, on developing attitudes and feelings about sex, and second, what kind of risks are inherent to the Internet? On the latter point, the question has been raised as to whether the Internet is a forum like a bookstore, which need only put up a sign to warn about sexually explicit materials so that young people can avoid them if they choose; or whether it is like a television channel where young people are more captive, and the supplier of the images is expected to provide a higher level of self-restraint to protect them. It is obvious that the Internet has aspects of both of these.

The findings of the Youth Safety Survey suggest that it is not a simple matter for young people who want to avoid sexual material to do so. Young people report harassing, threatening and offensive behaviour directed at them on the Internet. Of the youths surveyed, 6% reported harassment and a third of that group reported being very upset or afraid because of the episode. Of the cases where the harasser was known, 54% were male and 20% were reported female (26% did not know the gender). Nearly two thirds of the harassers (63%) were other juveniles. In contrast to youths receiving sexual solicitations and unwanted exposure to sexual materials, youths being harassed did tell their parents, slightly more than a third told friends, and 21% of the episodes were reported to Internet service providers, 6% to teachers, and 1% to law enforcement.

As regards remedies to this problem, the survey revealed a lack of knowledge about available resources to deal with disturbing Internet episodes. Furthermore, in spite of the high level of family concern about exposure to sexual material, only a minority of families had adopted filtering and blocking software.

The key conclusions of the Youth Internet Safety Survey findings are cited as follows (Finkelhor et al., 2000):

- A specific fraction of youth are encountering offensive experiences on the Internet.
- The offences and offenders are diverse; specifically, more female offenders are involved than previously understood.
- Most sexual solicitations fail, but their quantity is potentially alarming.
- The primary vulnerable population is teenagers.
- Sexual material is very difficult to avoid on the Internet.
- Most young people brush off these offences, but some are quite distressed.
- Many young people do not tell anyone.
- Young people and their parents do not report these experiences and do not know where to report them.

Internet friendships between teens and adults are not uncommon and seem to be mostly benign. We still know little about the incidence of traveller cases (where adults or youths travel to physically meet and have sex with someone they first came to know on the Internet), or any completed Internet seduction and Internet sexual exploitation cases including trafficking in child pornography.

COLLEGIATE STALKING AND CYBERSTALKING

Critical to the study of any behaviour is definition. Meloy (1996) made one of the first attempts to define stalking as "obsessive following". Using a similar concept, Cupach & Spitzberg (1998) define "obsessive relational intrusion" (ORI) as "repeated and unwanted pursuit and invasion of one's sense of physical or symbolic privacy by another person, either stranger or acquaintance, who desires and/or presumes an intimate relationship".

Definition aside, what is the impact on the victim of being stalked, whether online or offline? In the limited studies on victims of stalking, Mullen & Pathé (1994) noted victims to feel compelled to alter their lifestyle by moving, changing address, and/or giving up social activities. Hall (1998) found that 83% of victims surveyed reported their personalities changed as a result of being stalked. Hall's study also found that 85% of the respondents were more cautious, 40% often felt paranoid, 53% felt more easily frightened, and 30% were much more aggressive. Similarly, Sheridan et al. (2001) found that 59% of their sample reported feeling frightened, and 44% altered their behaviour as a result of being stalked. Indeed, being stalked over a period of time has been described as "psychological terrorism" (Spitzberg et al., 1998) and has been suggested to be a cause of posttraumatic stress disorder (Wallace & Silverman, 1996).

College and university student health and counselling staff have reported on changes in student mental health issues (Koplik & DeVito, 1986), coercive sex on campuses (Miller & Marshall, 1987), drug and alcohol abuse (Bowen, 1987) and problems related to stalking (Gallagher, 1988). In a 1992 survey of counselling centre directors, Gallagher (1992) found that 26% of the directors reported a definite increase in collegiate stalking while 74% reported the incidence of such cases was about the same as in the previous year. However, no director reported a decrease.

In an effort to better understand student affairs officers' perceptions of these problems, a survey was distributed among 1100 member institutions of the National Association of Student Personnel Administrators (NASPA). Data from the 504 four-year institutions reported that more than a third of the directors had to intervene in one or more stalking cases in the past year. The directors' response to the stalking behaviour in 15%

of the cases was a warning while 21% required a warning plus counselling. Other cases required stronger measures. Eighteen per cent of the pursuing students were denied access to halls of residence, 31% were brought before judicial boards for sanctions short of suspension or dismissal, and 15% were dismissed or suspended from school. Beyond these sanctions, 24% of the victims sought an external court order to force their pursuers to desist (Gallagher et al., 1994).

A study of offline and online stalking was undertaken on a college population of 656 students in an east coast university (Burgess et al., under editorial review). Eleven per cent (72) of the students responded "yes" to the question: Have you ever been stalked? The majority (44 or 61%) were female with 28 (39%) male. Ages ranged from 17 to 42 with 55% aged 20 or younger. Students were undergraduates (92%) and the majority were Caucasian (70%). The profile characteristics of these 72 students revealed the typical student to be an undergraduate, average age of 20, who began using the Internet at age $15\frac{1}{2}$ and who currently used it for about 5 hours a week but did not enter chat rooms. The majority of students had come across inappropriate material on the Internet and over half had received inappropriate email; a small number had received threats of physical violence and about half had been solicited for sex online. The majority agreed that sexually explicit material on the Internet was a growing problem and it was too easy to access sexually explicit material but they were divided as to whether the government should regulate Internet content.

The profile characteristics of the pursuer revealed that the majority were aged 20 or younger and were white males. The students being pursued usually first told a friend within a month of the stalking. Students initially tried to reason and then later ignored the pursuer, and in addition they had their telephone calls screened. The majority did not feel threatened or fearful of being in great danger, suggesting that the acts could be termed cyberharassment rather than cyberstalking. A number of the males who were targeted in this sample were high school or college athletes, suggesting a modification of the "celebrity stalker" concept.

ADULT CYBERSTALKING

The earliest publication that was found concerning the area of cyberstalking was a brief note by Christina Carmody in the *American Bar Association Journal* in 1994. She noted that women were complaining of relentless emails and jammed fax machines from obsessive admirers. Barton (1995) concluded that computer abuse was advancing as quickly as computer technology, but the laws addressing the problems of harassment by computer were lagging. At that point in time, he noted that the federally subsidised Internet connected more than 5000 networks and 1.7 million computers throughout the United States and abroad and was frequented by more than 20 million users. Growth on the Internet was estimated to be as high as 15% a month. However, emails were being sent for improper purposes, and Barton described "flaming", a general term describing vitriolic email. Flaming was a massive mailing of vituperative, sexually suggestive, or meaningless messages by a group acting either in concert or not and which was designed to intimidate one or more other users. Another form of email abuse was the mail bomb or letter bomb, a long email message that ties up a recipient's system by consuming its computer memory.

Concerning the application of law to this problem, Barton (1995) concluded that bills not specifically tailored to the nature and scope of email harassment were insufficient. He spelled out four standards for effective, enforceable cyberstalking laws:

• that there be specific intent;
• that the statute recognises technological differences in means of communication,
• that it specify anonymous emails and single, identified contact in mass flaming (sending vicious, negative messages) as being illegal; and
• that it also specify that a combination of harassment by telephone and other electronic communication constitutes repeated harassment.

It became apparent that the use of the Internet to engage in these behaviours presented unique legal questions, and the first cyberstalking provisions were enacted in the Michigan law in 1992, with the first successful prosecution in that state in 1995 (Ross, 1995). Andrew Archambeau pleaded no contest to having sent 20 emails over a two-month period to a woman after he had been asked by the victim and the police to stop. He claimed that he was pursuing the woman for romantic reasons and that the communication was non-threatening since the victim could have ignored it. Archambeau was sentenced to a year's probation and a psychiatric evaluation was ordered.

CYBERSTALKING STUDIES

The best compilation of information concerning the phenomenon of cyberstalking can be found in Reno (1999). This report explored the nature and extent of cyberstalking, surveyed the steps law enforcement, industry, victim groups and others were taking to address the problem, analysed the adequacy of current Federal and state laws, and provided recommendations on how to improve efforts to combat this growing problem. One large study cited by Reno was conducted on a random sample of 4446 college women. Fisher et al. (1999) reported that 25% of stalking incidents among college women could be classified as involving cyberstalking. The report also noted that the majority of police agencies in the United States had not investigated or prosecuted any cyberstalking cases. However, some agencies, particularly those with units dedicated to stalking or computer crime offences, have large cyberstalking caseloads, e.g. New York City and Los Angeles. On the matter of jurisdiction and statutory limitations, Reno urged the need for state, local and Federal officials to work closely together in addressing these questions. She also made recommendations to the Internet industry and to victims and their support groups concerning how they could assist in dealing with cyberstalking.

Several authors have addressed the question of cyberstalking in recent publications. Rebecca Lee (1998) discussed romantic and electronic stalking in a college context. In addition to reporting data on the extent of this behaviour, Lee suggested that, to a certain extent, it was "a socially-sanctioned behaviour, instituted and encouraged by Western courtship mores and ideas of romance". References to cyberstalking are also found in a comprehensive publication on the psychology of stalking, edited by J. Reid Meloy (1998). Meloy & Shana Gothard (1998) note that since the Internet allows communication with another person in an environment that is unconstrained by social reality, cyberstalking does have a certain psychodynamic appeal for the perpetrator. The lack of social constraint means that social anxiety, particularly as an inhibitor of aggression, is non-existent. Therefore, certain emotions and desires endemic to stalkers—anger, jealousy, envy, possessiveness, control—and the aggressive impulses they stimulate to devalue or injure can be coarsely and directly expressed toward the target. Lloyd-Goldstein (1998) suggested that the computer underworld, with its alternative universes, virtual realities and cyberpunk counterculture, with the blurring of lines between fantasy and fact that it nourishes, "will serve to quicken and potentiate the twisted fixations of the stalker, thereby creating a new and more challenging set of problems in the years to come".

THE JOVANOVIC TRIAL

In a highly publicised New York case that was reported in the *Sexual Assault Report* (2000), graduate student Oliver Jovanovic was convicted of kidnapping, sexual abuse and assault. Jovanovic and the complainant had met in an online chat room where, within a very short time, their email took on an "intimate" tone. Jovanovic described his interest in the occult, the bizarre and the grotesque, and the complainant indicated her interest in making a film in which a person is killed. Their communications also included discussions about sadomasochistic fantasies and the complainant's purported interest in being dismembered. Within several weeks of commencing email communication, the two agreed to meet for a date and following dinner, they returned to Jovanovic's apartment to watch a sexually violent video. Jovanovic then ordered the complainant to remove her clothes and lie on the bed, which she did, and she was then tied to the bed. She testified she did not protest because she did not know what to do. When hot wax was poured on her, she protested that he stop and demanded to be untied. The defendant refused and proceeded with sexual force. The complainant was finally able to escape the next day. Back at her dormitory, she replied to an email from Jovanovic that she was "quite bruised mentally and physically, but never so happy to be alive". They continued their online communications later that day.

Jovanovic appealed his conviction, arguing that the trial court improperly applied the Rape Shield Law to exclude certain statements made by the complainant in her email. The Supreme Court of New York, Appellate Division agreed, holding that the Rape Shield Law was inapplicable to much of the evidence precluded at trial and that this preclusion interfered with the defendant's right to confront the witness (*People v. Jovanovic*, 700 N.Y.,S,2d 156 (N.Y. App. Div. 1999)). The court wrote that the complainant presented a "one-sided" story of "a woman being drawn into a cyberspace intimacy that led her into the trap of a scheming man". The precluded evidence consisted of redacted statements from her emails in which she admitted she was a sadomasochist, that she was the slave of another man, and that she was a "pushy bottom"—a term for a submissive partner who pushes the dominant partner to inflict greater pain.

The court held that the redacted emails were not subject to the Rape Shield Law because they were "merely evidence of statements made by the complainant about herself to Jovanovic". The court also found that the defendant's purpose in offering the statements was not to undermine her character by implying she was unchaste. Rather, it was to highlight her state of mind on the issue of consent, and his state of mind regarding his own reasonable belief as to her intentions. Even if the Rape Shield Law were to apply, the court concluded that the emails fell within a number of the law's specific exceptions. First, because of the intimate nature of the messages, they should be viewed as equivalent of prior sexual conduct with the accused. In addition, the "history of intimacies" had the potential to shed light on the motive, intent and state of mind of both people. Second, the statements were admissible under the exception for evidence that tends to rebut that the accused is the cause of the "disease" of the victim. The court held that Jovanovic should have the right to inquire about other sadomasochistic relationships that would tend to disprove he was the cause of the bruises to the complainant. Third, the court believed that these statements fell into the exception for facts "essential" to the court's determination and admissible "in the interests of justice". The court found that the fact that the complainant made the statements to the defendant was highly relevant "to establish that she purposefully conveyed to Jovanovic an interest in engaging in sadomasochism with him".

The issue of consent was relegated to a footnote explaining that "as a matter of public policy, a person cannot avoid criminal responsibility for an assault that causes injury or carries a risk of serious harm, even if the victim asked for or consented to the act". Despite that rule, the court was not persuaded by the People's argument that it was irrelevant if the complainant initially consented if she withdrew her consent and Jovanovic continued to act. The court responded that "because the jury could have inferred from the redacted e-mail messages that the complainant had shown an interest in participating in sadomasochism with Jovanovic", the evidence was "clearly center" to the question of whether the complainant consented to the charged kidnapping and sexual abuse and whether she withdrew her consent.

Finally, the intermediate appellate court held that the trial court's rulings on the evidence were "errors of a constitutional dimension". Jovanovic's Sixth Amendment right to confront a primary witness was violated. The preclusion of the email messages "gutted Jovanovic's right to testify in his own defense" and resulted in his inability to adequately challenge the complainant's reliability and credibility. Having found such prejudice to the defence, the court reversed Jovanovic's conviction in its entirety and remanded the matter for a new trial (Sexual Assault Report, 2000).

The case was then appealed to the higher level Appelate Court. The prosecution argued that the intermediate Appelate missed the point that Jovanovic held that the sexual activity described by the complainant never happened. Thus, consent was not an issue. One year later the prosecution dropped the charges.

This case of sadomasochistic email between two university students illustrates that the Internet has become a new medium in which strangers can communicate anonymously, compare sexual scripts and subsequently meet in person. And, since Jovanovic's first trial was overturned and not retried, there was no opportunity to determine his guilt or innocence.

CHILD PORNOGRAPHY AND PAEDOPHILES

With millions of children having access to home computers and online services, the use of the Internet as a vehicle for procuring victims, distributing illegal material, including pornographic images, and promoting criminal sexual abuse of minors has become a major concern and will, inevitably, be of ever increasing concern. This darker side of the Internet permits criminals to meet, network, transfer illicit materials, and commit crimes across state and international borders. Criminal uses of computer technology range from the online solicitation of children for sexual purposes, the production and transmission of child pornography, and the distribution of pornographic materials.

Paedophiles are persons with sexual interest in underage children. One method to gain access to children is by watching and stalking them. Internet chat rooms are very attractive places for vulnerable children to meet "friendly" adults, making it easy for the online predator to anonymously lure children from the confines of their home. Online predators can use chat rooms to groom their potential victims. An online friendship may be initiated with the child, which includes shared hobbies and interests, possibly leading to the sending of pictures or gifts. In this way, the online predator can groom the child, build trust and eventually arrange a meeting. This process is well established in the modus operandi of paedophiles. What is new, however, is the vast limitless playground of the World Wide Web.

Computers provide child molesters with a highly efficient vehicle for meeting their needs in diverse ways, including:

- organising their collections, correspondence, and fantasy material;
- communicating with a much wider, larger and more diverse audience (both victim and offender);
- the storage, transfer, manipulation and creation of child pornography;
- the maintenance of financial records;
- the facilitation of efforts to elude apprehension relative to conventional techniques such as surface mail and telephone. This is particularly the case with public access computers, making it more difficult to trace the source to the offender.

Although the Internet has expanded the avenues available to paedophiles to view and collect child pornography, the gate swings both ways. The Internet also offers law enforcement officers an additional, powerful tool for identifying and apprehending offenders. The following case of a "Big Brother" reveals a host of different flags that should have been identified long before the eventual revelation of a past history of accessing child cyberporn. "Big Brother" is the name of a service provided to single mothers who request an adult male to act as a role model to a fatherless boy. A volunteer is matched with the child and provides a consistent programme of activities geared to the age level and interests of the individual child.

A single mother raising her two young sons applied to a Big Brother agency, and after an interview and evaluation was given Mr B. After about 5 months, she was contacted by the agency and informed that the "big brother" had been arrested for downloading pornography from the Internet. Mr B. pleaded guilty and a civil suit resulted. In reviewing the agency application form, many numerous flags (or questionable areas) were noted, as well as clear warning signs that were ignored once he had begun his "big brother" role.

Mr B's pattern included targeting young prepubescent boys, engaging them in oral sex, and videotaping the acts. He used sexually explicit foreign movies to normalise his sexually deviant behaviour prior to videotaping his sexual abuse of the boys. The photographs of the boys were later placed on the Internet and sent to other paedophiles. The agency application form provided ample evidence of his poor psychosocial adaptation as an adult, his lack of mature peer relationships, his tendency to be a "loner", his gravitation toward children, his clearly stated sexualised "preferences" when it came to children, and his ploys and manipulations when it came to accessing "preferred" children. Mr B's prior history of accessing child pornography over the Internet suggests both his long-standing sexualised interest in children, and possible evidence for escalation (i.e. moving from the realm of cyberporn-assisted fantasy to acting on the fantasy) (Prentky & Burgess, 2000; Burgess & Prentky, 2000).

The Reno Report (1999) on cyberstalking described the Federal Bureau of Investigation's 1995 undercover initiative, dubbed "Innocent Images", to combat the exploitation of children via commercial online services. As of 31 December 1998, the initiative had resulted in 232 convictions.

Several other articles concerning paedophiles and child pornography are of note for readers interested in further work in this area. Keith Durkin (1997) discussed how paedophiles exchanged pornography over the net, and about how they used Internet chat rooms to locate children to molest. He also discussed "Boy Lovers" newsgroups that shared information which tended to validate this activity. John Soma et al. (1997) discussed the need for transitional extradition treaties for abuse of the Internet by paedophiles. The topic of "virtual child pornography" was discussed by Debra Burke (1997) in her article, and finally, Daniel Armaugh (1998) discussed how children can be protected on the Internet.

US v. Reinhardt

In *US v. Reinhardt* (97-60030-01) the court granted the government's motion for pre-trial detention. The defendant was charged with producing and distributing child pornography. On the government's motion for pre-trial detention under the Bail Reform Act, the District Court held that, first, the defendant's case involved a crime of violence, second, there were no conditions of release which could reasonably assure safety of community and appearance of the defendant, and, third, the defendant also posed a risk of flight.

This case is critically important for its illustration of the use of the Internet as a tool for paedophiles and child pornographers. It clearly links a paedophile's use of technology to access children for sexual purposes, to gain control over the children and their families, to recruit new victims, and to communicate with other paedophiles. The amount of detail, care and compulsiveness that is demonstrated in the profile of a career paedophile is exemplified in this case.

Paedophile's social networks are other paedophiles. They socialise, telephone, write letters, email, network and share strategies for continuing their deviant relationships with children, even when in prison. In Florida, one convicted child pornographer used his prison post office box number to expand his distribution of child pornography until he was discovered. He was also using the Internet to communicate with other paedophiles.

Paedophiles can move from an isolated position of solo operator into a network of perpetrators: for example, Reinhardt had a co-defendant. It is no wonder that we now see the elaborate and organised networking that is well under way on the Internet both nationally and internationally. This case emphasises the Internet paedophile as an entrepreneur having a product line on his own home page. Reinhardt provided advice to a chat room correspondent on how to build a long-term relationship with a young boy, how to manipulate parents in order that they not "cause problems", and educated his victims on how to answer questions about the ongoing sexual relationship. Reinhardt videotaped instructions to his victim in how to type in responses to sexually oriented questions being sent from a chat room. His home page contained images of naked children and his victims as well as an image of his own penis wherein he had a minor assist in the scanning of his genitalia, an act serving as a permanent document of his sexual entrapment of the boy.

Paedophiles can be totally preoccupied with their sexual interest in children, and the Reinhardt case illustrates how the Internet can facilitate this obsession. The probation office identified nine jobs Reinhardt held between 1986 and 1997 in four states: he would move whenever a child complained to a parent. His obsession with the Internet was noted in his owning several computers while living in a trailer.

This case reveals the inner workings of paedophiles and child pornographers. The general public can now access all dimensions of child sexual exploitation through the Internet. They can call up a paedophile's home page or talk with him in a chat room. Although Internet paedophile activities are losing their clandestine nature, the technology that is available does allow the paedophile to be more discriminate in selecting and testing his victims by remaining anonymous. As with cases of adults who form romantic attachments over the Internet, paedophile–victim relationships can develop online before moving on to telephone calls, the sending of items through the mail, and to a physical meeting.

Internet paedophiles are sophisticated in the investigative aspects and have developed ways to bypass the restrictions, e.g. the growing use of encryption. Investigators report that such coded messages are sometimes impossible to decipher.

A critical question is whether children can be protected from the Internet paedophile. In March 1997, Senate hearings examined the risks of victimisation to children in cyberspace. The result was the establishment of the CyberTipline (www.missingkids.com/cybertip) in March 1998. The tipline has been created at the National Center for Missing and Exploited Children for parents to report suspicious or illegal Internet activity online. The intent is to ensure that the Internet not be allowed to become a sanctuary for paedophiles, child pornographers and others who prey upon children.

LAW ENFORCEMENT RESPONSE TO ILLEGAL SEX ON THE INTERNET

A valuable book for investigating cyber stalking is Clark and Dilberto's book 'Investigating Computer Crime' (1996). This is a practical book on collecting electronic evidence and investigating crimes that involve computers. It follows a step-by-step approach to the investigation, seizure and analysis of computer evidence. Topics like computer search warrants, interviews, sketches and photographs, physical search, security and arrest, and technical evidence seizure and logging are all covered extensively. Also addressed are the topics of the types of evidence, where it may be found, an examination of the evidence for criminal content, cautions and considerations, legal requirements, and evidence storage. The book explains how it is of particular importance that officers assessing the computer's hard drives know how to find materials that have been erased but may still be accessible to a trained person, that they are aware of how to get around security programmes which destroy certain materials when unauthorised access is attempted, and that they collect disks, particularly back-up disks that may contain crucial evidence.

The Reno Report (1999) noted above offers recommendations to law enforcement and criminal justice officials. These include the need to take this type of crime more seriously, the need for training, the need for specialised units, the need to share information with other jurisdictions, and the need to work more closely with victim groups.

In the area of child sexual abuse, Kenneth Lanning & Robert Farley (1997) wrote an excellent piece on "Understanding and investigating child sexual Exploitation". Describing the characteristics of paedophiles who stalk children on the Internet, they noted that because of the relationship that the victim establishes with the offender, the children often object to the intervention of law enforcement and may warn the paedophile concerning the investigation. The authors observed several major problems that make the investigation of child sexual abuse and exploitation difficult for the law enforcement officers and the criminal justice system, including: (1) the fact noted above that the victim is often a willing participant who is naturally curious, easily led by adults, often in need of attention and affection and often defiant of their parents, (2) that children do not make very good witnesses when being cross-examined by the defence, and have to be helped to get ready for this experience, (3) that law enforcement officers working in this area burn out quickly, and are often in need of assistance and support to do their job, (4) that it is often difficult to identify what constitutes sexual activity when talking about the relationship between children and adults, and (5) while societal attitudes are generally strong concerning the matter of child molestation, that groups like the North American Man-Boy Love Association (NAMBLA) try to portray police activity as the intrusion of the police into an area which they call "natural".

Grienti (1997) also wrote about paedophiles' use of the Internet. He noted how paedophiles were using the bulletin board system to make contact with children, often misrepresenting themselves in areas of age, sex, appearance and interests. Focusing on the problems in his native Canada, Grienti went on to note how it was difficult to control bulletin board systems, which connect a large number of groups of people with common interests. It is not surprising that those who have an interest in sexual materials, both hard- and soft-core pornography, and paedophiles find each other. Since many bulletin boards and chat rooms have developed to serve the needs of youthful users, these provide an excellent opportunity for paedophiles to make contact with youngsters. He also notes that this has become an international problem since the Internet is truly global. Finally, Grienti points out how it is in the best interests of the Internet service providers to actively intervene to try to control these problems before they get too far out of hand.

Finally, Pettinari (1998) discusses the FBI Innocent Images project, where police pose as children on the Internet. The author notes how the Internet provides paedophiles with a safe place for trading child pornography and to discuss with one another how to successfully molest underage children. There are also packaged tips to foreign countries for those interested in child prostitutes. Also, child-oriented chat rooms and bulletin boards provide an excellent place for the paedophile to meet children. In discussing the Innocent Images project, Pettinari points out how the police officers must take special care in developing believable profiles that would entice paedophiles to contact them, must earn the predator's trust, avoid entrapment, have the necessary equipment to download materials which the paedophile might send, be very careful in logging all activity, and set up contacts with law enforcement authorities in the location where the predator lives.

TIPS AND SERVICES TO VICTIMS

There has been a concerted effort, by the Internet industry, law enforcement and victims' groups, to get information out to victims and potential victims concerning what they should do both to protect themselves and to deal with situations which *can* happen to them. Appendix II of the Reno report (1999) presented a list of tips on "How you can protect against cyberstalking—and what to do if you are a victim". Reno also discussed the creation of victims' and support organisations which address these problems and provided the addresses of cyberstalking resources that can be accessed online.

The Reno report's recommendations focused primarily on victim services and support groups. The recommendations for victim service providers and advocates included:

1. A call for an increase in direct services and referrals to victims of cyberstalking.
2. The training of domestic violence and other victim service providers and advocates on Internet technology regarding the tactics used by cyberstalkers and how to respond to the needs of the victims.
3. Naming the behaviour as "cyberstalking" and validate that the crime is occurring when working with individual victims.
4. Raising public awareness of the crime.

Ellen Spertus (1996) wrote an excellent piece on "Social and technical means for fighting on-line harassment". Since many intrusive activities do not cross the line of being illegal, this can be valuable information for people wanting to stop such activity. They include blacklists, explicit reputations, secure authentication, private or moderated mailing lists, programs for filtering messages based on their contents and senders, and public replies to harassers.

Jessica Laughren also addressed the question of how victims should respond in her article on the University of Calgary's web site, "Cyberstalking awareness and education". The article focuses on the need of the stalker to gain control, and how the possible victim can guard against this. This can often prevent the situation from escalating to "real-life" stalking.

Finally, the National Center for Victims of Crime has a web site where victims and those concerned about this problem can get tips about how to avoid harassment and how to respond when harassed. Laughren emphasised the need for the victim to provide evidence to the authorities so that action can be take. She also recommends that users consider a gender-neutral email address, that they choose an unusual password and change it regularly, that they be careful about what chat rooms they use, that they consider using an anonymous remailer so that others in the chat room will not know their address, and particularly that they employ "common sense", being careful about what information they share with others online.

The National Center for Victims of Crime can be reached over the Internet at www.ncvc.org. This site has links to other US organisations focused on the problem at the state, national and international levels. Other valuable web addresses include: www.cyberangels.org, a non-profit group devoted to assisting victims, www.getnetwise.org, an online resource for families and caregivers to help children use the Internet in a safe and educational manner, and whoa.femail.com, Women Halting Online Abuse.

CONCLUSIONS

In conclusion, it is a misconception that cyberstalking is less serious than offline stalking (Lee, 1998). Stalkers can operate anonymously by using a false name, forging email messages, without revealing their handwriting or aspects of their personality. They can obtain a great deal of information about their target. Personal profiles that are completed for commercial online services may reveal an individual's name, age, marital status, and location. There is even a World Wide Web site titled "The stalker's home paged" that can aid a user in locating a local street map of a person's residence as well as his or her Social Security number and also provides information on how to stalk an individual discreetly (Lee, 1998). Cyberstalking is predicted to be a growing behaviour of the 21st century. Research is needed to provide direction and solutions for the problems and issues identified in this chapter.

REFERENCES

Armaugh D (1998) Safety net for the Internet: protecting our children. *Juvenile Justice* **5**(1):9–15.

Barton G (1995) Taking a byte out of crime: e-mail harassment and the inefficacy of existing law. *Washington Law Review* **465**:841.

Bowen O (1987) Campus alcohol uses. Paper presented at the National Conference on Alcohol Abuse and Alcoholism, November, Washington, DC.

Burgess AW (2000) US v Reinhardt. In *Violence Through a Forensic Lens*. King of Prussia, PA: Nursing Spectrum.

Burgess AW, Alexy E, Baker T & Smoyak S. (under editorial review) Offline and online stalking in college population.

Burgess AW & Prentky RA (2000) Big brother and cyberporn. *Sexual Assault Report* **3**(7):98.

Burke DD (1997) Criminalization of virtual child pornography: a Constitutional question. *Harvard Journal on Legislation* **34**(2):439–72.

Carmody C (1994) Stalking by computer. *American Bar Association Journal*, **80**:70.

Clark F & Diliberto K (1996) *Investigating Computer Crime*. Boca Raton, FL: CRC Press.

Cupach WR & Spitzberg BH (1998) Obsessive relational intrusions and stalking. In BH Spitzberg & WR Cupach (eds) *The Dark Side of Close Relationships* (pp. 233–63). Hillsdale, NJ: Lawrence Erlbaum.

Durkin KF (1997) Misuse of the Internet by pedophiles: implications for law enforcement and probation practice. *Federal Probation* **61**(3):14–18.

Fisher BS, Cullen FT, Belnap J & Turner MG (1999) *Being Pursued: Stalking Victimization in a National Study of College Women*. Report on Sexual Violence Against Women, Washington, DC: Department of Justice.

Finkelhor D, Mitchell KJ & Wolak J (2000) *Online Victimization: A Report on the Nation's Youth*. Alexandria, VA: National Center for Missing & Exploited Children.

Gallagher RP (1988) *National Survey of Counseling Center Directors*. Pittsburgh, PA: University of Pittsburgh.

Gallagher RP (1992) *National Survey of Counseling Center Directors*. Monograph Series. Alexandria, VA: International Association of Counseling Services.

Gallagher RP, Harmon WW & Lingenfelter CO (1994) CSAO's perceptions of the changing incidence of problematic college student behavior. *NASPA Journal* **32**:375.

Gregg J (2000) Foreword. In D Finkelhor, KJ Mitchell & J Wolak, *Online Victimization: A Report on the Nation's Youth*. Alexandria, VA: National Center for Missing & Exploited Children.

Grienti V (1997) Pedophiles on the Internet. *RCMP Gazette* **59**(10):14–15.

Hall A (1998) The victims of stalking. In J Melloy (ed.) *The Psychology of Stalking: Clinical and Forensic Perspectives*. San Diego, CA: Academic Press, pp. 113–37.

Hall A & Karl J (1999) Congress looks to end cyberstalking. 30 September 1999, CNN Morning News.

Koplik EK & DeVito AJ (1986) Problems of freshmen: comparison of classes of 1976 and 1986. *Journal of College Student Personnel* **27**(2):124–30.

Lanning K & Farley RH (1997) *Understanding and Investigating Child Sexual Exploitation*. US Department of Justice, Office of Justice Programs, Office of Juvenile Justice and Delinquency Prevention, Washington, DC. NCJ number: 162427.

Laughren J (n.d.) Cyberstalking awareness and education. http://www.ucalgary.ca/~dabrent/380/webproj/ jessica.html

Lee R (1998) Romantic and electronic stalking in a college context. *William and Mary Journal of Women and the Law* **4**:373–2.

Lloyd-Goldstein R (1998) De Clerambault on-line: a survey of erotomania and stalking from the old world to the World Wide Web. In JR Meloy (ed.) *The Psychology of Stalking: Clinical and Forensic Perspectives* (pp. 193–212). San Diego, CA: Academic Press.

Miller R & Marshall J (1987) Coercive sex on the university campus. *Journal of College Student Personnel* **28**(1):38–47.

Meloy JR (1996) Stalking (obsessional following): a review of some preliminary findings. *Aggression and Violent Behavior* **1**:147–62.

Meloy JR (ed.) (1998) *The Psychology of Stalking: Clinical and Forensic Perspectives*. San Diego, CA: Academic Press.

Meloy JR & Gothard S (1998) The psychology of stalking. In JR Meloy (ed.) *The Psychology of Stalking: Clinical and Forensic Perspectives* (pp. 1–23). San Diego, CA: Academic Press.

Mullen PE & Pathé M (1994) Stalking and the pathologies of love. *Australian and New Zealand Journal of Psychiatry* **28**:469–77.

Pettinari D (1998) Investigating Internet crimes against children. *Sheriff* **50**(6): 10–15.

Prentky RA & Burgess AW (2000) *Forensic Management of Sexual Offenders*. New York: Kluwer.

Reno J (1999) *Cyberstalking: A New Challenge for Law Enforcement and Industry*. A report from the Attorney General to the Vice President, Washington, DC.

Romans, JSC, Hays, JR, White, TK (1996) Stalking and related behaviors experienced by counseling center staff members from current or former clients. *Professional Psychology, Research and Pratice* **27**(6):595.

Ross ES (1995) E-mail stalking: Is adequate legal protection available? *John Marshall Journal of Computer and Information Law* **23**(3):405.

Sexual Assault Report (2000) Jovanovic trial, April/May 2000, Kingston, NJ: Civic Research Institute, PO Box 585.

Sheridan L, Davies GM & Boon JCW (2001) The course and nature of stalking: a victim perspective. *The Howard Journal of Criminal Justice* **40**:215–34.

Spertus E (1996) Social and technical means for fighting on-line harassment. http://www.ai.mit.edu/people/ellens/gender/glc

Spitzberg BH, Nicastro A & Cousins A (1998) Exploring the interactional phenomenon of stalking and obsessive relational intrusion. *Communication Reports* **11**(1):33–47.

Soma JT, Muther TF & Brissette H (1997) Transnational extradition for computer crimes: are new treaties and laws needed? *Harvard Journal of Legislation* **34**:317.

Wallace H & Silverman J (1996) Stalking and post-traumatic stress syndrome. *The Police Journal* **69**:203–6.

CHAPTER 13

Stalking and the Law

PAUL INFIELD and GRAHAM PLATFORD, BARRISTERS

5 Paper Buildings, London

INTRODUCTION

Over the past few years stalking appears to have become increasingly prevalent. Hardly a week goes by without the media reporting some new case of stalking or some new manifestation of it. Some are comparatively trivial; others end in rape, serious assault or murder. For those who are subject to the full attentions of a committed, obsessed stalker the effects can irrevocably alter their lives. As the Home Office said July 1996:

> Stalkers can have a devastating effect on the lives of their victims, who can be subjected to constant harassment at home, in public places, and at work, to the extent that they can feel that they are no longer in control of their lives. It is not unknown for a stalker to harass a victim for many years (paragraph 1.4).

It is not for nothing that it has been described as "rape without sex".

It has now become clear that stalking is a real, pernicious social problem, the manifestations of which affect many people. In 1998 the British Crime Survey (BCS) reported that 11.8% of adults aged 16 to 59 recalled being the subject of "persistent and unwanted attention" on at least one occasion since the age of 16. The fact that 73% of those were women indicates that the problem is predominantly, though not exclusively, a female one. That bias was repeated when the BCS looked at people's experiences over the past year (the 12-month period starting sometime between January

Stalking and Psychosexual Obsession: Psychological Perspectives for Prevention, Policing and Treatment. Edited by J. Boon and L. Sheridan. © 2002 John Wiley & Sons, Ltd.

and June 1997). Of those surveyed, 2.9% had experienced persistent and unwanted attention during that period, a figure which the BCS calculated as representing 880 000 people. The figure was higher for women (4%) than for men (1.7%), and highest for women aged 16 to 19 (16.8%). Even if one acknowledges that the definition "persistent and unwanted attention" is a wide one for stalking, those statistics are still very worrying.

THE LAW BEFORE THE PROTECTION FROM HARASSMENT ACT 1997

Legal systems have long experience of regulating how and when people are allowed to affect each other.

In England and Wales the law against nuisance, which has been part of the common law for centuries, has, until recently, been the main weapon against such wrongs. Cases on private nuisance encompass almost all imaginable forms of annoyance of people in the enjoyment of their own land, including the making of excessive noise and smell, encouraging excessive traffic over a private road, telephoning excessively or at unsocial hours, making unpleasant telephone calls and sending offensive mail. Some of those annoyances would amount to stalking; arguably, all of them also amount to harassment.

In the past 20 or so years before the passing of the Protection from Harassment Act 1997 there were a number of attempts to use the law against nuisance as a law against harassment or to recognise a discrete but parallel personal right not to be harassed. However, no consensus emerged in the courts. In *Thomas v. National Union of Mineworkers*[1] Scott J. said[2]:

> Nuisance is strictly concerned with, and may be regarded as confined to, activity which unduly interferes with the use or enjoyment of land or of easements. But there is no reason why the law should not protect on a similar basis the enjoyment of other rights. All citizens have the right to use the public highway. Suppose an individual were persistently to follow another on a public highway, making rude gestures or remarks in order to annoy or vex. If continuance of such conduct were threatened no one can doubt but that a civil court would, at the suit of the victim, restrain by injunction the continuance of the conduct. The tort might be described as a species of private nuisance, namely unreasonable interference with the victim's right to use the highway. But the label for the tort does not, in my view, matter.

That passage was criticised in subsequent cases on the ground that it elevated harassment into a general tort (i.e. civil wrong). In *Patel v. Patel*[3]

---

[1][1986] Ch 20, [1985] 2 All ER 1
[2][1986] Ch 20 at 64, [1985] 2 All ER 1 at 22
[3][1988] 2 FLR 179, CA

Waterhouse J. said baldly[4] "in the present state of the law there is no tort of harassment". It was also criticised in *Khorasandjian v. Bush*[5], where Peter Gibson J., in a dissenting judgment, said[6] "to the extent that Scott J. was holding that there is now a tort of unreasonable harassment . . . I cannot agree with him. There is no tort of harassment . . . and I do not think that the addition of the adjective 'unreasonable' would convert harassing conduct into tortious conduct." However, the majority of the Court of Appeal in *Khorasandjian* held that a tort of harassment did exist at common law.

Those differing views about the existence of a common law tort of harassment were resolved in the case of *Hunter v. Canary Wharf*[7], where the House of Lords made clear that the law against nuisance only protects those who own or have an interest in property against interference with their enjoyment of that property and that there is no tort of harassment in common law. As Lord Hoffman said in that case:[8]

> Nuisance is a tort against land, including interests in land such as easements and profits. A plaintiff must therefore have an interest in the land affected by the nuisance.

And in a passage which showed the need for the statutory intervention of the Protection from Harassment Act 1997 he added:[9]

> If a plaintiff, such as the daughter of the householder in *Khorasandjian v. Bush*, is harassed by abusive telephone calls, the gravamen of the complaint lies in the harassment which is just as much an abuse, or indeed an invasion of her privacy, whether she is pestered in this way in her mother's or her husband's house, or she is staying with a friend, or is at her place of work, or even in her car with a mobile phone. In truth, what the Court of Appeal appears to have been doing was to exploit the law of private nuisance in order to create by the back door a tort of harassment which was only partially effective in that it was artificially limited to harassment which takes place in her home.

Other than the law against nuisance the pre-1997 law in England and Wales had, in effect, three types of protection against harassment: laws against particular acts, laws against harassment in particular places, and

---

[4][1988] 2 FLR 179 at 182, CA
[5][1993] QB 727, [1993] 3 All ER 669, CA
[6][1993] QB 727 at 744A, CA
[7][1997] A.C. 655; [1997] 2 W.L.R. 684; [1997] 2 All E.R. 426; (1998) 30 H.L.R. 409; [1997] 2 F.L.R. 342; [1997] Env. L.R. 488; [1997] C.L.C. 1045; 84 B.L.R. 1; 54 Con. L.R. 12; [1997] Fam. Law 601; (1997) 147 N.L.J. 634; [1997] E.G.C.S. 59; [1997] N.P.C. 64; (1997) 94(19) L.S.G. 25; (1997) 141 S.J.L.B. 108
[8][1997] AC 655 at 702H, HL
[9][1997] AC 655 at 691G, HL

laws against harassment by particular people. Laws against particular acts included the prohibitions on acts such as assault (Offences against the Person Act 1861), rape (Sexual Offences Act 1956), silent or abusive telephone calls (Telecommunications Act 1984), "poison pen letters" (Malicious Communications Act 1988) and the making of defamatory statements; laws against harassment in particular places include prohibitions on harassment at work, including sexual (Sex Discrimination Act 1975) and racial (Race Relations Act 1976) harassment[10]) and in the home (Protection from Eviction Act 1977, Housing Act 1996); and laws against harassment by particular people include anti-social behaviour orders (which can be made by Magistrates Courts under the Crime and Disorder Act 1998) and, most importantly, prohibitions on harassment by family members under the "domestic violence" legislation (Part IV Family Law Act 1996).

Viewed in terms of preventing the increasing menace of stalking these laws were, at best, piecemeal. Some of those laws were enforced by the criminal courts alone, some only by the civil courts, and some by both. Each of those laws provided for different remedies: the criminal offences could be punished by fines or imprisonment, the civil torts could be restrained by injunctions (breach of which is punishable by up to two years' imprisonment for contempt of court) or compensated by damages. Some of the criminal penalties were widely seen as derisory: the maximum sentence for sending an indecent or grossly offensive letter is now a fine of £2500, for making an abusive telephone the maximum fine is £5000.

As the prevalence of stalking, or at least the level of interest in it, increased through the 1980s and early 1990s it became increasingly clear, therefore, that the courts could not provide a coherent response and that there was a need for Parliament to legislate against it. As the Home Office Consultation Paper said in 1996:

> The Government therefore considers that there should be a statutory tort of molestation. This would recognise that everybody has the right not to be caused distress as a result of molestation. The remedy would not depend on the existence of a relationship or on property rights, as current remedies do, but on the right to physical integrity, extending protection to cases where the harm suffered falls short of a recognised personal injury. It would be for the court in each case to decide whether the conduct complained of amounted to molestation; the term would not be defined in legislation (paragraph 5.5).

---

[10] Though both the Sex Discrimination Act 1975 and the Race Relations Act 1976 use the term "harassment" even for offensive behaviour committed on one occasion it is arguable that this is not really harassment, for that term indicates behaviour on more than one occasion

THE PROTECTION FROM HARASSMENT ACT 1997

When it came to legislate, the Government was faced with two basic legislative models which had been used around the—mostly English-speaking—world. The most common model was what we call the "list method". This method simply lists acts which, if carried out by a person, amount to harassment or stalking. Section 264 of the Canadian Criminal Code passed in, 1993, for instance, prohibits "criminal harassment" in this way:

1. No person shall, without lawful authority and knowing that another person is harassed or recklessly as to whether the other person is harassed, engage in conduct referred to in subsection (2) that causes that other person reasonably, in all the circumstances, to fear for their safety or the safety of anyone known to them.
2. The conduct mentioned in subsection (1) consists of:
    a. repeatedly following from place to place the other person or anyone known to them;
    b. repeatedly communicating with, either directly or indirectly, the other person or anyone known to them;
    c. besetting or watching the dwelling house, or place where the other person, or anyone known to them resides, works, carries on business or happens to be; or
    d. engaging in threatening conduct directed at the other person or any member of their family.

Most jurisdictions, including most of the states of the USA, appear to have adopted this model. Some, however, have chosen the other "general prohibition" model, as exemplified by Florida's anti-stalking law, which provides the following definitions:

STALKING is committed when a person willfully, maliciously, and repeatedly follows or harasses another person.
AGGRAVATED STALKING which is a felony, may be committed in one of two ways:
a. When the stalker makes a credible threat to cause physical harm or death;
   or
b. When the stalker continues after an injunction for protection or any other court imposed prohibition that has been filed for protection.

The problem with which both these models labour—and the problem which has bedevilled this new area of the law—is how to define the words "stalking" and "harassment" in a way which satisfies the law's requirements for precision, coherence and consistency. Dictionaries tend to define "stalking" in terms of hunting, something along the lines of "to pursue stealthily", and they define "harassment" as "vexing by repeated attacks, to trouble or to worry". Neither of these is entirely satisfactory: the modern-day stalker may be anything but "stealthy" and "pursuit", of itself, cannot be made against the law without catching in its net every budding Romeo; harassment, on the other hand, is often carried out without "attacks" per se, while to define it as merely "to trouble" or "to worry" is to risk demonising many activities of daily life including the customer who shouts at the shopkeeper or the driver who "carves up" another. As the Home Office Consultation Paper put it in 1996:

> The greatest difficulty in extending the criminal law to deal with the activity of stalkers is one of definition. The term "stalking" does not apply to a particular action or kind of action which can easily be defined in legal terms and prohibited. There is a risk that if the scope of any new legislation to deal with stalking is not carefully defined it will criminalize the everyday behaviour of innocent people. The law applies to everyone and must be certain and exact; it cannot be tailored so as to apply only to certain individuals ... Many of the actions of stalkers are, in themselves, harmless—walking up and down a street, or standing on a street corner for example. There is a need for care to ensure that new laws against stalking do not, for example, catch investigative journalists, religious activists, debt collectors or even political canvassers. The challenge is to catch stalkers without putting in jeopardy the liberty of others to pursue innocent activities or those sincerely seeks to start a relationship with someone where their actions could not reasonably be considered to be a nuisance (paragraphs 4.1 and 4.2).

The essential difficulty in defining both stalking and harassment is that, while we know them when we see or hear them, their means are difficult to put into words. They are well understood but hard to define. The law, however, cannot operate without some definition which can be understood both by the courts and by those who may appear before them. Fair law demands definitions which are both readily understood and reasonably certain. The law does not operate on the basis which the fictional Lord Chief Justice, Lord Light, set out in A.P. Herbert's "Rex v. addock: Is it a free country?" (Herbert, 1935):

> It is a principle of English law that a person who appears in a police court has done something undesirable, and citizens who take it upon themselves to do unusual actions which attract the attention of the police should be careful to bring these actions into one of the recognised categories of crimes and offences, for it is intolerable that the police should be put to the pains of inventing reasons for finding them undesirable.

The "list method" and the "general prohibition" model deal with these definitional difficulties in different ways. The list method sets out a list of specific, defined activities which it prohibits, while the general prohibition method does not define harassment or stalking but, in effect, leaves it to the common sense of the court to decide in each case. The list method has the advantage of certainty and makes it easy for the courts, the potential offender and the victim to ascertain whether certain activities will amount to a breach of the prohibition. But it suffers from the disadvantage that its very certainty creates rigidity, for it defines stalking and/or harassment by reference to what activities those phrases are understood to encompass by the legislators at the time of the passing of the law and it does not have the flexibility to change, for instance to take account of new methods such as stalking over the Internet. The general prohibition, on the other hand, trades certainty for flexibility. Each case is decided afresh by reference to what the court hearing it decides is understood as stalking or harassment at that time. However, it achieves this at the expense of some uncertainty.

When the British Parliament came to decide which of these methods to use for its proposed legislation it had behind it the ill-fated Private Members bill presented by Janet Anderson MP, which had used the list method. The Government decided instead to opt for the general prohibition, ostensibly because it felt that that method gave more protection to the victims of stalking. As David MacLean, then Home Office Junior Minister, said during the debate:

> Stalkers do not stick to activities on a list. Stalkers and other weirdos who pursue women, cause racial harassment and annoy their neighbours have a wide range of activity which it is impossible to define (*Hansard*, 17 December 1996, col. 827).

So it was that the Protection from Harassment Act 1997 passed into law. . It came into force in England and Wales on 16th June 1997 and all of its section were finally implemented on 1st September 1998.

Sections 1 and 7 of the Act set out so much definition of harassment as there is in the Act:

1. Prohibition of harassment
(1) A person must not pursue a course of conduct—
    (a) which amounts to harassment of another, and
    (b) which he knows or ought to know amounts to harassment of the other.
(2) For the purposes of this section, the person whose course of conduct is in question ought to know that it amounts to harassment of another if a reasonable person in possession of the same information would think the course of conduct amounted to harassment of the other.
(3) Subsection (1) does not apply to a course of conduct if the person who pursued it shows—

(a) that it was pursued for the purpose of preventing or detecting crime,

(b) that it was pursued under any enactment or rule of law or to comply with any condition or requirement imposed by any person under any enactment, or

(c) that in the particular circumstances the pursuit of the course of conduct was reasonable.

7.   Interpretation of this group of sections

(1) This section applies for the interpretation of sections 1 to 5.

(2) References to harassing a person include alarming the person or causing the person distress.

(3) A "course of conduct" must involve conduct on at least two occasions.

(4) "Conduct" includes speech

There are a number of things which are worth noting about these sections and the Act in general:

- First, the word "stalking" does not appear anywhere in the Act. One can only assume that it was thought—probably rightly—that stalking was a sub-species of harassment and could, therefore, be encompassed within it.

- Second, there is no definition of harassment. The closest the Act gets to one is section 7(2), but that is an enlargement not a definition. (Curiously, that subsection uses the phrase "harassing a person", a phrase which does not appear elsewhere in the Act. Presumably, it is meant to be read as referring to "harassment of another"). The question of what is harassment appears to be one that is left to the court in each case.

- Third, the offence/tort is not simply "harassment" but "pursuing a course of conduct which amounts to harassment of another" which the perpetrator "knew or ought to know" amounted to harassment. The word "pursuit" appears to indicate that some deliberate act is required to be proved or implied from the defendant's conduct. The words "course of conduct" are defined by section 7 as meaning conduct on two or more occasions, though the Act does not define what is an "occasion". (Presumably harassment at different meals would be two occasions but at different courses of the same meal would not be.) The phrase "ought to know" is defined by section 1(2), the effect of which is to make the test what a reasonable man would think if he had the same information as the defendant.

- Fourth, once the prosecution or claimant has proved the pursuit of the course of conduct amounting harassment and the requisite knowledge the burden of proof appears to shift to the defendant to prove, if he can, that one or more of the three defences set out in section 1(3) applies. This is an important safeguard: the prosecution does not have to prove that the defendant was acting unreasonably; the defendant has to prove the contrary. The standard of proof he has to satisfy is the civil standard, that is "the balance of probabilities". Those defences provide protection for defendants such as law enforcement agencies, those acting pursuant to other enactments or rules of law, and those who can prove that they were acting reasonably.

- Finally, there is nothing in the Act about motive. It does not matter why the defendant has harassed his victim: the only questions under the Act are whether he has harassed another person, whether he knew or ought to know that he has done so and whether any of the defences in section 1(3) apply. This is unusual in English criminal law, for most offences involve a *mens rea* or mental element, such as intent or recklessness, and few serious offences involving public odium have no such element. In practice, however, to require the prosecution, for instance, to prove that a stalker intended to stalk would render the offence toothless, for many stalkers harass their victims not out of malevolent intent but from other motives.

The 1997 Act creates two criminal offences and a civil tort. The criminal offences are "Harassment" (Section 2) (which is triable only in the Magistrates Court and is punishable by up to 6 months imprisonment or a fine of £5000 or both) and "Putting a person in fear of violence" (Section 4) (which can be tried either in the Magistrates Court or the Crown Court and is punishable in the latter by up to 5 years in prison or an unlimited fine or both). The civil tort is "Harassment" and there is no tort akin to "Putting a person in fear of violence". The civil court can grant an injunction and award damages (including damages for anxiety caused by the harassment and any financial loss resulting from it; Section 3(2)). The Act is probably unique in creating, under the same umbrella, both criminal offences and civil torts.

There are two other unique aspects of the Act:

- A court sentencing a defendant for an offence under the Act may make a "restraining order" (Section 5). This unique order, the like of which is unknown in any other area of the criminal law, is designed to protect the victim of the harassment or any other person named in the order from further conduct which amounts to harassment or will cause a fear of violence. Under it the court may prohibit the defendant from doing anything described in the order. The language indicates that it may only prohibit certain conduct, not require the defendant to anything positive. The order may have effect for a specific period or until the court makes a further order. So a defendant may be prohibited from contacting the victim ever again, or from going to her home or place of work. If a defendant breaches a restraining order that breach is a criminal offence for which he can be imprisoned for up to 5 years or be fined or both.

- A defendant who breaches an injunction made against him by a civil court not only commits a contempt of court (punishable by up to 2 years imprisonment) but can, alternatively, be prosecuted for an offence under the Act (Section 3(6)) (punishable by up to 5 years imprisonment or a fine or both). This cross-over between the civil and criminal law is unique in English law.

THE EFFECT OF THE PROTECTION FROM HARASSMENT ACT 1997

If the creators of the Act thought of it as a panacea for the problems of stalking and harassment they will have been disappointed. For, though it has undoubtedly provided legal remedies which were either previously unavailable or difficult to obtain, it has, in practice, had rather fewer teeth than had been thought. It has also been used in ways which were probably unintended.

Perhaps the most striking thing about the use of the Act in practice has been that it has been used mostly against people other than archetypal stalkers. As a Home Office research study (Harris, 2000) said:

> There is a widespread perception that the Protection from Harassment Act was introduced to deal with the problem of stalking. However, this study has shown that it is in fact rarely being used for what might be described as 'classic' stalking cases in which a stranger obsessively follows and harasses a person with whom they have become fixated. It is far more often used to deal with a range of lower-level harassment by neighbours and former partners.

That wide ambit of the Act was not accidental and appears to have been expected by the government. The Home Office Consultation Paper produced in July 1996 prior to the passing of the Act said this:

> A general tort of molestation on these lines might also catch a wider range of activities than those of stalkers, such as harassment in disputes between neighbours or at work. The provisions of remedies to deter stalkers may therefore give further protection to people in these wider areas (paragraph 5.15).

In practice, as Harris (2000) suggests, the Act is being used in family and neighbour disputes and against landlords and employers far more than against "classic" stalkers. That this is possible is due to the wide, general wording of the Act, something which Parliament felt was necessary in order to combat stalkers. In the cases studied by Harris (2000), in 98% of cases the suspect and victim were known to each other either as partners, ex-partners or relatives (41%), acquaintances (41%) or neighbours (16%), and in only a small percentage of cases were the parties strangers. The most common reason for harassment was that the complainant had ended an intimate relationship with the suspect.

There is an obvious danger in this: if the Act is used as a sort of panacea against a wide range of social and perceived legal ills it may become seen as a low-level piece of legislation incorporating offences and torts which carry little or no social opprobrium. If that were to happen, it seems likely that the police would become less interested in dealing with offences under the Act, the Crown Prosecution Service (CPS) would become less likely to prosecute and the courts would become less likely to give condign punishments—thereby leading to a sort of vicious circle in which the Act is further devalued.

On the other hand, of course, the fact that the Act is being used to remedy a wide range of ills indicates that there is no other remedy for them. Finding appropriate definitions or legal strategies to separating the "harassing" ex-husband from the "classic" stalker is probably an impossible task.

For most victims the police and the criminal courts are the first port of call, and relatively few appear to take proceedings through the civil courts. There are undoubtedly good reasons for this: the police can act quickly and impose immediate sanctions, such as arrest and imprisonment (even if only overnight), on a stalker; studies have shown that quick, severe intervention often stops stalking behaviour if carried out early enough in the behaviour cycle; and, to the victim at least, the criminal route is cheaper than the civil route, which, particularly with the recent reduction in the availability of Public Funding (formerly Legal Aid), a victim will almost always have to pay for herself; and the penalties available in the criminal courts, both in terms of sentence and restraining orders, are much more severe, and are widely perceived as much more effective, than those available to the civil courts. On the other hand, of course, by initiating criminal proceedings a victim effectively loses control of the case, handing it over to the police and the CPS.

For the majority of victims who take initiate proceedings via the police and the criminal courts the reality of the Act differs markedly depending on where they are harassed, for the practices of police forces (and even of districts within the same force) vary widely. In some districts of the Metropolitan Police, for instance, we know that victims have been treated with great kindness, taken to special suites, supported by trained officers and given appropriate information throughout the investigation and subsequent court proceedings. In other districts of the same force we have been told of untrained officers behaving wholly inappropriately, for instance telling victims to have a chat with the stalker to tell him to go away and stop pestering them. For those of us old enough to remember them, the ways in which the police currently deal with stalking cases is all too often reminiscent of the early days of the first domestic violence legislation.

There may, of course, be good reasons why police officers sometimes deal badly with cases of stalking. The Act is often regarded as difficult to understand (largely because it does not define "harassment") and guidance on it has not been available to police forces until recently. There are also clear resource implications for many forces. Most importantly, perhaps, it needs to be remembered that cases under the Act are often difficult to pursue. For, as the above figures show, many cases under the Act involve the aftermath of the breakdown of relationships or neighbours disputes, both of which are situations where it is often difficult, if not impossible, to divine the truth, and where allegations and counter-allegations abound. Indeed, as our own experience in the courts indicates, an allegation by one person in such situations is very often met with similar counter-allegations, neither party having any real evidence to support their assertions. It is, perhaps, little wonder than some police officers and police forces appear reluctant to deal with such cases.

The statistics tend to support that impression. Home Office figures for 1998 and the first nine months of 1999 show that in 1998 693 people were cautioned for an offence under Section 2 and 173 for an offence under Section 4. The 1999 figures were 983 and 165 respectively. In 1998, 4304 people had proceedings under Section 2 (ordinary harassment) taken against them in Magistrates Courts; the 1999 figure was 3813. In 1998, 1505 people appeared before Magistrates Courts for Section 4 offences (putting a person in fear of violence) while the corresponding figure in 1999 was 1176. Given the widespread perception that stalking is prevalent, those figures seem low.

The CPS, which decides whether to prosecute and carries out that process, often appears equally reluctant to pursue harassment cases, though possibly for good reason. Out of the 4304 cases brought under Section 2 (harassment) in Magistrates Courts in 1998 1812 (42%) were "terminated early", while the 1999 figure was 1700 out of 3813 (44.5%). Of Section 4 charges (putting a person in fear of violence) 852 out of 1505 (56.6%) were "terminated early" in 1998 and 684 out of 1176 (58.1%) in 1999. Harris (2000) says that 39% of harassment cases were terminated by the CPS, compared with the national average for all offences of 14% (including bind-overs). In nearly half of terminated cases the defendant agreed to be bound over. Cases involving neighbour disputes were the most likely to be dropped, accounting for nearly half of such cases. The great majority of terminations were on the grounds of insufficient evidence, most commonly where the victim retracted their complaint. Those are worrying statistics, for where a type of case creates a disproportionate number of terminations for such reasons the police are, in time, less likely to arrest and charge and the CPS are less likely to initiate prosecutions.

As we have indicated above, most stalking cases are dealt with only in the criminal courts. There are three practical concerns about the way in which the criminal courts deal with harassment and stalking cases. First, victims are often prevented from giving evidence about previous occasions on which they have been stalked by the defendant. That has the effect of preventing evidence from being given to the effect that the defendant knew or ought to have known that his conduct amounted to harassment under Section 1 of the Act. Second, when it comes to sentencing, courts often appear simply to deal with the conduct included in the charge before them rather than with the effect of that conduct taken as a culmination of the previous stalking behaviour. Thus, a stalker who has telephoned his victim and shouted abuse at her 100 times may be sentenced only for the five occasions in respect of which he appears before the court and the court will not take account of the effect of the previous 95 occasions of such conduct. Thus, the fact that stalking is a cumulative crime, the effects of which increase, almost exponentially, with each new manifestation—that the one-hundredth occasion is incomparably worse than the first precisely because there have been ninety-nine previous occasions—is something which often appears to be ignored. That often makes victims feel very aggrieved, and they often say that they feel as though their feelings and their suffering have been disregarded. Finally, when defendants breach restraining orders—as seems often to occur, even though the statistics give a different picture—the sentences they receive often appear to be anything but condign. That demoralises victims and police and weakens the system of restraining orders.

There are often good reasons for victims to take proceedings in the civil courts: they can initiate proceedings when the police or CPS are unwilling to do so;[11] they retain control of the proceedings and do not have to rely on the judgments of the police and the CPS; they may not wish to stigmatize an ex-partner or spouse with a criminal conviction; and the standard of proof is lower than in the criminal courts. However, they face a number of difficulties in taking that route. First, they often have to pay for those proceedings themselves since the availability of Public Funding is now very limited. Second, the procedure in the civil courts is often perceived—with some justification notwithstanding the introduction of the new Civil Procedure Rules in 1999—to be unduly complex and slow. Finally, the only remedies available to the civil courts in such cases are injunctions

---

[11] Private people can pursue criminal proceedings themselves but this is very unusual.

and awards of damages. In practice, few, if any, victim is interested in damages; what they want is for the stalking behaviour to stop. Hence, what they seek is an injunction, an order of the court breach of which is punishable by up to two years imprisonment.

Finally, we turn to the question of punishment. In 1998 10% of those charged with Section 2 offences and 15% of those charged with Section 4 offences in the Magistrates Courts were imprisoned. In 1999 the figures were 11% and 14% respectively. For those defendants who were sentenced in the Crown Court in 1998 38% of those charged with Section 2 offences found themselves in prison while in 1999 that figure had reduced to 21%; for Section 4 offences the figures were 50% in 1998 and 46% in 1999. Whether or not these sentences are appropriate is, perhaps, a matter of personal judgment. What is clear, however, is that those sentences are often merely blunt instruments which do not deal with the core of the stalking problem. Once in prison no stalker is subjected to any regime which challenges his behaviour, to psychological or psychiatric assessment or treatment, and nothing is done to cause him to consider the obsessive nature of his behaviour. Indeed, to the contrary, there is anecdotal evidence to show that some stalkers swap details of their victims and there have been so many instances of stalkers continuing to stalk their victims by letter and telephone from inside prison that the Prison Service has published an Instruction to Governors setting out ways of combatting the problem.

CONCLUSION

The Protection from Harassment Act 1997 is a wide-ranging and effective law intended to prevent stalking and other forms of harassment. It enables the courts to deal with those who stalk and harass under one legal umbrella rather than under a host of disparate laws, as was the case before the 1997 Act came into force. Its terminology is deliberately general so as to enable it to catch all likely forms of stalking in its net, but that has caused the Act to be used by many victims of behaviour other than "classic" stalking.

In practice, the Act has been used more against other ills of society, such as family and neighbours' disputes, than against "classic" stalkers. That, and difficulties over the use and perception of the Act, have lead to problems in the police, CPS and courts operating it. One must hope that, just as happened with the domestic violence legislation after the difficult early days of the late 1970s, those difficulties will be ironed out and the Act will start to be used increasingly as an effective weapon against the pernicious crime of stalking.

REFERENCES

Harris, J. (2000). *An Evaluation of the Use and Effectiveness of the Protection from Harassment Act 1997*, Home Office Research Study 203. Research, Development and Statistics Directorate, Home Office: London.

Herbert, A.P. (1935). *Uncommon Law*. Methuen, London.

Home Office (1996). *Stalking: The Solution—A Consultation Paper*. Home Office: London.

CHAPTER 14

Conclusions

Julian Boon

and

Lorraine Sheridan

University of Leicester

The assembled contributions of this book represent an international show-case of that which is currently known about stalking and psychosexual harassment. While highly informative, the picture that emerges is both encouraging and disturbing.

Perhaps one of the most encouraging aspects is that of international awareness. In the first paragraph of the preface to this book a victim was quoted as believing that although stalking represented one of the most serious crimes of the 1990s, no one other than the victims understood its seriousness. It is clear from the subsequent chapters that this is no longer the case. Professionals from all over the world have shown that awareness has now been markedly raised. Encouragingly, this is the case from all orientations of professional interest, be they rooted in law enforcement, victim support, the legal field, academia or disciplines involved with the aetiology and treatment of offenders.

A consistent theme throughout the book has been to tap into research and professional experience to articulate ways of combating stalking. For example, Pathé & Mullen (Chapter 1), the editors (Chapter 5), Baldry (Chapter 6) and Kropp et al. (Chapter 9) each address practical issues of case management. Also of major practical value in prophylactic terms is De Becker's contribution (Chapter 3). In helping potential victims understand the role of seemingly innocuous conventions in the onset and

Stalking and Psychosexual Obsession: Psychological Perspectives for Prevention, Policing and Treatment.
Edited by J. Boon and L. Sheridan. © 2002 John Wiley & Sons, Ltd.

maintenance of stalking behaviour, they can be forearmed to avoid being selected as victims. Copson & Marshall (Chapter 4) provide the other side of the coin by providing practical suggestions for approaching and interacting with victims where stalking has already gone beyond the onset stage. Probably the most encouraging aspect of this volume is the comprehensive and practical nature of all the contributions—something which would not have been remotely possible in the early 1990s.

Encouraging too is the comprehensive coverage of risk assessment factors. Meloy's chapter in particular provides in-depth consideration of violence in the context of stalking (Chapter 7). In partitioning victims into public and private figures and distinguishing between affective and predatory violence, the chapter does much to articulate the different motivational forces that underpin stalking violence. In so doing, it also articulates key relationships between risk, behavioural characteristics and victimology. Taking a different line, though still looking at violence, Baldry's chapter concentrates on stalking violence and its strong link with domestic violence. Looking at this particular type of harassment, different motivation patterns emerged, with different risk indicators and intervention strategies being suggested. This also underlines the complexity which has emerged and how far we have come in developing our understanding of what is not so much a single entity of "stalking" but a collection of related phenomena. It is the emergent recognition of this point which goes a considerable way towards understanding why it is that there has been such difficulty in developing a consensus definition of what "stalking" actually is.

Further confirmation of the complexities and the different forms which stalking and psychosexual harassment can take comes from the contributions of Fitzgerald & Seeman (Chapter 10) and of Badcock (Chapter 8). The former contribution serves as an important reminder that stalking offences in whatever form are not solely a male preserve while the latter provides insight into the different approaches which can be employed in case management and the treatment of stalkers. Again, on a positive note, both contributions do provide some hope that psychotherapeutic and psychopharmacological intervention can have utility in the treatment of offenders.

Although in many ways the book undoubtedly provides encouragement for those who in the 1990s were lost in feelings of helplessness and despair, the implications of the text are in many ways more disturbing than ever. While there has been enhanced awareness and the contingent introduction of legislation to address the problem (see, for example, Infield & Platford, Chapter 14), the prevalence rates of stalking in its various forms remain high. This may be for several reasons. First, in domestic harassment—the most prevalent category—it may be that the majority of the cases do not reach the attention of the relevant authorities (see Baldry, Chapter 6).

Furthermore, of the contributors who advanced practical suggestions for victims and case management, all were clear for the need to acknowledge that none can be regarded as being fail-safe. Prevalence rates are also likely to remain high because of the way that some categories of stalking offender use social convention and their victims' kindness to ensnare them. While all who have read Gavin de Becker's chapter on this topic will be better equipped to guard against becoming a stalking victim, it is a simple matter for the perpetrator to move on to another victim who has not had the benefit of it. Additionally, as several of the contributors pointed out, mounting a successful prosecution in legal terms is far removed from successfully intervening to prevent further stalking. Collectively, for a variety of reasons, professional and public awareness combined with legislation do not provide guarantees for curbing prevalence rates per se.

Two specific aspects of concern were juvenile stalking and cyberstalking. McCann's work on late-childhood/early adolescent offenders and victims has revealed that the problem may be starting markedly earlier than had previously been widely recognised (Chapter 11). If future research confirms this to be widespread in the biographies of stalkers, then as his chapter states, there is a clear need to explore ways of intervention very early on. Burgess & Baker's coverage of cyberstalking also conveyed worrying points which rendered it every bit as serious a problem as more conventional stalking techniques (Chapter 12). The relative potential for the perpetrator to remain anonymous and their ability to use search engines to acquire personal information are particularly empowering techniques for individual stalkers. These points together with the sheer speed of technological change are of grave concern.

What are the overall implications of this edited text? The main lesson of course is that we have advanced awareness of the course and nature of stalking. In addition to this more basic advancement, we now possess practical suggestions on how to combat stalking and aid both its victims and its perpetrators. In addition to this, the preceding chapters have raised several new areas of concern. Such knowledge alone does not, of course, mean that we will be able to eradicate stalking overnight. What it does point to, however, is an increased understanding of this nebulous crime. As has been argued throughout the book, stalking is extremely difficult to define, legislate against and ultimately prevent. It is hoped that academics and appropriate professionals working towards these ends can use the research reported here. Beyond these groups, the population at large needs to be educated on what stalking constitutes, how it develops over time, and how it may be detected and hopefully avoided. A few years ago stalking was labelled by journalists as the crime of the 1990s: we hope that this book means the situation stays that way.

Index

Index compiled by Roisin Turner